"My friendship [with the Goodes] has never ~~share the same commitment to the poor and n...~~ ~~flicts~~, and those fleeing from both natural disasters and war. Even today, as we meet, there is no distance, no doubt that as servants of the living God we are part of His great plan of love for the world."

JOSIANE ANDRÉ, M.D.
Cofounder, Medair, Switzerland

"The path that the Goodes take us down in this book is exhilarating. Their practical blend of justice and spirituality propel them to Afghanistan, Thailand, India, Africa, and a thousand destinations in-between. Readers better prepare to have their hearts broken and their spirits lifted at the same time."

DAVID BATSTONE
Cofounder and president, Not For Sale; professor, University of San Francisco

"In this book we get a glimpse of Steve and Marie's amazing journey with the Lord, a journey that took the couple to places many of us will never get to go, but when reading along we are allowed to see some of what the Lord is doing in and through them."

ADRIENNE BLOMBERG
Director, Siam-Care Foundation, Bangkok, Thailand

"This world desperately needs more leaders like [the Goodes], bringing the light and hope of Christ in places of darkness and injustice."

DAVID AND SUSAN COLE
Board of regents chairman, University of the Nations

"Steve and Marie's story begins with vulnerability and openness, a mark of their ministry. Throughout the book there are wonderful tales of acts of compassion often linked with courage and always carried through with humility. The humanity of this extraordinary couple shines through each chapter."

THE REVEREND PETER COOK
Vicar, Christ Church Bangkok, Thailand

"Gripping your heart, this story is one of those books you can hardly put down. As you walk through Steve and Marie's journey, you'll see that the couple deserves your attention."

LOREN CUNNINGHAM
Founder, Youth With A Mission

"Steve and Marie Goode are world changers. Their story is full of the practical outworking of God's Word and ways, woven throughout their lives in missions. It is laced with humor and honesty that all of us can learn from."

LYNN AND MARTI GREEN
Youth With A Mission

"Steve and Marie's hearts have always beat with compassion for the poorest and most vulnerable. The story is of a couple who made themselves available, first to see with God's eyes of compassion and then to obey—no matter how crazy it might have seemed. In the process the authors have touched thousands of lives with God's mercy."

MICHAEL GREEN
Youth With A Mission

"Steve and Marie's account demonstrates where simple obedience to God's calling can lead: fulfilled lives, firm hope and assurance in the midst of pain and disappointment, countless lives changed by the free flow of God's love through human vessels, and global impact on the issues that burn on God's heart."

DR. TONI GROSSHAUSER
Development consultant

"Have you ever wondered what your life would look like if you lived as though you were the hands and feet of Jesus? This book is chock-full of real stories that will inspire you to seek God's call for your life."

PETER J. ILIYN
North American director, YWAM

"Steve and Marie invite us to join them on their spiritual journey as servants to the servants of the Lord. No land is too dangerous and no journey too far to bring words of love and encouragement."

MARY LOS BANOS
President, The Children's House, Hawaii
The Good Shepherd Program, Myanmar

"I loved this book. What captures me is the clear, relentless commitment of Jesus to the poorest, weakest, neediest, and most vulnerable. It showcases how, as we are willing to walk with Him among the poor, He invades communities and forever changes lives."

COLLEEN MILSTEIN
Director, Advocacy and Engagement, LOOM International

"I've known Steve and Marie for thirty years. Steve married me and my wife in a refugee camp. But I didn't know half of what they've been a part of. This, their life story, reads like a thirty-five-year roller-coaster ride, but a ride with a destination: to make known the love of Jesus to some of the most threatened and needy of our hurting world."

JOHN PADDON
YWAM Norway

"Steve and Marie are not attempting to fill the shoes of God but cry out for the real thing, and He shows up. Those who know them testify that the love of God has rubbed off on them."

KARIN RAMACHANDRA
Counselor and Bible teacher, Colombo, Sri Lanka

"[The Goodes'] commitment to follow wherever God leads has thrust them into the most extreme challenges of social crisis, danger, and suffering, only to see God glorified through miraculous expressions of compassion and ministry."

JERRY RANKIN
President emeritus, International Mission Board, SBC

International Adventures

Adventures in Naked Faith

Against All Odds

Bring Your Eyes and See

Cell 58

A Cry from the Streets

Dayuma

Living on the Devil's Doorstep

The Man with the Bird on His Head

The Narrow Road

Taking On Giants

Taking the High Places

Tomorrow You Die

Torches of Joy

Totally Surrounded

Walking Miracle

A Way Beyond Death

BRING YOUR EYES AND SEE

Our Journey into Justice, Compassion, and Action

STEVE AND MARIE GOODE
WITH JEMIMAH WRIGHT

YWAM PUBLISHING
Seattle, Washington

YWAM Publishing is the publishing ministry of Youth With A Mission (YWAM), an international missionary organization of Christians from many denominations dedicated to presenting Jesus Christ to this generation. To this end, YWAM has focused its efforts in three main areas: (1) training and equipping believers for their part in fulfilling the Great Commission (Matthew 28:19), (2) personal evangelism, and (3) mercy ministry (medical and relief work).

For a free catalog of books and materials, call (425) 771-1153 or (800) 922-2143. Visit us online at www.ywampublishing.com.

Bring Your Eyes and See: Our Journey into Justice, Compassion, and Action
Copyright © 2015 by Steve and Marie Goode

Published by YWAM Publishing
a ministry of Youth With A Mission
P.O. Box 55787, Seattle, WA 98155-0787

All rights reserved. No part of this book may be reproduced in any form without permission in writing from the publisher, except in the case of brief quotations embodied in critical articles or reviews.

Library of Congress Cataloging-in-Publication Data
Goode, Steve.
  Bring your eyes and see : our journey into justice, compassion, and action / Steve and Marie Goode, with Jemimah Wright.
    pages cm. — (International adventures)
  1. Goode, Steve. 2. Goode, Marie. 3. Missionaries—Biography. 4. Missions, American. 5. Youth with a Mission, Inc. I. Title.
  BV2121.U6G66 2014
  266.0092'2—dc23
  [B]   2014029865

Unless otherwise noted, Scripture quotations are taken from the Common English Bible®, CEB® Copyright © 2010, 2011 by Common English Bible.™ Used by permission. All rights reserved worldwide. Verses marked *The Message* are copyright © 1993, 1994, 1995, 1996, 2000, 2001, 2002. Used by permission of NavPress Publishing Group. Verses marked NIV are taken from the Holy Bible, New International Version®, NIV® Copyright © 1973, 1978, 1984, 2011 by Biblica, Inc.® Used by permission. All rights reserved worldwide.

"Blessed Be Your Name" written by Beth Redman and Matt Redman. Copyright © 2002 Thankyou Music (PRS) (adm. worldwide at CapitolCMGPublishing.com excluding Europe which is adm. by Integritymusic.com) All rights reserved. Used by permission. "God of This City" written by Aaron Boyd, Andrew Mccann, Ian Jordan, Peter Comfort, Peter Kernaghan, Richard Bleakley. Copyright © 2008 Thankyou Music (PRS) (adm. worldwide at CapitolCMGPublishing.com excluding Europe which is adm. by Integritymusic.com) / worshiptogether.com Songs (ASCAP) sixsteps Music (ASCAP) (adm. at CapitolCMGPublishing.com) All rights reserved. Used by permission.

Some names have been changed to protect identity.

ISBN 978-1-57658-561-0

First printing 2015

Printed in the United States of America

Bring your eyes and see, and then you will believe.
—SOMALI PROVERB

To the six hundred-plus staff of the various YWAM Relief Services teams who served with us in Thailand through the fifteen years of the Indo-Chinese refugee crisis: We learned together about suffering, injustice, history, politics, and trusting, worshiping, and obeying God in the midst of challenge—through the Khmer Rouge genocide, the Vietnamese land and boat people exodus, and the flood of Lao refugees from the valleys and mountains. You set your own lives and careers aside to serve others. You obeyed God and used your skills during this incredible time of history as crisis brought us together. We worked hard and had fun. Together we laughed and cried. We are forever indebted to you.

Contents

PART THREE: CENTRAL AND SOUTH ASIA AND AFRICA

Acknowledgments

IT HAS CERTAINLY taken a team to bring this book together. Thank you to everyone who has encouraged us for many years to write this book. A special thanks to Tom and Terry Bragg for continuing to pursue us and encourage us that we had a story to tell and for opening the door to YWAM Publishing and your talented staff. Our editor, Luann Anderson, was a model of patience and encouragement—thank you for staying with us through all the delays of our schedule and life.

Jemimah Wright, you won a special place in our hearts during the month we relived our lives with you. You are a gifted writer, you know how to ask great questions, and you are an empathetic listener. You left an amazing hole when you departed Thailand. If you had not come, this book would not be in print today. Thank you for getting us started.

Thanks to the many who read, edited, suggested changes, and contributed to this project. Thanks to Victoria Smith, Phyllis Buckley, Michael Green, Toni Grosshauser, Adrienne Blomberg, and Karol Svoboda for taking the time to read the very rough draft and give us detailed input. Special thanks to Ian and Gabrielle Talbot, Anjali Kanagaratnam, and Joanna Geiger for helping us see the finish line in completing this book.

Yvonne Dos Santos, you have lived so much of this with us. Thank you for reading and rereading this manuscript and for all the ways you served us with your encouragement, your loyalty and faithfulness, your anticipation of need, meals and snacks, special treats, running errands, covering for us so we could write, and continually filling in the blanks and gaps—and not least, for your prayers. Your friendship of over forty years has been a great gift to us.

To all of our friends and coworkers, thank you for walking with us. You have made the journey *so* rich and given us great things to live, to learn, and to write about. We had joy in being reminded of each of you, and we listed everyone's name in the first draft, wanting you to know we remembered. But we were encouraged by several to remove the names, since they broke the flow of the story. But you know who you are, and be assured, we do too!

Foreword

MY WIFE, DEYON, and I first met Steve and Marie in 1974. We traveled and worked closely that year for six weeks, presenting "The Last Commandment," a cutting-edge multimedia presentation, in Zimbabwe and South Africa as we recruited African young people for a European youth festival in Belgium sponsored by the Billy Graham Association. Then in 1975 Marie became my assistant for missions in Europe, the Middle East, and Africa, and Steve became the leader of our English-speaking schools in Lausanne, Switzerland, that included practical outreach into Southern and Eastern Europe and the Middle East. Steve also cofounded ProclaMedia along with Larry Wright while working in Lausanne.

The Goodes were a central part of our leadership team, expanding YWAM growth in Switzerland and Europe in the mid- to late-70s. In 1976, they were a great strength to us personally shortly after the birth of our third child, John Paul. Deyon was hospitalized for emergency surgery at the time. The Goodes' response to our health challenges and those of raising a special-needs child bonded them even more deeply to us. This demonstrated how they engage practically when almost any crisis comes their way. To this day John Paul remains very special to Steve and Marie.

Steve and Marie were key in the founding of Mercy Ships. Marie led the team to Venice, Italy, where the first inventory of the M/V *Victoria* was completed, while Steve was leading the outreach in Venice. I learned that Steve and Marie were capable of great responsibility. YWAM was just beginning a decades-long global emphasis of God's heart for the poor and needy of our world. Steve also served in leadership on the board of directors of Mercy Ships until 2006.

It was the Indo-Chinese refugee crisis in Thailand in 1979, and particularly the genocide of the Khmer Rouge, that moved the Goodes into lifelong service to those in crisis, the poor and vulnerable, and the exploited of our world. In this book you will read practical implications about what happens when a couple says yes to God, not knowing where that is going to lead them. The Goodes would be the first to say that it was the teams of talented people with marketable skills brought together through crisis that played a key part in this sixteen-year response.

We continued to work closely with the Goodes in the Mercy Ministries (MM) area. Steve took on the role of Mercy Ministries in Asia and the Pacific in 1992. He accepted the global responsibility for MM in September 1995. I could then devote 100 percent of my attention to Mercy Ships.

Steve and Marie are some of our closest friends. That is what crisis does for relationships. We have seen them grow, develop, and serve tens of thousands. Their heart for God and for the poor of our world has taken them around the globe in service. Deyon and I count it a privilege to have served with them.

DON STEPHENS
President and Founder, Mercy Ships

Foreword

TWO REALITIES ARE woven in word and action throughout this book. The first is that God's fundamental purpose for man is unequivocally relational, toward God and toward his neighbor. The second is that this same relational God is relentless in His commitment to addressing the plight of the poor and needy. Most of us would engage in the former but distance ourselves from the latter. Not the Goodes. They are a people of unusual obedience, aligned to a loving God and their neighbor, wherever that has taken them. Their journey of engaging the impossible evidences that reality. We have known the Goodes intimately and have experienced the profound and immeasurable impact of their lives, on our children and on the poor to the powerful.

This book will unsettle you about who *your* neighbor is. Steve and Marie discovered their neighbors in such places as refugee camps and among the trafficked and those disenfranchised by war and poverty. That quest took them to the nations, to places and conditions they never expected to go. In simple and at times tenacious obedience, they discovered a brokenhearted God and His dream for addressing the desperation they faced. They didn't judge or alienate their neighbors but got to know them. In turn, they have modeled for their generation the Word becoming flesh: "The Word became flesh and blood and moved into the neighborhood. We saw the glory with our own eyes, the one-of-a-kind glory, like Father, like Son, generous inside and out, true from start to finish" (John 1:14, *The Message*).

God is still moving into neighborhoods that least expect Him. These stories are incontrovertible evidence of this fact and are true from start to finish. Be careful. More than a cursory read will challenge your perception of a God who is really there and the extent to which He will go to demonstrate His love to your neighbor.

CAROL AND DAVID BOYD
US National Prayer Breakfast Movement

Preface

Sow a thought and you reap an action; sow an act and you reap a habit; sow a habit and you reap a character; sow a character and you reap a destiny.

—Ralph Waldo Emerson

LIFE IS A SERIES of steps and choices that become like threads that are woven together. Sometimes it is difficult to see these woven threads until we step back and take a look at the pattern being created. The journey of steps that we walk is simple yet incredible, and we do not walk alone. We are born into a locality, into a family and extended family, into a culture of friends and background, into ways of looking at things and ideas that help shape us as individuals.

Some of us have been exposed to faith in God, while others have not. This book is about two people who found each other at a young age and committed to the journey of life together. The golden thread in our lives is a God of relationship, who loves us and wants us to love Him, others, and even our enemies. We do not know where this journey will end, but God has asked us to walk with Him step-by-step. He has promised that He will lead and guide us. We continue to listen and obey to the best of our understanding.

Our prayer is that this book will encourage those considering their next step. May you understand that although we do not always see where we are headed, we live one step at a time. Bring your eyes and see that God is faithful to lead us as we are obedient to take that first step. Then we will believe.

PART ONE

United States and Europe

The Bike and the Motorcycle

Conversion, like wisdom, takes a lifetime.
—Scot McKnight, *The Jesus Creed*

AT THREE IN the morning my mother softly nudged my shoulder to wake me up. Bleary-eyed, I got out of bed and grabbed my clothes, trying not to rouse my younger brother, John, sleeping next to me. Forty minutes later I was peddling my red Schwinn bicycle through the cool morning air to pick up a bundle of newspapers from the gas station on Highway 51, a few blocks from my home.

I had been delivering papers for a year, and now at fourteen I had a good routine. I would pack as many papers as I could—about 120—into bags slung over my small frame, fill the basket on the front and the double baskets on the rear of my bicycle, and make the journey to where my paper route started in the Frayser area of Memphis, Tennessee.

The more papers you delivered, the more money you could earn, and the only way to increase this income would be to have a motorcycle.

I liked the small Honda, the one my friend Dennis had. Dennis could deliver over two hundred papers, finishing earlier and making more money than me. I knew my dad would never allow it. He was very clear. I was not even allowed to *ride* a motorcycle, let alone operate one. This was before helmet laws were introduced in our city. My father had been a medic in the army and had later worked as an ambulance driver. He had seen too many injuries and deaths from motorcycles to allow his sons to ride them. I knew enough to let it go.

I met Dennis that morning at the gas station, and he said he would come over to help me finish my route. We would then go back to his house and sleep for a couple of hours before going out to enjoy our summer break from school. It was July 15, 1965, the day before my dad's forty-sixth birthday.

I was tired that morning and was looking forward to finishing my route and getting a little sleep at Dennis's house. I heard the sound of his motorcycle coming down the road.

"Hey, hand me some papers," he shouted. I gratefully passed over my last ones for the remaining houses. In no time all the newspapers were delivered and Dennis came back to meet me.

"I'll follow you home," I said, knowing he would get back to his house faster than I would.

"Why don't you just leave your bike here and hop on the back?" he suggested matter-of-factly.

This made sense. It would be so much quicker, I reasoned. But all of a sudden I heard my dad's voice in my head: "Son, I don't want you riding motorcycles."

What should I do? I thought.

I stifled a yawn. I was exhausted. Desire for sleep won out. I ignored my conscience and disobeyed my dad. He'd never even know, right?

Grabbing my empty bags, I left my bike behind a fence and jumped on behind Dennis as he revved the engine and pulled away.

We were nearly home when we saw the fifty-passenger Memphis city bus. To turn right onto an intersecting road, the driver had to make a wide, sweeping left turn on the narrow S-curve in the road. As the driver came to our side of the street, Dennis tried to swerve right to get out of the way of the bus. Instead, the motorcycle hit some loose gravel in the center of the intersection and started sliding. As Dennis was slowly braking, leaning to the right to avoid hitting the bus head-on, the back end of the motorcycle where I was sitting rotated closest to it.

As if in slow motion, I slipped off the back of the motorcycle, terrified. I was headed straight under the bus and passed out on impact. The back double wheels ran over the right side of my torso, hip, and thigh. The brakes screeched as the bus driver realized a human body was under his vehicle. Because the driver thought the wheels were still on top of me, he reversed the bus, running back over my leg, tearing up my body as the weight of the wheels crushed my right leg from knee to pelvis. Dennis escaped uninjured.

As I regained consciousness, I was lying on the street next to the back wheels of the bus, people standing over me. The first thing I remember was the sound of Dennis's mother's voice. We were only a few hundred yards from Dennis's home.

"He's dead! He's dead!" she screamed.

I remember thinking, *I can't be dead . . . uh . . . if I can think!* At the same time I was crying out in pain, losing a lot of blood. I just wanted someone to lift my head up off the ground so I could see what had happened to me. When eventually someone did lift my head, I passed out from shock at what I saw.

An ambulance arrived, and I was rushed to the hospital. My dad worked nights for a trucking company, and my mother had been waiting for the very bus that ran over me. She was on her way to work as a bookkeeper at a wholesale company on Main Street in Memphis. When the bus did not arrive, she had walked back home and asked my older brother David to drive her to work. Later, it was David who took the call from the hospital and contacted Mom and Dad to tell them what had happened. My parents came to the hospital as soon as they received the news. When I regained consciousness, I was lying on an emergency-room bed, my father standing over me with tears streaking his face.

"Sorry, Dad. Please don't be mad at me. I am really sorry. Will you forgive me for riding on that motorcycle?" I said weakly.

"Sure, son," Dad replied, taking my hand and giving it a squeeze. "Is there anything that I can get for you?" he asked. I thought for a moment and said, "Dad, I am so thirsty. Could you get me a big Pepsi-Cola and a candy bar?" My dad, holding back his tears, tried to calm and assure me, but he knew I was in critical condition and what was ahead of me. He had seen many similar life-threatening accidents during his days as an army medic.

I was taken to surgery as soon as the doctors stabilized me and replenished my blood loss. My dad later told me he had asked the team—led by general surgeon Schayel Scheinberg, urologist Joseph Orman, and orthopedic surgeon Leo Hay—what the chances of saving my leg were.

"We have to save his life first," the doctors had said grimly. Each doctor came to Mom and Dad over the next few hours, not to give them hope, but to update them on my condition. The first surgery lasted five hours. Dad asked Dr. Scheinberg not to keep anything from the family. He also told the doctor that scores of people were praying, that they had put me fully into the hands of God, and that they trusted Him for a miracle. Dr. Scheinberg could only reply, "Your son is in *very* critical condition."

I was in intensive care for two weeks, and my parents did not know from day to day whether I would survive. The huge loss of blood threatened to end my life. My pelvis was fractured in three places. My bladder was displaced several inches from its normal position, and the urethra was torn loose from it. The mutilation of my right thigh from the hip to the kneecap would require removal of sections of the quadriceps muscles. Grit, dirt, and sand had fused into the area so deeply that the doctors had to cut away infected flesh, making suturing of the thigh impossible. Three times, I returned to the operating room for removal of infected flesh.

My doctors had differing views on the course of treatment. A few of them believed that amputation of my leg was necessary to save my life, while others thought getting the thigh infection under control could save my life *and* my leg.

I underwent six surgeries in three months. I was confined to a special circular electric bed with a Stryker frame that rotated 360 degrees, slowly enabling my fractured pelvis to bear body weight, allowing movement to prevent bed sores, and aiding the nurses and orderlies who tried to rotate me without touching or lifting. The surgeries included skin grafts, with skin taken from my left thigh and my chest. The smell of freshly transferred skin on my injured leg was sickening, as was the antiseptic smell of the iodine. Because nothing could touch my grafted skin as it healed, a cage was placed over my body with the blanket on top of that. A heat lamp was put under the blanket to dry out the skin.

My doctors were worried about additional infection and prescribed strong intravenous antibiotics. At one point two bags were taken straight from a cold refrigerator and hooked up to my IV. My whole body began shivering violently, as if my blood had turned to ice. Once my body could tolerate the weight of blankets, I must have had a dozen of them on top of me. But it seemed to make no difference. My lips turned blue, and I wondered if I would ever feel warm again.

"He can't take this," my dad said, trying to reason with the nurses, who insisted I needed the antibiotics but allowed my dad to take the second bag from the fridge and place it on the windowsill for the sun to warm it a bit. That didn't help much.

Each night in the hospital, Mom would rub my feet, and then when I could not take the pain any longer, she would call the nurses to give me a shot of pain medication. Only then could I fall into a fitful sleep. This pattern went on for my entire hospital stay.

I was finding recovery slow and difficult and often cried because of the intense pain and the frustration of being confined to bed for so long. My room was on the third floor of the hospital. I was able to look out the window and see children in a park playing sports, running, and jumping. *I won't ever be able to do that again,* I told myself as I wept alone in my room. I thought my life was over, and I didn't know how long I could stand the constant pain.

Many people were unable to see me in this condition and thus could not visit me. Just after the accident one of the pastors from my church, Jerry Sandidge, visited me. He left shocked and ill at the sight and smell of my mangled body and was moved to compassion by the amount of my pain. Leaving the hospital, he returned to the church just as the choir was beginning their weekly practice. Interrupting the singing, he told them about me. "We have to pray for this boy right now," he said. He told me later that he'd felt there was a battle going on for my life and that through prayer the church was willing to fight for me.

My family prayed for my recovery night and day. My mother spent every night at my side, and my father stayed with me during the daytime. My parents were both Christians and trusted God for my life, but it was one of the most difficult times of their lives.

As the weeks went by, it looked like I wasn't going to lose my leg. Slowly I began to show improvement.

"We'll have you walking out of this hospital," Dr. Scheinberg said, pleased with my progress. In 1965, skin grafts had a 50 percent success rate. But 100 percent of the skin that was transplanted onto my leg lived. Dr. Scheinberg told my father that he knew people were praying, because he felt someone else in the operating room helping and guiding him as they worked on my body.

In the last month of my hospital stay I was moved from the circular bed to a regular one. I continued rehab, began whirlpool baths, and started to move around in a wheelchair. While lying in bed for two months, I had lost a lot of muscle strength. During my first trip in the hallway I was able to move about forty yards, but I was so tired that the nurse had to wheel me back to the room. However, the more I got up and moved in the chair, the more my strength came back.

I also had a tutor, since I was missing the first weeks of high school. I was eventually wheeled out of the hospital in mid-October and given an aluminum walker to help me get around. This didn't work well in our small home, however. Because the walker banged into doorjambs and made movement difficult, I graduated to crutches pretty quickly.

My dad tried to encourage me, saying over and over, "Stevie, it's a miracle you are alive. God saved your life. You can trust Him. He saved your life for a reason. Ask Him what He wants you to do." At one point in Dad's life when he was a soldier in Korea, he had thought about being a missionary or being in full-time Christian service of some kind. That never worked out, however, and Dad did not want me to miss anything God had for me. I knew he was right—this was a miracle. God had spared my life, and I wanted to know what His plan for me was.

For two weeks I used crutches to get around our house and then started to ride my bike to school. I tried to walk as normally as I could without limping and without the use of the crutches. All I wanted was to be normal like everybody else. I had lost all feeling above my right knee and thigh and would often hit my leg on some object and not realize the damage until I saw the blood seeping through my trousers. I had a lot of physical therapy to get stronger and more flexible. It seemed like I had grown a foot that summer while confined to a hospital bed. Improvements came day by day, and when I went back for a checkup, Dr. Scheinberg didn't recognize me. I walked into his office with hardly a limp.

Even though I was confident and popular in school, after the accident I became more self-conscious about my appearance. My body was a patchwork of lighter and darker skin from the grafts. If I was swimming or wearing shorts, children would come up to me and ask, "Wow, what happened to your leg? And your chest?" They were fascinated with my story of the motorcycle (and children still are). They are not afraid to ask questions and to inquire about my scars.

Despite being saved from death, I had not discovered my purpose in life and had questions about giving my life to God. I was independent, and my perceptions of God and questions about Him affected my trust in Him. It somehow seemed safer to try to control my life, even when it went horribly wrong. I did not yet understand that this humble Creator of the universe died so that I could be free, that He was loving, kind, and faithful to a thousand generations, that He was patient, and that true love does not force itself on any of us. God simply waits.

I enjoyed playing basketball, baseball, and tennis and really did not have much time for God in my remaining years of high school, even though I went to church on Sundays. Those close to me often reminded me that God had saved my life for a reason, without saying, "Maybe you should figure out what His purpose is." I was starting to listen to the words of my peers rather than what I felt were narrow dos and don'ts of those in authority. Whenever my parents, my grandmother, my two older brothers, or other authority figures suggested or told me what I should do, I struggled with their perspective and thus struggled to obey. I was independent, strong willed, and resistant, but somehow I stayed out of serious trouble.

My family attended First Assembly of God, Memphis—the same church Elvis Presley attended once or twice a year. The church was about twenty-five minutes from our home. At the end of our street was a little Baptist church, a congregation where a girl named Marie Bentley worshiped. On the Sunday after my accident Marie had heard about me from a friend who had been riding the bus that hit me, and she had been praying for my recovery. Little did either of us know at the time that the boy for whom she was praying would one day serve God and others with her on the other side of the world.

Love at First Sight

Each life is not just a journey through time, but a sacred journey.

—Frederick Buechner, *The Sacred Journey*

SHONEY'S BIG BOY was the place to hang out in our part of town. It was a restaurant with a drive-in area where you could park and order your meal, which would then be brought out to the car. All the high school kids hung out there, and one Saturday night I got the prize of being able to use my parents' car—a blue Rambler—having somehow been given permission over my older brother Ron. I parked at Shoney's and then hopped out to talk to some friends. As I strolled past one of the cars, I noticed a pretty blonde-haired girl in the backseat of a convertible.

"Well, hi there," she said with a big smile.

"Well, hi," I replied before walking on. I didn't think I knew her, but I knew I wanted to. She was beautiful.

Later I found out she was as surprised as I was that she had spoken to me. She didn't think I would actually hear her and was a little embarrassed that she had been so forward.

Over the next few weeks I saw Marie at Shoney's, and we would smile and wave casually from a distance. I had to figure out a way to meet her, since we didn't go to the same high school. I didn't have to wait long. One Friday night at Shoney's I got into the car with a school friend and his girlfriend, who happened to attend the rival school, Frayser High. My friend's girlfriend was chatting through the open car window with a girl in a car next to us. I was very happy to see that the girl was none other than the pretty blonde I had been waving to over the past few weeks.

"Hey, Steve, this is Marie Bentley," my friend said. Marie and I smiled nonchalantly at each other, and my heart skipped a beat. We had been officially introduced, and now I just had to find a way to ask her out. The next week I was in my parents' car, again at Shoney's, when I saw Marie walk past.

"Hey, come on over and talk," I shouted out. Marie turned and smiled and said she'd be right back. She seemed cool and collected, but I would have been very happy to have known that actually she was shaking as she walked into the restaurant, overjoyed that I had spoken to her.

That night in the car we talked and talked, and I wasted no time in asking Marie out for the following Friday. Every evening that week I phoned Marie as she got home from school and then just before she went to bed. I simply wanted to hear her voice but was soon told it was enough to call once a night. I found out later that Marie's mother had disapproved of the twice-a-day calls and told Marie to tell me that one was sufficient.

On our first date, I think I spent all the money I had. I took Marie to see *The Dirty Dozen* at a nice movie theater and then back to Shoney's, where we sat inside the restaurant for a change and ate their famous strawberry pie.

Marie and I started dating just as the fall semester of our senior year began in August 1967. I learned that Marie had given her heart to the Lord at age eight. While listening to a Sunday sermon, she had had a revelation of sin for the first time and started weeping quietly. When an invitation was given to invite Jesus into one's heart, Marie knew she wanted to do it.

"I have to go up," she said, looking up at her dad, who turned to his wife. Her parents wondered if their daughter was too young to really know what she was doing.

"I have to go up," Marie said again, more insistently.

"Okay, sweetie," her dad replied before taking her hand. Together they walked down the aisle to the front of church.

"Why are you here?" the pastor asked kindly when he met Marie.

"I want to give my heart to Jesus," Marie said.

"Let's pray together. Tell Jesus what's on your heart."

Quietly Marie poured out her heart to the Lord, repenting of her sin and asking Him to come into her life and lead her.

Now in high school, Marie was a friend to everyone and was well liked, though she struggled inwardly with how to live out her faith among her peer group. She was the captain of her cheerleading squad, while I had fought back from the accident to become captain of our basketball team, wearing a football thigh pad on my right thigh to protect myself from injury.

One week our schools were playing against each other in a basketball game. The odds were not good, since my school had a modest basketball record and I, being barely six feet, was taller than most of the guys on my team. The poor quality of our team may have added to the fact that our coach had lost interest and often seemed to nap during the games. Marie's school, which had about two hundred more students in each year's class, had state basketball players on its team. I realized this game was not going to be pretty.

Marie had been very nervous in the weeks leading up to the game. Just to get a reaction out of her, all the boys on her school team who knew she was dating me would say, "We're going to hurt Goode." She couldn't bear to watch me being defeated.

As the referee blew the starting whistle, the ball was tipped to one of the Frayser players and I stole it, dribbled down the court, and made a layup. The first two points were on the board.

Marie, who had been thinking we were going to get annihilated, instinctively stood up and let out a cheer of joy. Since she was leader, the rest of the cheerleading squad followed, cheering my scored points.

Their school supporters in the bleachers laughingly shouted, "Sit down, Bentley—wrong team!"

Marie turned bright red when she realized what she had done. She was able to laugh about it later, but it was hard to live down, because the incident was written about in the school paper.

At the end of the school year Marie was nominated "Miss Frayser," a senior class honor celebrating good grades and community service that was voted on by teachers and fellow students. I was able to sneak out of school and drive over to her ceremony to see her crowned.

"*Wow!*" I thought as I watched her, with her beautiful blue eyes and blonde hair, parading out in a long white dress. Marie was stunning. I felt proud that I knew her and that she was my girlfriend. A week later, our roles were reversed when the same ceremony was held at Westside. Marie convinced her guidance counselor to take her to watch, and she was in the audience to see me crowned "Mr. Westside."

After graduating in May 1968 we talked about our decision to attend different universities. Although we decided we could date other people, we still anticipated that we would marry when we finished college. I had been accepted at the University of Tennessee at Martin, and Marie would attend Middle Tennessee State University in Murfreesboro.

For two years we wrote to each other every day. Although Marie was intent on getting a degree in business education and finishing college in four years, I was considering college in the same way I had high school, hoping to do as little as possible to get by. That did not work very well.

One of the highlights of my first year at the university was the opportunity to play tennis on a regular basis. I enjoyed the game and even won the singles intramural tournament. You can imagine how thrilled I was when Marie came home over a school break having earned an A in tennis. I could not wait to get on the court to enjoy another thing we had in common. After warming up for twenty minutes, I called Marie to the net and asked her if her tennis teacher was a guy. She said, "Ah, yes. Why?"

"Well," I said, smiling, "the way that you are spraying those balls all over the court, I was just wondering how you got an A." (Turns out that even though Marie had aced the written tests and knew the rules of tennis, her execution needed some practice. Tennis became one of our favorite pastimes.)

Eventually my grades revealed my intentions. I had no guidance or purpose in life and wanted to find something that would fulfill me. I looked down different avenues—first at sports and then partying. Too late, I realized they were both dead ends. I failed my first year at the university.

My parents said they would not continue to support me to waste my time. I moved back home and got a job before transferring to the University of Memphis in my hometown. I still had to pay back my parents for the loan they had given me for the first year, which was humbling.

Back under my parents' watchful eye, I continued to struggle, trying to find out who I was. I still resisted those in authority. Part of the problem could have been that Dad, because of his service in the army, wasn't around much when we were growing up. My brothers, Ron, David, and John, and I were really raised by my mother and her mother, Josie Pickard, or Mama Jojo, as we called her. This was the 1960s, and I guess I was mimicking what was going on in the culture around me. I was a rebel, always questioning everything. This caused much conflict with my parents.

I suspect it was Mama Jojo's prayers that saved me many times over the years. Mama Jojo did not finish high school, but she was a woman of God, a woman who prayed and met with Him daily. Every morning about ten o'clock, she would lie across the bed on her back with her large Bible on her chest and wave her white hanky in the air, lifting up her grandsons and others in prayer loudly before the Lord. Her praying was so loud that all the neighbors knew our lives inside out. Sometimes I wondered if she thought God had a hearing problem.

The four of us boys unintentionally put serious pressure on our mother, so much so that Dad left the army early for the sake of the family. Children growing up do not often see the richness of heritage and relationship in family and extended family and the sacrifices that are made. Dad had been in the armed services for seventeen years, and if he had completed just three more years, he would have had a full pension and benefits. But because he knew he was losing connection, influence, and relationship with us, he sacrificed the pension for the sake of the family. (In 2006 my brother Ron wrote the US government to ask them to send any medals that our dad had received while he was in the army. Dad had entered the army right before Pearl Harbor and while in service was given nine medals that he never talked about with his sons: a medal for good conduct, a marksman medal, a Combat Medical Badge, and medals for European campaigns such as the Battle of the Bulge and the Elbe River battle. We had no idea of the challenges he had faced, and I had little appreciation for the sacrifices he had made, for the country and for our family.)

It was only when I took a world civilization class in my first semester back in Memphis that everything changed for me. My professor was a staunch atheist. He seemed to take pleasure in using class time to contest Christianity and to try to shake the faith of students. Disabled from polio, he had a bitter attitude. He would smoke cigars in class, often dropping ashes on students' feet as we sat captive to his caustic diatribes.

I disliked this man and didn't agree with what he was saying, yet my limited understanding of God and His character was not strong enough to refute him. I wondered how my professor had become so bitter, and it caused me to think that if I did not, somehow, change the direction I was headed, I could end up just like him—resentful and mad at the world.

As I sat listening to his faith barrages day after day, I realized that either this professor was right—and therefore I needed to agree with him wholeheartedly—or he was wrong, which meant I needed to radically alter the direction of my life. Right there in the class I prayed quietly, "God, if You are here, and if You are real, please show Yourself to me."

I can't explain what happened except to say, as the Brits do, the penny dropped. The lights suddenly went on and I understood there was a God who was knowable. I knew that Jesus was real, and all that I had been exposed to in my years at First Assembly of God began to make sense.

"Okay, my life is Yours," I prayed right there in the lecture. "Tell me what You want me to do, and I will do it." Despite my good intentions over the years, this time I meant it.

Go and ask your parents' forgiveness popped into my mind.

I knew that this had to be God, as it would not have come from me. Suddenly I had a glimpse of the disrespect, pain, and suffering that I had caused my parents. My brothers often complained that after the accident, I had become a spoiled brat who could get away with almost anything. I remembered how once, when I had been rude to Mom, she took a thick ruler to spank me. The ruler broke. I laughed at her and at the same time saw the fear in her eyes as she realized she could no longer control me. Another time, my dad did something that I deemed unjust. I decided to ignore him, only saying "Yes, sir" and "No, sir" in communication. I kept up this twisted disrespect for days, stubbornly driving a wedge between my father and me. It broke my mom's heart.

One day my mom came to me in tears. "Stevie, you are tearing this family apart," she said. "You cannot continue to treat Dad like this." I simply replied that I did not have to talk to Dad if I didn't want to.

Now, sitting in class and considering my sin, I started to see the awful pain I had caused my parents. I would return home and ask their forgiveness with a heavy and contrite heart.

Back at the house, my parents and I talked and cried together. The prodigal son had returned home. We wept together for a long time, and through that, something deep happened. God was helping me take steps to overcome my rebellious and independent nature. There would be much more to come.

My life was now being completely changed, the fruit of becoming a follower of Jesus immediately evident. I became a voracious reader, devouring books and taking my studies seriously. I went from being on academic probation and just scraping by to being on the dean's list or honor roll. This heart change also saved my relationship with Marie. We had agreed to see other people while we were at different universities. Marie had met a Southern Baptist guy who had pursued her and convinced her to go out with him. He was a musician who loved the Lord and wanted to be in full-time ministry when he graduated. One night he even went over to Marie's house with a stool and his guitar to serenade her. This was serious competition, and because of the life I had been living, he was causing Marie to think about what she wanted for her future. Marie and I loved each other, but she knew that she could not be married to someone who was living a life without values, purpose, direction, or God. The Lord used that young man to challenge Marie's faith and encourage her toward a deeper and more intimate walk with Him. And once God had my attention, Marie became convinced that I was still the man she wanted to marry.

About this time my older brothers, Ron and David, and their wives, Sheila and Pam, were attending a First Assembly Sunday-school class for newlyweds. Marie and I started attending the group even though we were not yet engaged. We could see the couples' own peer group deeply impacting their lives. The group laughed a lot, had fun together, studied Scripture, prayed for one another, and talked about serious issues and subjects affecting their lives. Marie and I were quickly challenged in our faith. God was teaching us what love looked like and about openness and communication and putting the Lord first in our relationship.

After two years in college, Marie's summer job at Memphis Light, Gas and Water turned into a permanent one. Marie stayed on to work rather than return to school. I knew marriage was the next step for us, but after reading Paul's writings in the New Testament, I had questions, particularly regarding the issue of being single or married and serving God. I didn't know what was best for us. I was also reticent in making a commitment to Marie, since a few friends had married straight out of high school and were already divorced. I wanted to take time to make sure marriage was the right decision, but I was getting pressure from every side of my family to ask her to be my wife.

"When are you going to ask that girl to marry you?" my exasperated mother asked.

Eventually I put a halt to the use of the word *marriage* among my family—it was a closed subject. That stake in the ground helped me make my own decision. It took only a few more months before I was ready to ask for Marie's hand, although the way I did it was far short of memorable.

Marie and I were driving down Frayser Boulevard, singing along with the radio.

"How about October?" I suddenly asked out of the blue.

"For what?" Marie replied, turning to me with a confused expression.

"To get married," I said as if it were obvious.

"What about June?" she said, trying to hide her disappointment at the casual way I had asked.

That was it. No thoughtful proposal, romantic venue, or flowers. It was not making the memory that we had often talked about. As you can imagine, it would take a long time for me to live that one down. I have counseled many young men not to follow my proposal model but to make a memory that will be fun and romantic and will bring great joy as the story is retold . . . and it *will* be retold again and again!

Marie and I agreed on plain wedding bands. We were two twenty-year-olds with very little to our names, but that didn't matter. After I asked Marie's dad for his daughter's hand in marriage, he handed her a savings account book. As he sensed our relationship becoming serious, he had opened an account for his daughter. It held $500 for us to spend on the wedding.

Our wedding day of August 14, 1971, was beautiful. The ceremony was held in West Frayser Baptist Church, where I, Gary Stephen, married Delores Marie. (In the south, people are often called by both first and second names.) After the ceremony we spent the night at one of the nicest hotels in Memphis, the Rivermont Hotel, overlooking the Mississippi River. When we were dating, we used to sit on a nearby park bench, longingly dreaming of spending our wedding night there. Our dream had come true.

Usually wedding pranks involve a car. Because we wanted to avoid anyone messing with my golden lime Javelin, I had made a plan before arriving at the hotel. My dad's workplace was a few miles from the Rivermont Hotel, and Dad had parked my Javelin there for safekeeping. We would use his car to leave the wedding and then exchange it for the Javelin afterward. Somehow the word got out. Marie's older brother Thomas had driven a long way for this wedding and planned some fun at his sister's expense. He found the Javelin and maneuvered the frame onto small blocks so that the wheels were off the ground. Marie and I arrived at the parking lot, got in the car, and thought we had fooled everyone. I gave my new bride a kiss, started the engine, and put the car in gear. Nothing happened—except the spinning of wheels!

"What's wrong?" Marie asked as I got out of the Javelin to see what was going on. I could hear Thomas laughing as he sat in his car a few yards away. Then promptly, after he had seen his little sister's face, he moved the car off the blocks, and we were off for our honeymoon.

After our time at the hotel, we spent three days in Branson, Missouri, in the foothills of the Ozark Mountains, before returning home. Marie supported me through two more years of college, where I studied radio, TV, and film, with a minor in journalism.

Just three months into our marriage we were hit with the sadness and grief of the death of Marie's father. He was only fifty-nine, but we were thankful that he had seen us married. Happy Bentley, or Hap, as he was called, had survived a heart attack when Marie was three. Another attack came a few months before our wedding, and Hap recovered from that one. The third and fatal one came on November 15, 1971. Happy had lived up to his name: he was loved by all who knew him. His death left a deep hole in Marie's heart.

Despite the sadness of losing Hap, our first months of marriage were exciting, and we sensed that God had something special for us. It didn't take long to find out what that was.

"CAROL BOYD IS back, and we're having a baby shower for her at the church. Can you come?" my mom asked Marie one Sunday about five months into our marriage. Carol Herzog had grown up at First Assembly. She had attended college in Memphis and then in California, where on the first day of registration she had met David Boyd. The couple had returned to Memphis for a short visit to introduce their six-week-old daughter, Gretchen, to Carol's family. Marie agreed to attend, and I agreed to play basketball with David while the women showered his wife with gifts. It was at this gathering that Marie realized Gretchen was born on the same day Hap had died, which created a strong emotional connection as she remembered the verse "The Lord has given; the Lord has taken; bless the Lord's name" (Job 1:21).

Grabbing the ball, David and I headed for the basketball court. He told me that he and Carol had joined an organization called Youth With A Mission (YWAM) after hearing YWAM leader Floyd McClung speak in California. YWAM was a short-term volunteer organization led by an international council. It had twenty bases of operation and three training schools in the United States, Europe, and Asia/Pacific. The couple had had no intention of moving, but when a YWAM staff member made a special effort to deliver the organization's first brochure to their home, they realized God was calling them to Europe. They had completed two years of service, helping to establish YWAM Germany.

David was a talented and competitive basketball player. I immediately liked him. After we ran around the court, shooting baskets and having fun, we talked more about faith, missions, and hearing God's voice.

"What? You mean God speaks?" I asked, incredulous.

"Sure He does. You just have to learn to listen."

This began a whole new way of walking in and living by faith. We were eager to have the Boyds over for dinner as often as we could to hear their stories of encouragement. They were in love with each other and with God. I was afraid that we monopolized their time, spending hours and hours with them. The more time Marie and I spent with David and Carol, the more our world was opened. They told us about teaching tapes and other books and resources from missionary leaders—Loren Cunningham from America and Winkie Pratney and Joy Dawson from New Zealand. The Boyds' faith was so real to them, affecting everything they did. We hungered for the same.

As their time in Memphis came to an end, David told us what was next. "We are going back to Europe to prepare for the summer Olympic Games in Munich to host hundreds of young people to practically share their faith. Why don't you guys come?" he asked one night at the dinner table.

"We'll pray about it," I said, looking at Marie for her reaction. I could tell that she was indeed open and willing to pray about it but that her mind was wondering how it could possibly work.

We ended up not going to Munich, but we corresponded with David and Carol when they returned to Europe and soon became even closer friends with them. Two things about the couple captivated Marie. First, Carol wasn't just enduring alongside David and the call to missions. She was called just as much as he was and loved the work the same as he did. Marie was also struck by the Boyds' generous hearts and the sacrificial way they gave. They never asked for money, even though we found out later they had very little support and trusted God to provide their needs. One time we sent them $75, quite a lot for us at the time, since we were living on one salary plus occasional part-time jobs. They wrote back right away in total amazement—it was the exact amount they had been praying for, and it had arrived on the exact day they needed it. How puzzling to us, yet encouraging, to hear that we were used by God without even knowing it.

We were taking small steps but had not yet fully learned how to listen and to hear from God. At the same time, we had been deciding whether to be involved in the outreach ministry at the Munich Olympics. It would be a costly venture, for which we did not have the finances, and Marie would have to take unpaid leave from work. Despite this, we were open about going. When David was in Memphis again, we talked to and prayed with him about this. I had a sense that we were not supposed to go, and Psalm 138:8 came to Marie's mind: "Don't let go of what your hands have made." We were both surprised that on this, the first time we asked God for specific direction, the answer seemed to be no. Yet David in his wisdom felt confirmation that indeed we had heard from God. Our decision was now made. Instead of going, we raised awareness for the Olympic outreach and encouraged people to pray.

Prayer turned out to be very important, because a horrendous event occurred at the Olympics that summer. Eleven members of the Israeli Olympic team, along with a German police officer, were taken hostage and killed by the Palestinian group Black September. We were concerned for everyone involved in Munich, including our friends on outreach, and we knew this incident would affect all that they were doing. We learned later that this Munich outreach was historic. Palestinians were asking forgiveness of Israelis, and Israelis were offering forgiveness to Arabs. Thousands of Christians from more than fifty nations marched for peace, distributing long-stem roses (provided by the city authorities) to people on the streets. This led to many conversations about what the YWAM group were doing. The Olympic outreaches continue to this day.

This practice of hearing from God was interesting and encouraging. We found God was slowly drawing us toward missions, but we didn't know what it would look like. I was actually thinking about it more than I was communicating to Marie. One Wednesday night I announced to the church that God had called us to serve Him in other lands. Marie and my family were all sitting next to me in the pew. As I spoke, the family looked at Marie with wide eyes.

"Why didn't you tell us?" our sister-in-law Pam mouthed to Marie.

"I didn't know!" Marie whispered back, shrugging her shoulders.

I had to eat humble pie later that day and ask Marie to forgive me for making the announcement without talking to her first. These were early days of my learning to plan and to work with Marie as a couple.

THREE

Hearing God's Voice

My entire journey comes down to a series of unplanned promptings from heaven that have charted a course for my life even I never could have foreseen.
—Bill Hybels, *The Power of a Whisper*

MY HEART WAS in the right place in wanting God's best, but I really didn't have a clue about sharing my faith. As I approached college graduation in August 1973, my involvement in campus outreach consisted mostly of distributing tracts or getting into conversations about dos and don'ts from the Bible. One day when David Boyd was visiting Memphis, I asked him to come with me for some campus outreach.

"How do you speak about your faith in Germany?" I asked, eager to be given new ideas or tools.

"We just pray and ask God to lead us to who He has prepared for us to speak to," he said matter-of-factly.

Since I wasn't sure what that meant, I asked David to lead and told him I would be the silent prayer partner. We arrived on campus and began to pray in a spot in the center of the university as students milled around.

"You see that guy over on that wall? I think God said to go and talk to him," David said, pointing to a young man with brown hair.

It all sounded a bit strange to me, but I tried to act casual, as if I was totally comfortable with what he was suggesting.

"Okay, I'm with you. I'll pray and you lead," I said, having no idea what was about to happen. We walked over to the student, and David greeted him.

"Hey, man, what's happening?" David said, striking up a natural conversation.

We were chatting when suddenly the guy became suspicious.

"Did my mother send you two to speak to me?" he asked.

"No, not at all. Why?" I said.

"I had a conversation with her this morning. She was concerned about my spiritual well-being. She told me she was going to pray for God to bring someone to talk to me today, and now you two are here. That's weird."

I was about to faint from shock.

"Okay. Well, how is your spiritual life?" David asked, following up from what the guy had said. The student opened up to us and shared some things he was struggling with and asked us to pray for him.

The encounter left me walking on air. It had been so normal and easy to hear from God and to share in a relaxed, natural way.

"Where did you learn how to do this?" I asked David excitedly.

David went on to talk about the YWAM School of Evangelism (much of this course is now taught in the present-day Discipleship Training School, or DTS), a place to learn about hearing God's voice, understanding His character, and sharing His heart.

Even though Marie and I had grown up in the church, we both recognized our need for more training, input, and spiritual depth. Because I had majored in radio, TV, and film in college, we wondered if our future involved media and missions. But first we wanted to go deeper spiritually. The School of Evangelism (SOE) was just what we needed.

After all our talk about missions, however, Marie had some doubts. She wondered whether I had married the wrong woman since she was gifted practically as an administrative type and wasn't a nurse, a musician, or even a teacher—the only professions she thought would be useful on the mission field. "How will I be of any use?" she worried to herself.

Marie told no one this secret concern. She was shocked, then, while listening to David speak one Sunday at our church. David spoke about how God wants to use *everyone*—dentists, cooks, drivers, preachers, musicians, and more.

"God also needs secretaries, administrators, and accountants on the mission field," David said, seeming to look straight at Marie.

Marie knew it was God speaking to her heart. She knew she was the right wife for me and that God had a job for her as well.

We sent off an SOE application and were accepted for the eight months of training. When David told Loren Cunningham, the founder of YWAM, about my background and that we were coming, Loren wrote us a letter describing his vision for how media and missions fit together. Loren's vision sounded interesting, but at this point we didn't see the big picture. We were only making a commitment to an eight-month school.

The biggest sacrifice in preparing for the trip was selling my Javelin sports car to pay for our tuition and travel. Thankfully we were not in debt from college. I had received a disability scholarship because of my accident, and that helped pay college fees. (Even though I was able to play sports, because of my disability—scarring on my right leg and internal injuries from my accident—the army had rejected me when I was called up to serve in Vietnam.)

As we were moving ahead toward the SOE, confusion arose. Out of the blue Christian Broadcasting Network (CBN), located in Virginia Beach, Virginia, offered me a job with a great salary and benefits. My family was overjoyed, and it seemed like an easy decision for me to take this job rather than serve in YWAM with no salary, no benefits, and no retirement. Marie and I were confused.

I called David for counsel. When I told him about the dream job offer, he burst out laughing—so loud and hard that he couldn't stop.

"David, this is not funny. Why are you laughing? What do I do?" I asked, exasperated.

When David calmed down, he told me that something similar had happened to him when he made a commitment to obey the call of God to missions. "Every word of the Lord is tested," he said. "So you need to know what God has said to you."

We knew God was telling us to go to SOE, and when we realized that this job offer was a test, I happily wrote back to CBN declining it. I felt as light as a feather.

We were twenty-three years old, and because we had traveled only west to Texas and south to Florida, packing for nine months in Europe was a serious challenge. Our friend Julie, who had lived in Austria for two years with her husband, came to our rescue. She came into the bedroom of my parents' home, where we had moved after selling everything we owned. She saw the suitcases Marie had spread open on the bed and asked what she had chosen to take. Marie innocently pointed to the closet and Julie said, "Marie, you can't take all of that!" There came a rude awakening that we would be living out of a suitcase, not a closet. Julie was a godsend in giving us radical orientation to this new season of life. Forty years and many international trips later, we still laugh about that day. We had so much to learn.

We set off for Lausanne, Switzerland, where the school was starting on December 30, 1973. We flew first to New York, where my brother Ron and his wife had moved three months earlier. After our visit, we caught an Icelandic Air flight to Luxembourg, the cheapest flight to Europe. Marie and I were feeling a little apprehensive. This was our first flight outside the United States. God encouraged us from Joshua 1:3–8:

> I will give you every place where you set your foot, as I promised Moses. . . . No one will be able to stand against you all the days of your life. As I was with Moses, so I will be with you; I will never leave you nor forsake you. Be strong and courageous, because you will lead these people to inherit the land I swore to their ancestors to give them. Be strong and very courageous. Be careful to obey all the law my servant Moses gave you; do not turn from it to the right or to the left, that you may be successful wherever you go. Keep this

Book of the Law always on your lips; meditate on it day and night, so that you may be careful to do everything written in it. Then you will be prosperous and successful.

The plane headed to Luxembourg, but inclement weather and lack of radar for the conditions diverted it to Brussels. By the time we landed, we had missed our train to Switzerland and had to wait hours for the next one. It was the first time either of us had ridden a train. All I knew about trains in Europe was what I had read in a book by Corrie ten Boom about World War II—how trains were used to take people to concentration camps. This image was still quite vivid in my mind. Marie and I found our cabin and promptly fell asleep, but minutes later we were awakened by an impatient ticket collector. I was in such a delirium that it took a while to understand what he was saying. Not knowing about jet lag or its effect on the body and mind, a part of me thought we were on our way to the concentration camps. Our international travel adventures had begun!

FOUR

Whole Hearts for Ministry

Christ calls us to be His partners in changing our world, just as He called the Twelve to change their world two thousand years ago.

—RICHARD STEARNS, *The Hole in Our Gospel*

THE LAUSANNE YWAM BASE was called École La Forêt at Chalet-à-Gobet and was in the French-speaking part of Switzerland. About seventy-five students and staff were taking part in the SOE, which included a three-month lecture phase, a three-month Europe and Middle East field trip, and a Summer of Service (SOS) for two months. Loren Cunningham, YWAM's founder, was leading the school.

Much of what we learned in the first few weeks was new informa-tion about pursuing God with a whole heart. Marie and I had gone to church all our lives, sitting through services, eating lunch with fam-ily and friends, and then getting on with our week. We loved God and tried to apply biblical principles and teaching to our everyday life. Now we were learning about personal devotion, spending regular time with God, and practical repentance. We also learned from incredible men and women of God about various worldviews, including their presuppositions and influences on society.

The lectures were life changing. After each lecture, before going to lunch, we would pray and wait on God for what He was personally telling us. Marie and I skipped many lunches, often in tears of repentance, as God was dealing with us and helping us to change our thinking. We thought we were good people; we hadn't turned to crime or drugs. But God wanted to deal with us about the little things—the heart attitudes. However, His love came through loud and clear. His encouragement and affirmation to us was foundational to all that we were hearing and learning.

The staff began teaching us about intercession. We were soon praying together for nations around the world, our faith growing in the understanding that our prayers could actually make a difference and change nations. We were praying for such things as the international peace talks taking place in Paris between America and Vietnam, and for people, situations, and countries we had never heard of.

During the SOE lecture phase, teachers would share insights about humility, rebellion, and independence. Teacher Joy Dawson spoke about there being no differentiation of sin and pointed out that delayed obedience was still disobedience. I learned that rebellion was also sin. Satan was the first rebel, and I wanted nothing to do with continued rebellion or independence.

This school was also a lot of fun, and we experienced lighter moments in our time in Lausanne. During the second week, Loren Cunningham spoke on the topic "relinquishing your rights." Somkiat Kittipongse, the first Thai man to attend an SOE, was in our school. Because he had not been in a total English-speaking environment before, sometimes things were lost in translation. He was struggling with the cold weather in Switzerland, having come from the tropics to a snowy winter in the Alps. He also missed rice, which at home he would have had three times a day. In Lausanne he was lucky to have a brown rice equivalent once a week, if at all.

Somkiat sat through Loren's lecture with a glum expression on his face. It was obvious that something Loren said had hit him hard. The message was dynamic, and many of us were weeping as we laid everything before God. Slowly Somkiat got to his knees and prayed. A few of the students had offered to go over recorded tapes of the lectures with him to make sure he understood everything that was taught. It was only then, a few days later, that they realized Somkiat had thought Loren was teaching on "relinquishing your *rice*." He had been surprised at the topic, but he knew if that was what God was asking of him, that was what he would do.

Our lecture phase included opportunities for small outreaches before we embarked on a larger one. We heard that Maharishi Mahesh Yogi, the founder of Transcendental Meditation (TM), was speaking nearby at the University of Lausanne. Half the students were assigned to attend the lecture and silently pray and speak with people in the hall. The other half would stay at Chalet-à-Gobet asking God how they were to pray for this event.

Marie and I were part of the group that went to the university. The hall was packed with a few hundred people, all having heard of the reputation of the speaker and his ability to levitate (at that time TMers believed they could fly—more like hop—in the lotus position). At first the speaker showed a rather boring film, but the projector broke down fifteen minutes into it, causing some confusion. A lot of people left at that point.

"I feel some spiritual activity going on that does not want us to succeed," the yogi complained as he finished the evening ahead of schedule. We were then able to chat with the people who remained. Marie and I shared our faith with a man named Robert and with the woman who had organized the event. When we got back to the chalet, we told everyone what had happened.

"That is amazing," one of the women remarked. She showed us a list of what they had prayed for. The students had prayed that the film would not work and that there would be confusion in the room. They had also felt they should pray for a man named Robert and a woman wearing a large necklace. We told the students that the woman who organized the event wore a large necklace and that we had spoken with her. All the students were encouraged by how exact God had been in showing them how to pray and how to listen.

Our time at the school deeply impacted every area of our lives. At the end of the lecture phase we set out on our field trip, driving through Europe, the Middle East, and Eastern Europe. Mark Spengler, our trip leader, appointed me and a friend named Tom Bloomer as student leaders. We were traveling on a fifty-seat bus, followed by a van and a food truck, which transported tents, sleeping gear, and provisions. We camped together for the entire trip except in Germany, where it was so cold that the plastic of our tents froze and the single women had to spend the night in a chapel. Because Tom and I were busy leading the group, Marie and Cynthia (Tom's wife) learned to set up tents like professionals, though at times a couple of the single guys came to their rescue!

Our trip through Europe included praying together, hearing reports on the different countries we were driving through, and speaking to the people in the places we stayed. We learned about the Catholic world and the life of Paul in Italy, the Orthodox world and the early church in Greece, the Judaic world and the life of Jesus in Israel, the Muslim world and history in Egypt, and Turkey and the communist world in Eastern Europe. Moving to a new location every day was exciting yet challenging. The strain of putting up and taking down tents came to a head for Marie and me when we arrived at Masada, a site of ancient palaces and fortifications overlooking the Dead Sea in Israel. Arriving too late to secure a campsite, all we could do was pump up our air mattresses and stretch out on our sleeping bags in a local car park. There happened to be a party that night, and we got no sleep thanks to drunken people wandering through the parking lot, laughing and shouting. Marie and I kept all our valuables between us and pulled our sleeping bag over our heads. We had been traveling all day and were tired and overheated, and now this noise was preventing adequate sleep.

"I am not made to live like this, and I am not going to live like this," Marie hissed angrily under the covers. I tried to soothe her, but there was nothing much I could say. Traveling in tents had taught us how to have arguments very quietly, and in a situation like this, there were not too many good responses or easy answers to give her.

A hike up Masada before dawn was planned for the next day. Some chose not to make the climb, Marie included. In fact, she informed me that she might not even be there when I returned. She was pretty upset.

I had confidence she wouldn't go too far, since we didn't have much money, but after climbing Masada at 5:00 a.m., I raced down quickly to see if she was still there. Our leader's wife, Eva, had spent some time with Marie talking and praying through issues that were on her heart.

The hardest thing for Marie in joining YWAM was giving up her rights to what was "normal." Normal was not living in tents and traveling on a bus through ten countries with a hundred other people. Though this was a short-term outreach for some, Marie sensed the calling of God to something longer and was struggling with what form that would take. To this southern belle, normal was a house with a white picket fence and lots of children—this was what Marie had dreamed of all her life. Her parents had not traveled far in their lives (and neither had mine, apart from military service). Her mom always did the laundry, grocery shopping, and the ironing on specific days each week. Life was predictable, safe, and centered around family.

Our life was now not predictable, not safe, and we were far from our families. The one thing we both knew was that soon we would have children—something normal—which would help make up for the brothers, sisters, nephews, and nieces that we missed back home. Marie and I had already picked out names, and it was just a matter of time before we would have two or three little Goodes running around—or so we thought.

At the beginning of the Summer of Service I became sick. We had just returned to Germany when I started to have excruciating pain. We were with David and Carol Boyd, and when I described the symptoms, they recognized them right away.

"That sounds like epididymitis. It's worse than a bladder infection. I was in the hospital for that a month ago," David said.

I groaned, thinking he was taking this mentoring a step too far.

Marie and I found a doctor who confirmed David's diagnosis. Epididymitis involves inflammation, and it can also be associated with urinary tract infection. I took antibiotics and waited for the pain to subside. I also felt God speak to me through this difficult time, telling me this trial was preparation for future suffering—suffering that might help me understand and minister to the challenges of others.

Carol knew how serious my condition could be, since the doctor had told her and David that the infection could lead to sterility. (For them it did not; in fact, they chose us as godparents for their children, Gretchen, Aaron, and Jon Marc.) We were on a tight schedule, and all we could do was pray, but in the meantime, we would be traveling with the school to Holland. I was able to partially lie down on the backseat of the bus and try to cope with the pain. I was given bottles to empty my bladder, but as the miles went by, the pain increased and I realized I was getting worse. My urine was white and cloudy, indicating serious infection. The antibiotics weren't working.

After what seemed like a lifetime, we arrived at a campground in the Netherlands, and I was able to stretch out in our tent. At the same time, we received a telex (a modern telegram) from Loren inviting us to Lausanne for the first International Congress on World Evangelization, headed up by Billy Graham. I was asked to be a cameraman. I couldn't even think about walking, much less traveling and working. I was in agony, my body was swollen with infection, and my face was ashen. The pain was unbearable, and Marie and I prayed to God for mercy. It was pouring rain. After a long, sleepless night, Marie went to our school outreach leader, Mark Spengler, and told him I had to get to a hospital.

We arrived at the nearest emergency ward, Marie sighing with relief that I was somewhere dry and clean and was receiving proper medical treatment. It was a weight off her shoulders. Slowly the infection was brought under control by a change of antibiotics, but the doctors thought that scar tissue from the accident when I was fourteen was blocking urine—the true cause of the infection.

With the help of a new antibiotic I recovered enough to work at the Congress on World Evangelization. There, Marie and I heard about "unreached peoples" for the first time and signed the Lausanne Covenant, committing ourselves to concrete and sacrificial action. Point five of that covenant, Christian Social Responsibility, was particularly important for us: "God's concern throughout society for justice and reconciliation and liberation of men and women from every form of oppression." We decided to start praying regularly for two of the poorest countries in the world with very few believers—Afghanistan and Nepal.

When the congress finished, we were tempted to return to the United States. The combination of sickness, fatigue, and twinges of homesickness were making a strong case. However, when we prayed, we felt that we were to complete our two-month Summer of Service. We headed to Germany and worked at a US military base near the Czechoslovakian border with YWAMers Tom and Terry Bragg (who later pioneered YWAM Publishing). When the summer was finished, we began our journey back to Memphis. On our way home, I became sick again and was in serious pain by the time we landed.

My brother Ron arranged an appointment with a urology specialist, Dr. Dale. I was told I needed a two-part surgery to reroute my urine and remove serious scar tissue that had formed like concrete inside of me. The first surgery would take place immediately, the second in four to six months. These were the first surgeries of their type in Memphis. A challenge, yes, but we had an even bigger one before us—no insurance and no money to pay medical bills. This was our first major test of faith and finances. We prayed for God to provide, and upon hearing what we were doing, Dr. Dale provided his services for free. But we still needed to cover the remaining hospital bills.

I remember well coming out of surgery. When Marie saw my pallid face, she nearly fainted and had to sit in the corner with her head between her knees.

"Where's Marie?" I asked my dad through the pain.

"She's here, son."

Marie had never seen anyone come out of surgery and was shocked at the sight of me.

It took me a few weeks to slowly regain my strength. We began to seek the Lord for whatever was next. The doctor told us the surgery might have affected our ability to have children. All we could do was wait and see.

While I was recovering from the first surgery, God was speaking to us about the next thing—continuing with YWAM and returning to Lausanne and on to South Africa—but we didn't want to leave in debt. We had outstanding hospital bills and needed air tickets.

"Lord, if we are going to serve You with our lives, we need to know now that You will provide. We don't want to leave the States while in debt," Marie and I prayed earnestly. Eventually we believed we were to move in faith and make preparations for the trip.

We did not feel that we were to publicly speak of our need but believed we were to trust God to bring in the funds. As people asked, we would explain what we felt God was showing for our next step. We were blessed to see our family and friends come together and offer money to help pay the medical bills, and then my parents gave us money for our airfare to Johannesburg. It was hard for us to receive from them because we were now an independent family and because we didn't want to be a burden to them. We had specific ideas of how we thought God should provide. After we prayed, the Lord spoke clearly about not discouraging those who wanted to give to us, especially those close to us. We realized that blessings would come to those who gave, so why would we deny those blessings to our own family?

In the end, it was difficult for loved ones to see us leave while I was going through so much physically. But they never stood in the way of what we thought God was saying to us. Instead, they did everything they could to encourage us to be obedient.

We had been attending our First Assembly Sunday-school class during this time at home, and Fred and Becky Morgan, the leaders of the class, had an offering taken for us on the last Sunday before we headed back overseas. Those in the class were very generous, and what they gave covered the outstanding hospital bills, except for $138 for an anesthesiologist bill.

We were flying out to New York in a few days to stay with Ron and Sheila before catching our onward flight. We boarded the plane, praying for God to provide the final amount needed. When we arrived in New York, Ron said he had arranged for us to speak at his church on Wednesday night and hoped we didn't mind. We were happy to speak. We talked about the ways God had led us and told some of the stories from our SOE travels. At the end of the evening the church took an offering for us. We nearly cried when we saw the amount: exactly $138. We left the States the next day debt-free. God had said He would provide for us, and He was faithful to His promise.

The Greatest Commandment

A chastity, or honesty, or mercy, which yields to danger will be chaste or honest or merciful only on conditions. Pilate was merciful till it became risky.

—C. S. Lewis, *The Screwtape Letters*

WE HAD BEEN BACK in Lausanne only four days before we flew to South Africa to work with YWAM South Africa, traveling all over the country with Don Stephens, the YWAM director for Europe, the Middle East, and Africa. Marie and I were the technical team for "The Last Commandment," a multimedia presentation. "The Last Commandment" had premiered at the Lausanne Congress and was quite high-tech for the time, with eight slide projectors run by a small computer and all set up for rear projection behind a nine-by-twenty-one-foot screen. The production helped create momentum for Eurofest '75 (a Great Commission convention for youth) taking place in August in Brussels.

Many were concerned about the timing of this trip so soon after surgery, but the doctor had said it was safe for me to travel. We believed that we had been given a green light by God, and we were again trying to be obedient step-by-step. It was not an easy time for my recuperation, since I couldn't lift anything heavy and had to stand back and let the rest of the team do all the physical work. Marie even had to carry the luggage. It was humbling, humiliating, and scary for the two of us, since we were concerned about stitches, infection, and not wanting to go through another bout of illness—especially in Africa, where we didn't know much about the hospitals. We completed the six-week project in good health and returned to Lausanne.

At the beginning of 1975 we were scheduled to take "The Last Commandment" to Australia and New Zealand. We traveled to England, where the equipment had arrived from South Africa, and planned to continue onward once we had purchased airline tickets. We knew this was another important step in our decision to trust God. When the time was upon us to purchase tickets, we could not see where the money would come from. We were in a YWAM England staff meeting and heard the leader explain to the group that he believed God wanted them to be part of our next mission step. This group of people were living without funds, just like us (no one in YWAM receives a salary). We were overwhelmed and humbled at their giving and encouragement to us. The tickets were purchased.

We were to travel with Loren and Darlene Cunningham to Australia and New Zealand for what Loren called the Repentance Tour. This trip had to do with the loss of a ship YWAM had tried to purchase in New Zealand called the M/V Maori, reports of which made the front pages of many newspapers down under. The ship had been obtained with a deposit donated by a British businessman, although YWAM was not able to fulfill the conditions. In the end, YWAM lost the ship, which was sold for scrap. Loren felt that the vision for a ship was still from God but that we had focused on a vessel instead of the Lord and had made a presumption regarding the timing of its release.

Loren wanted to personally ask forgiveness from the pastors in New Zealand who had supported the vision of the ship and given financially. We had a lesson in humility as we witnessed him repenting, requesting meetings, and being brokenhearted when some pastors refused to even meet with him. We learned much as we sent Loren off to these meetings and spent the time in prayer with Darlene and other members of our team. At our young age of twenty-four this was a deep life lesson of worship and trusting God in the midst of challenge, particularly when things did not turn out the way we expected, hoped for, or prayed about. We will never forget Loren's model of openness, taking responsibility for one's actions and repentance, as well as his follow-through to communicate with pastors and with the public.

For the next three months, we traveled with "The Last Commandment" in the United States with a worship group called The Family. The group had come together during our Lausanne SOE. Two couples, four single men, and a two-year-old traveled through twenty states in a van. We visited more than eighty churches, staying with families from those churches. Despite the crazy schedule, we formed lasting friendships within the group and saw many respond to the call of missions. In 1956 Loren had had a vision of waves of young people moving across the globe. YWAM was mobilizing young people into missions who were international and interdenominational at a time when very few mission agencies were doing this.

When our commitment with "The Last Commandment" finished, we returned to Memphis for my second surgery. The surgery went well, and I had a portable catheter for two weeks without incident. Dr. Dale arranged the surgery at the city hospital, where the fees were minimal, and he again gave us his services at no cost. I then had several medical tests, which showed that there still seemed to be a blockage. Dr. Dale said more surgery would be needed, but not for another year, since my body was traumatized and needed a break.

As we rested, we sought the Lord for our next step. We received two invitations: to continue with YWAM USA and to return to Switzerland and work with Don Stephens in the training schools in Lausanne.

We returned to Lausanne in the autumn of 1975 to study French. Our meager efforts were a great source of amusement to the French SOE students there. Our teacher was clothed in amazing patience and had a great sense of humor. She did lose it with laughter the day I tried to describe a traffic jam and called it un traffic confiture (traffic jelly).

I will forever be famous for this. The language school was responsible in November for performing a skit for the French SOE explaining the meaning of Thanksgiving. It all had to be done in French after about only seven weeks of study. Those poor students are probably still wondering what American Thanksgiving is all about.

My other jobs amounted to being a gopher (as in "go for"—someone who runs errands), filling in the gaps and running around after everyone. I really wanted to work with Don, who had taken over from Loren as leader of the Lausanne base. I respected Don as a man of God and was eager to work with him and to be mentored and coached by him. Instead, my first job was to repair the cement wall of the annex to the chalet where we all lived. I had no idea what I was doing and was working alone. Because the building's stonework was crumbling, what were once hairline cracks soon became gaping holes as I chipped away with my hammer.

"Lord Jesus, I didn't come here to rebuild this building!" I said out loud, as I let out my aggression on the cement wall.

My dear wife meanwhile was privileged to spend lots of time with Don, since she had become his personal assistant in his role of YWAM director of Europe, the Middle East, and Africa. I had to choose to rejoice with her and try to learn what God was teaching me as I worked on the wall of the annex.

God taught me many lessons in humility and serving, and in the process we both became very close to Don and his wife, Deyon, who also introduced us to a couple with whom we ended up spending a lot of time—Merryl and Pierre Christen. Merryl was from Australia and had been a spiritual medium. She was invited to a Bible study at the Christian Women's group in Lausanne. She went along and saw a table full of books to borrow. She picked up one called *The Screwtape Letters* by C. S. Lewis and took it home with her. Merryl was changed simply by reading the book.

"I am serving Screwtape!" Merryl exclaimed in horror to her friend, referring to the devil character in the book. She soon gave her life to the Lord, but her husband, Pierre, was not too happy about it. He was Swiss, and the couple had married after meeting in Canada. Pierre had been married before and was fourteen years older than his new wife. He liked the fact that Merryl was a medium because he felt that it gave him some sort of power and insight into his business and connections in Central Asia. He was a high-powered businessman with many contacts. He always had a deal going somewhere and was now working on selling chalets to the Iranian royal family.

One evening while Don was traveling, Deyon invited us to dinner to meet the Christens. We had prayed beforehand that Pierre would be touched and come to know Jesus, just as his wife had done about six months before. When I met Pierre, I realized it wasn't going to happen as quickly for him as it had for Merryl.

Pierre cut right through the conversation about faith and questioned, "How can you believe Jesus is God? How can you believe the Bible is the Word of God? It is ridiculous to think blood can bring the forgiveness of sin!" he exclaimed.

Week by week I would meet with Pierre, trying to answer his questions, explaining why and what we believed. He was a fiery man, raising questions every time we met, but I learned to love him and listen to him. He had some sort of joy refuting faith in God by showing me his books on spiritualism, the Qur'an, eastern religions, and the occult—anything that was not about Jesus. At this point he wanted relationship with God only if God could get him out of trouble financially and sell his chalets.

Merryl told us later what had happened to Pierre. One night Pierre was particularly enraged in a conversation with her and their daughter. He went on a tirade for thirty minutes, mad and frustrated at everyone and furious about everything he had been hearing from Don and me about faith in Jesus and what it meant to become a follower.

Merryl was at a loss but simply sent up a quick "Help me, Lord" prayer. She then asked Pierre, "Are you finished?"

When he answered that he was, she went on to point out to him that everything in his life was falling apart: their housing situation was disastrous, his job was going badly, relationships with his children were not good, and their marriage was strained. She then asked him, "Can you give me a good reason for refusing to accept what you heard from Don and Steve about faith in the Lord, seeing that everything in your life is a complete mess?"

Pierre paused for a moment and said, "All right, I'll give God a month." He went to the phone and called me, telling me that he had given God a month but that if nothing changed, he would go back to his own beliefs. He asked me what was the next step, and I told him to get all his occult books out of the house immediately. Pierre thought I was crazy, but with Merryl that evening he put as many occult books as he could find into a box and out into the garden shed.

Don and I kept meeting with Pierre, and by the end of the month Pierre had invited Jesus Christ into his heart. His life was radically changed forever, although it was not all smooth sailing. Pierre traveled an arduous, sometimes rocky journey, since he had much to deal with because of his many investigations into eastern religions and occult practices. Nonetheless, once he had understood who his real enemy was, the multiple burning sessions of books and other valuables and getting rid of objects and pictures that held occult motifs followed, until the house was cleared and free to be used for God. Pierre had been radical in his opposition to Jesus but was now just as radical in his pursuit of God.

God brought Pierre to faith and discipleship using all of us in different ways. The last time we saw Pierre was in September 2009 in Switzerland as we celebrated YWAM Lausanne's fortieth anniversary, just before he died from cancer in 2010. Merryl wrote to us, saying, "Pierre was a rebel heavyweight and needed a young lion who could roar just like him but who had the gentleness of a lamb and could reach right into his little boy's hurting heart and prepare it to open up to the Lord Jesus. And you did. Wonderfully. Thank you for being the willing tool in God's hand to bring another prodigal home. You know how dearly Pierre loved you for it."

During the time Marie and I were learning French, I started working for the media arm of YWAM, later called ProclaMedia Productions. At first this was very practical, mundane work—sitting for hours through lectures, taping the speakers at our training schools on audio or video. But it also meant that I had a front-row seat on great teaching. For example, we were asked to videotape ten hours of Corrie ten Boom's talks. Corrie had survived a WWII concentration camp and was a wonderful woman of God. Marie and I had read her books and seen

The Hiding Place movie and could not believe that she was at the chalet with us. We spent a beautiful Swiss summer week, and we would have our midday meals on the front lawn, enjoying the view of the Swiss Alps, listening to the sound of the Swiss cowbells from the farm across the street while enthralled with the conversation of Tante Corrie in her strong Dutch accent. Corrie very humbly asked me to pray for her before she spoke one day on the subject of forgiveness. I was blown away, just a young man from Memphis, who was trying to follow God step-by-step, being asked to pray for this incredible woman. The only thing that I remember about that prayer is that I held her hand.

Corrie went on to tell the story of how God had asked her to forgive the guard who was responsible for her sister's death in the camp when she had met him at a conference in Germany. She had struggled with this as the guard held out his hand for her to shake. Yet when she heard the quiet voice of the Lord say, "Forgive him for My sake," she was able to reach out and shake his hand. Forgiveness brought great freedom, and Corrie ten Boom taught powerfully around the world on this subject.

Another event on our agenda became the 1976 Summer Olympic Games outreach in Montreal, Quebec. As the gopher I had been given the task of arranging transport. This was no easy feat since we believed that one thousand young people from the UK, Germany, Denmark, France, Slavic countries, India, Finland, Norway, South Africa, and Egypt would attend. In the end I had to charter two large airplanes, negotiating contracts with the various airlines. It was a huge job, made trickier by the fact that we did not have any money.

One day I had a meeting with four officials from Pan Am Airways. They looked at me, an inexperienced twenty-five-year old, with strange expressions, as if they didn't believe I was serious.

One of my challenges was giving students a set ticket price. We had to pay in US dollars, which was difficult because the exchange rate was constantly changing. Finally, we thought all was settled. The first plane was a Pan Am round-trip flight from Geneva to Philadelphia, destined for a three-day conference on prayer called "If My People," an outreach for the bicentennial celebration of America's independence, and then on to the Montreal Olympics. The second plane was a Sabena Air round-trip flight from Brussels to Montreal. We were about to sign when the Pan Am executive realized a "little" mistake: the price did not include the airfare onward from Philadelphia to Montreal, an additional $44,000. We arranged to bus the group from Philadelphia to Montreal.

All of the money came in on time, along with the complexity of multiple currencies. Both planes were filled with YWAMers. The flight crew had never seen a group like this pray, give thanks, and worship, filling the cabin with a beautiful sound. They were touched to see how we treated each other.

Two thousand of us were staying about an hour outside of Montreal at the YWAM base in Dunham. With that big a group, half would stay at the base for one day and have teaching from Loren, Don, and other leaders while the other half took buses into Montreal for the outreach. For food, we all ate at a local school cafeteria made available to us during the summer break.

Our two weeks in Montreal were very successful. We prayed and talked to thousands of people about the love of Jesus and even flew hot-air balloons with "Jesus is Lord" on the side in huge letters.

One evening Marie and I were walking back to the bus after a day of outreach. Suddenly a car with a TV station logo on the side pulled up alongside us.

"Hey, do you want tickets to the high-dive event?" the driver asked.

Marie and I looked at each other.

"Let's do it!" I said, and we took the tickets.

The only problem was the hour-long journey to get back to where we were staying, and we would have no way of getting home if we missed the YWAM buses. But still, we couldn't throw away this chance. We would think about getting home later.

The event was wonderful. We had excellent seats and watched the American swim team dive its way to a gold medal. Marie had tears in her eyes as they raised the American flag and our national anthem was sung. It was the only Olympics event we went to, and it was better than we could have asked or imagined. We chatted with a Canadian couple next to us, and when the event ended at about 11:00 p.m., they asked us where we were staying and how we were getting home.

"We are staying in Dunham, and I'm not sure how we are getting home!" I replied, smiling.

The couple said they would help us out, giving us a lift part of the way back. There came a point in the road where they had to go a different direction to their home, and they left us on the highway to hitchhike the rest of the way. It was about midnight by this point, but we amazingly got another couple of rides. Marie marveled at how natural it was for her to do things like hitchhike now. A young woman from Memphis, Tennessee, would normally never dream of hitchhiking. We were definitely being changed!

We arrived back at Dunham about two o'clock in the morning, still jazzed from our experience.

"You made it back!" our friends exclaimed later in the morning.

We felt it had been a little gift from God. As we are obedient to Him, He gives us surprise treats on the side. We could never have planned having the best and most expensive tickets or seeing our country win an Olympic gold medal. It couldn't have been better.

The last week of our outreach Ron and Sheila drove up from New York to visit for a night, camping with us at the base. They were amazed and a little concerned, I think, at how we lived with the freezing cold outdoor showers and basic conditions. In the morning we went out for breakfast to catch up, and I wanted to impress them with my French language skills. "Let me order. I can order for everyone!" I said expansively. But when the waitress arrived, my brain froze and I suddenly couldn't even remember the French words for cup of coffee. "*Je voudrais une cup de coffee*," I said fast, hoping no one would pick up my mistake.

Sheila burst out laughing. "Cup de coffee? That's not French!" she said. Marie and Ron were in hysterics. I smiled sheepishly, humbled again.

After two weeks of outreach we traveled back to Lausanne with a quick detour and short break in Memphis to see family. We were both feeling fit and healthy and had begun to think seriously about starting our family. It was September 1976, and I checked in with Dr. Dale for a follow-up to my surgery from the previous year. After some testing, Dr. Dale confirmed that, medically speaking, it didn't seem possible that I would be able to produce children. We left his office devastated, but in our discouragement God spoke to us from Psalm 113:9: "God nests the once barren woman at home—now a joyful mother with children!"

Another specific scripture was given to us from Deuteronomy 7:14: "No one will be sterile or infertile." Marie wrote in her diary: "This is the first time that I have seen it say or refer specifically to man. This is the promise to the children of Israel, and we can claim it for ourselves today."

A few days later we were again praying with David, Carol, and our youth pastor from Memphis. After hearing the doctor's report, Carol was reminded of Isaiah 61:8–9: "I will . . . make with them an enduring covenant. Their offspring will be known among the nations, and their descendants among the peoples. All who see them will recognize that they are a people blessed by the Lord."

At that time we claimed the verse for our physical children, since that was the context in which we were praying. Looking back, however, it has definitely come to pass regarding spiritual children.

A few days later I received Psalm 104:30: "When you let loose your breath, they are created," and I said, "We need not worry about the medical report but will trust in the Lord because our times are in His hands."

In January 1977 we led an English-speaking SOE followed by a Middle East field trip. During the first month of the journey we ended up back at the foot of Masada, where Marie had had her meltdown. This time her attitude was completely different, and she was encouraging all the women to make the dawn trek to the top of Masada.

"Why are you so keen to do this?" one of the women asked.

"Because I dropped my axe head here, and I am going to pick it up again," smiled Marie, thinking about the scripture in 2 Kings 6:1–7, where God, through the prophet Elisha, helped a despairing man rectify a mistake. Marie wanted to return to the place where she had despaired and run up that mountain in victory, and she did.

When we got to Egypt, Mark and Eva Spengler, who headed back to Switzerland, turned the leadership of the group—ninety people—over to Marie and me. It would have been fine, apart from the fact that just after they left, I woke in the sweltering desert heat with another bout of incredible pain.

Marie nursed me as best she could. I was in agony from the pain in my lower back, and even though I needed medical help, we had to travel on by van, since we were supposed to catch a ferry early in the morning.

One of the nurses in the group gave me some pills that helped me sleep. I lay at the back of the van unaware of what was going on as everyone prayed like crazy.

Miraculously, by the time we reached the ferry, I was awake and completely fine. This happened three different times—I would suddenly be overtaken with debilitating pain, always in the middle of the night, always in an unfamiliar place where we didn't speak the language, and always when we were stepping into a major ministry time. When it happened, Marie said it was as if blackness had descended on her and she felt very alone and helpless to do anything for me. She would be frightened and would pray every prayer she could, crying out to God to save her husband. As the attacks continued, however, Marie realized what was happening—she was believing a lie from the enemy of our souls. The last time this happened she literally stomped her feet and said, "I am not alone! That is a lie. God is with me." As she did this, the blackness disappeared. Though she struggles emotionally when I suffer physically, she is careful to hang on to what is true, and that is that God is with us at all times and will never leave us, even though it seems very dark and lonely.

Back in Lausanne, God began to resurrect the vision of the ship. The M/V *Maori* was no more, but we prayed in faith that there would be another vessel. The staff in Lausanne started a twenty-four-hour prayer vigil, meeting in the sauna that doubled as a prayer room in the chalet. Months went by and Don Stephens viewed and evaluated many ships. As we prayed, we got word that a ship was available in Italy.

In early 1978, Don and YWAM leaders took a train to Italy to talk to the owners and negotiate a purchase. The ship was called the M/V *Victoria* and had been a first-class passenger ship, traveling from Venice, Italy, to Australia. It was twenty-five years old and needed extensive repairs to make it seaworthy, a task that would involve hundreds of YWAM volunteers. But for now, we excitedly awaited the news of their trip, hoping that this time, with the lessons we had learned from the failure to launch the M/V *Maori*, things would work out.

The 1978 World Cup soccer games were to be held in Argentina in June that year. Plans were made for all European YWAM training schools to come together for a major outreach in Venice, where the ship was, and then "all aboard" to sail to Argentina. In our naïveté we thought it would be that easy, like chartering the airplanes to Montreal. What we didn't take into account was that this ship hadn't moved under its own steam in quite a while, and it wasn't going to move for some time to come. We were still praying for the funds to complete the purchase of the M/V *Victoria,* but we had faith that God was in this vision and He would do it.

In April, Marie and I traveled down with our team from Lausanne to set up our tents once again, this time in Camping Jolly, an inexpensive campground outside Venice, in the industrial town of Marghera. We would stay there until it was time to leave for Argentina.

Three hundred of us from all over Europe were divided into groups according to which city in Argentina we felt we should go to. The football matches were being held in Mendoza, Córdoba, Rosario, Buenos Aires, and Mar del Plata. We had bought tents from Holland: big blue ones for the singles, smaller ones for families, and large ones for cooking. It was the Middle East field trip revisited, only staying in one location. The campground was empty apart from us, since Venice in April is rainy and cold. It wasn't too comfortable, but we began immediately organizing outreach and marches, Bible studies, intercession, and street meetings.

One of the exciting events on this outreach was bringing Colin Harbinson's theater production *Toymaker & Son* to the streets of Venice. A group was trained and started to perform the story through music and drama of Father God and Jesus, showing how sin entered the world and how Jesus came to redeem us. The venue we chose for the forty-five minute performance was outside the Venice Santa Lucia train station, the main station where travelers arrive and depart. The natural amphitheater with stairs allowed people to sit and look down on the performance. The allegory provoked many conversations from locals and tourists, and we were able to speak to people in their own languages, since we had so many different nationalities represented on our teams.

After the first month I was put in charge of our temporary camp, and Marie continued her work with Don by leading teams to make the first inventory of the ship. Volunteer work crews came aboard to scrape, sand, paint, and repair. There was no electricity, and the engines ran for only one hour in the morning and again in the evening, but the ship was fully stocked with cutlery, linens, chairs, and tables. Food was still on the griddle when we arrived on board. Those who had been on the ship previously must have left in a hurry.

The closer we got to the departure date to Argentina, the more obvious it was that the M/V *Victoria* was not going to leave Venice, not least because we still didn't own it. Some of the group left Venice to fly to Argentina, but Marie and I stayed at Camping Jolly to continue to lead the smaller outreach. From the majority of people who chose to remain, we sent teams to Greece and Turkey.

We ended up living in a tent in Camping Jolly for several months. In October 1978, Don arranged for a loan of $900,000 from Union Bank of Switzerland (UBS) to complete the purchase. Fifteen years later Don found out that the loan was made possible only because a director of UBS provided a quiet guarantee.

The ship was renamed the M/V *Anastasis,* which means "resurrection." We believed this ship was the resurrection of the vision that had died when YWAM lost the *Maori.*

IN JANUARY 1979 I led the lecture phase of the SOE followed by another lecture phase of Lausanne's first Discipleship Training School (DTS). The DTS program developed in several locations around the world and eventually became the entry-level requirement for YWAM staff, and the SOE became a second-level school. We took twenty-five DTS students on outreach, again camping our way down to Greece.

At the end of the outreach, God lined up a special treat for us. We had met an American military couple who had been involved in YWAM and were living in Greece. The couple were going to a leadership conference in Cyprus and offered their apartment to Marie and me. We gratefully accepted, and while the rest of the team went back to Switzerland by bus at the end of the outreach, we stayed on for an extra week.

It was one of our best holidays and a time of refreshing. Greece is beautiful. A beach was just ten minutes away, and we spent time snorkeling and enjoying the sun, food, and people. The cupboards were stocked with the American goodies we had missed, and we were offered use of a car to experience the wonders of Greece—all free of charge. We were reenergized and returned to Lausanne ready for the next challenge. What a gift from God!

PART TWO

Southeast Asia

A New Call

The only difference, maybe, is that with Cambodians the grief leaves the face quickly, but it goes inside and stays there for a long time.

—DITH PRAN, Cambodian journalist and genocide survivor

A CONVERGENCE OF people, prayer, and God's leading brought about dramatic life changes for us as 1979 drew to a close. Before returning to Lausanne, we had attended a French-speaking staff conference in Paris in September. Don Stephens told us of his recent trip with Loren Cunningham and Joy Dawson to Southeast Asia, where they had been shocked to see the devastation of war in the region and challenged by all the refugees fleeing the Khmer Rouge in Cambodia. His words and photos moved us deeply.

The majority of the world's Khmer people live in Cambodia. They are the predominant ethnic group in the country, accounting for the vast majority of the nearly eight million people living there at that time.

They speak the Khmer language, part of the larger Mon-Khmer language family found throughout Southeast Asia. The Khmer are Buddhist and animist. Sadly, the Khmer people have suffered tragic losses in the face of war from within and without.

Cambodia's history is complex, marred by years of terror and violence. In the 1960s, during the Vietnam War, the country served as a transport route between North and South Vietnam. Because of Cambodia's nearness to Vietnam, the communist Viet Cong army set up bases there. Although Cambodia remained neutral during the war, the presence of these bases caused American military forces to bomb the country heavily, launching secret campaigns beginning in 1969.

Between 1972 and 1975, communist forces known as the Khmer Rouge took control of the weakened country, instigating one of the most radical restructurings of a society ever attempted. The Khmer Rouge believed in creating an agrarian utopia, dubbing their first year in power "Year Zero." Within days, entire cities were evacuated and destroyed, money and property were deemed worthless, and hundreds of thousands were executed in what are now called "the killing fields." Led by Pol Pot, the Khmer Rouge murdered over two million Cambodians—15–20 percent of the country's population—over the next four years in one of the most brutal and disastrous regimes in modern history. Darkness descended upon Cambodia. When the Vietnamese army invaded and overthrew the Khmer Rouge in 1979, Cambodians fled the country, escaping to the border and refugee camps in Thailand.

Don showed photographic slides of his trip to the Thai-Cambodian border. Refugees were fleeing for their lives with just the clothes on their backs, rushing into Thailand. Marie and I were heartbroken to hear Don's reports of people so weak and in such terrible state that when they made it to the border, they collapsed and died.

Later that night we prayed together and talked about what we could do. God spoke to us that when we returned to Lausanne, we were to take another step: start an early-morning prayer gathering to pray for the refugees. Our prayer time was from 6:15 to 7:15 every weekday morning. We started that prayer meeting in the basement library of the chalet, not only for the Khmer refugees but also for the whole of Southeast Asia. It wasn't a hard thing to do. With Don's pictures still in our minds, of course we wanted to pray! What we did not yet know, however, was that we would soon want to be an answer to our own prayers and to go.

Everyone on the base also prayed and fasted once a week, sending the money saved from not purchasing food to help the refugees. We kept informed about the situation as much as we could in order to pray intelligently. We learned that World Vision and other relief agencies had arrived in Cambodia and along the Thai-Cambodian border, providing emergency relief and health-care services to desperate people.

The first YWAM team to arrive in Thailand was led by ministry pioneer Joe Portale. In late October 1979, he and Gary Stephens (Don's brother) set out for Thailand and Hong Kong, looking for ministry opportunities to help in the refugee crisis. Gary later returned to Hong Kong with more than thirty people who were volunteering at Jubilee Camp, a former police barracks built to house nine hundred people.

Refugees in both Thailand and Hong Kong were in dire need. In Hong Kong, more than eight thousand Vietnamese (known as boat people because of how they traveled from Vietnam on the treacherous, pirate-infested seas) had arrived after fleeing their country and were now squeezed into Jubilee Camp. In Thailand, Joe was struck by the needs in a just-opened camp for refugees escaping from the Khmer Rouge in Cambodia—hundreds of sick and dying refugees lying on grass mats. "The experience of that trip deeply etched a commissioning into my heart," Joe said later. Indeed, many of us were finding ourselves called to bring comfort to the least of these whom Jesus loved and whose cries He had heard.

At the same time as we were learning about the refugees in Southeast Asia, an organization called Terre des Hommes had airlifted thirty children from the Thai-Cambodian border. The children were flown to Switzerland, where they received treatment in Swiss hospitals. They looked like they had come from a concentration camp: they were skin and bones and in deep shock from the horrors they had witnessed over the past few years. They had been found alone, with no knowledge of whether family members had survived.

A Swiss family in Lausanne were about to make the refugee situation even more real to us. Bruno and Margret Cavassini lived in Epalinges, about ten minutes from our training school at Chalet-à-Gobet.

We had first met them in 1974. Bruno is of Eritrean-Italian origin, and Margret was originally from Germany. They had three biological children, Scarlet, Tania, and Matthias, and in 1977 they adopted a Korean-African American boy, Janny.

Margret began daily visits to children rescued by Terre des Hommes in a nearby hospital. Something about one of the girls grabbed her attention. The little girl, Lem, was small, had a sweet face, and was very timid. Margret started spending a lot of time with Lem, and after a few weeks, Margret and her family were deeply attached to her. They felt she had been placed in their path for a specific purpose. It took only a couple of months for Bruno and Margret to legally adopt Lem and welcome her into their family.

One Sunday we were invited to the Cavassini home to meet their new daughter. For the first time we had a face to put to all the stories and statistics from Cambodia we were praying for. Marie and I simultaneously felt God speak to us, and what we heard was very specific.

"I want you to go and serve the refugees," we heard Him say.

Marie and I wanted to prepare to leave right away and make an immediate move, but we were committed to staff the January School of Evangelism. We went to Don to submit to him what we thought God was saying. "We think we need to go now," we said, not wanting to waste any time.

After careful consideration Don had a different idea. "I think you should wait. Fulfill your responsibility here and then ask people from this SOE to go with you."

Those words were difficult to receive, but there was so much wisdom in Don's advice. We would complete the SOE, communicating the vision to twelve other YWAM schools from all over Europe. This would help us gather a team to travel to Thailand in April. Marie and I completed a fruitful SOE. We ended up with thirty-two people who wanted to travel to Thailand and serve with us.

Momentum was building as my April departure neared. I flew from Athens to Thailand on April 10 to get things ready for the team, who would be arriving in a week. Marie would follow five weeks later. We planned to be in Thailand three to five months to support Joe Portale, who had committed to serving the refugees for one year. We would return to Lausanne in October to begin preparations for the next January SOE.

While I landed in Bangkok, Marie was still in Lausanne sorting our earthly things. She went through all our possessions, giving and throwing away what we didn't need. She did a thorough job—not really necessary, since we were planning to be back by the end of the year, though something in Marie nudged her to get our affairs in order. She was also handing everything over to her good friend Janet Potter, including her duties as Don Stephens's personal assistant. Having given Janet the rundown of her responsibilities, Marie stood at the door before departing the office. "Well, Janet, see you in three to five months—or who knows!" she said with a big grin on her face. We would later find out that "who knows" would be the more accurate description.

I arrived in Bangkok straight from the snow in Switzerland to the hottest hot season in twenty-five years. My shirt stuck to my back with perspiration, and I felt lethargic from the intense heat as I was taken to the newly established YWAM house ten minutes from the airport. Bangkok was a noisy major city—quite a shock to the senses after orderly and serene Lausanne.

The YWAM house had sporadic running water and simple fans that brought little relief from the intense heat—no air conditioning in those early years. I stayed in Bangkok for a week, acclimatizing and getting prepared for the incoming team of thirty-two people. At the first opportunity I boarded a bus for the six-hour journey to the Thai-Cambodian border town of Aranyaprathet, or "Aran," as it came to be known. We lovingly called the buses going out to the border the "Orange Crush" because of their color and the fact that they drove at breakneck speed while packed full of passengers.

Situated 150 miles east of Bangkok, Aran was the closest town to the border and the refugee camp where Joe and his team were working. The camp was called Khao-I-Dang Holding Center (KID). Twenty kilometers (twelve miles) north of Aran in Prachinburi Province (now in Sa Kaeo Province) and a few kilometers from the Cambodian border, KID was built by the UNHCR (United Nations High Commissioner for Refugees). The camp encompassed three square kilometers of bamboo and thatch houses and by March 1980 had become home to 160,000

Khmer refugees. Water was trucked in every day, and each refugee was allowed twelve liters for all of his or her needs. Food, education, and medical services were also provided in the camp. In the beginning, KID was an open camp with free movement from border refugee camps, but by January 1980 it was closed to new arrivals.

I arrived at Aran in the early afternoon and with the directions that I had been given was able to pick up a "taxi" and make my way to the houses YWAM had rented. What I didn't know was that it was Songkran—the Thai New Year and Water Festival. Songkran is a major holiday in Thailand that has evolved into a national water fight, particularly with Thais throwing water on *farangs* (foreigners). My taxi was a motorcycle with a buggy type of attachment on the back, offering space for two people to sit. As we started moving, people in the streets doused me with water, smiling and laughing. *This is some crazy town,* I thought as I arrived soaking wet at the YWAM houses.

The tradition of Songkran is a time of honoring elders by pouring a small handful of scented water over their shoulder and receiving a blessing from them in return. Since I knew nothing about this festival, I did not know how to react to everyone throwing water at me and laughing. The water wasn't so bad; it gave short relief from the stifling heat. Years later at one of our YWAM staff meetings, the Thai staff modeled the real meaning of Songkran: they honored a number of us as leaders. This annual tradition reminds us of God's intention of respecting our elders and the blessing they can have on community.

The YWAM house was three miles from the Thai-Cambodian border, where Vietnamese troops in Cambodia were attacking Thailand. Having launched a full-scale invasion of Cambodia and ousted the Khmer Rouge, Vietnam now occupied the country. There was fear that the Vietnamese would invade Thailand as well. In fact, the Thai government had begun turning away refugees, sending them back over minefields planted earlier by the Khmer Rouge. US president Jimmy Carter, along with leaders of other countries, pledged international aid for the refugees. This enabled the once-closed border to be opened up again.

God had spoken earlier to Joe Portale's YWAM team to come to the border, but when the team arrived in Bangkok, the UN said they did not need them. "Everything is under control," the YWAM team was told.

The UN was making the KID camp smaller, meaning no more refugees would be allowed. They were also closing the door on agencies coming to help.

Because nothing we said seemed to work, all we could do was pray. We asked God again in a prayer meeting if we should be working with the refugees, and again we felt His answer was a clear yes. By now the team from Europe had arrived in Bangkok and were going to Aran by an Orange Crush and then hitchhiking to KID on water trucks or going by "baht bus" (a trucklike taxi with people crammed in the back that cost only a few Thai *baht*). I had to find something for them to do.

At this time the only way we could communicate with Bangkok and the rest of the world was to write a letter, send a telegram, or reserve a chance to use the town's only telephone. I decided to phone, eventually getting through to Joe and the others, letting them know that they needed to help us pray for an opening in KID. God heard our prayers. He showed me that several agencies working in the refugee camp all needed more help. In the end, our YWAMers—many of whom were doctors, nurses, and teachers—were placed with fourteen NGOs (nongovernmental organizations).

Five weeks later we had a routine going, and things were working as well as could be expected in a war zone. Marie would arrive on May 9, and as the date came closer, I started to get concerned about what she would think about our living conditions. We had no electricity, no running water, occasional poisonous snakes on the roads and paths we traveled, and monsoon season flooding that necessitated our house to reside on stilts. When May 8 arrived, I set off on the Orange Crush to Bangkok, so excited to see Marie but also nervous. What would she think? How would she handle this situation? What would she do?

SEVEN

Light Appearing

It's not a coincidence that in the Scriptures poverty is mentioned more than twenty-one hundred times. It's not an accident.

—BONO, National Prayer Breakfast, 2006

MY HEART SKIPPED a beat as I saw Marie coming. I had missed her so much.

"Look at you!" Marie said, smiling as she breezed through the arrivals entrance at Don Mueang airport. She was admiring the new white safari suit I had had custom made while I was in Bangkok. The suit helped me to stay cool and also looked smart for meetings I attended with the UN, government embassies, and other agencies.

Arm in arm we made our way to the parking lot and the old vehicle I was driving—newly purchased by YWAM. I was talking nonstop on this short ride back to the team house, filling Marie in on all that had happened.

The Portales and Wally and Norma Wenge greeted us at the house. Wally and Norma had arrived in Thailand to help for a couple of months with logistics in the expanding mission.

After catching up with the team, I went out and hailed a taxi to whisk Marie to the Bangkok Christian Guest House for the night. As we jumped into the taxi, the heavens opened and a Thai monsoon poured down rain. The taxi driver's windshield wipers didn't work—he had his window open and was leaning out cleaning the windshield with a dirty rag, allowing the rain to pour in on us in the backseat, which was actually slightly refreshing in the heat. Marie smiled, commenting on how different Bangkok was from Switzerland, where everything seemed to work perfectly.

Thankfully the guesthouse had air conditioning, giving some respite from the suffocating heat outside. Despite the noise from the streets below, we both woke up refreshed and glad to be together after our five-week separation. Marie had arrived during the hottest time of the year, and I realized we needed to do something outside to get Marie acclimatized to the tropical heat.

"Let's go to the Bangkok zoo!" I suggested after talking to the guesthouse receptionist. Marie agreed, but when we got there, we felt like animals on view. We were *farangs* (foreigners), tall and blond, and as we turned from admiring a monkey, we saw a crowd had formed around us. They were staring at us more than the animals they had come to view.

"Let's go!" Marie said under her breath. We made a quick exit.

The next morning it was time to head to Aran and to our little house on stilts. Splurging, we took the air-conditioned bus for the four- to five-hour ride, but as we traveled I suddenly remembered to what and where I was taking Marie. I felt the need to prepare her for our basic housing and living situation. As we drove past rice fields and palm trees, I looked for houses similar to ours so she would be prepared.

"It's better than that one. Oh, not as good as that one," I said, pointing to different dwellings along the way.

Marie just smiled. I had not given her enough credit. She was going to do just fine. When we arrived in Aran, we felt hot and sticky as soon as we stepped off the bus. The torrential rain had subsided, and steam was slowly rising from the steps up to the wooden home we would be sharing with Cindy Albrecht, Dorothea Hoffmann, Marilyn Ahrens, and Paula Kirby. We lovingly called Paula, our Trinidadian sister, "Fro" because of her great hairdo. God had already grafted her into our family tree since our first meeting in the mid-70s.

"Welcome, welcome!" came the cries of the YWAMers as they ran out to meet Marie. They had heard about the wife who was coming, and now here she was, slightly overwhelmed but keeping a brave face.

Sometimes our beginnings are not always what we expect. The toilet in our house was a squatty potty. These ceramic-molded bowls are normally at floor level, but ours was raised off the ground with cement. We had a bucket of water from our next-door neighbors' well so that we could "flush" our toilet, and the floor was wet most of the time. On her second evening at the house, Marie was wearing her rubber sandals when suddenly both feet slipped and she fell, scraping the insides of her legs and ankles. One of the Swiss nurses on the team cleaned the wounds, applied antiseptic cream, and bandaged both legs. Marie hobbled to our bed.

To prepare for bed, I showed Marie how to take a "dip shower" and then quickly jump under our mosquito net with the fan on us (if we had electricity), hoping to fall asleep before we dried. The bullfrogs, crickets, and *tukays* (big Asian lizards) tried their best to stop that from happening. The next morning Marie inspected her grazed legs and found they were already infected despite the good job the nurse had done cleaning the wounds. It was very hard to keep things hygienic in our living conditions, and this meant that Marie couldn't come to KID for a couple of days. With all the dirt and disease in the camp, the infection would have just gotten worse. This was not exactly the best introduction to the team and project that Marie had hoped for.

It took about twenty-five minutes to drive to the KID camp from our home in Aran, stopping at checkpoints along the way to have our passes inspected. We had obtained the passes from the UNHCR and later UNBRO (United Nations Border Relief Operations), who worked closely with the Royal Thai Army.

After a few days Marie was able to enter the camp. She had heard all about KID: the red dust, the blue water towers, and the refugees who greeted us with "okay, okay, bye-bye." Her first impression was being overwhelmed by how the refugees had suffered so much. They had each lost someone dear to them, and it showed in the sadness of their eyes. Marie teamed up with Tove Pedersen, a YWAMer from Norway. The two of them assisted the overworked nurses of the Catholic Relief Service pediatric center. Marie helped feed malnourished babies and sat with depressed mothers, encouraging them by holding their hands and crying with them in their vulnerability. She often used the French she had learned in Lausanne to talk with refugees, many of whom were fluent in the language.

Through the night and during the day we heard machine guns and bomb explosions from the fighting between Vietnamese and Khmer Rouge forces on the border. When bombs came into Thai territory, the Thai army responded by firing from their tanks only a few miles from where we lived. We became adept at distinguishing between outgoing and incoming shelling. Sometimes a land mine exploded, which was always heartbreaking. More often than not, the explosion involved a tragic end for a farmer or someone walking unknowingly over mined land.

Our daily schedule for the first few months included very few days off. The days were long, starting early each morning as we were awakened by the black marketeers as they played their music loudly sometimes as early as 3:00 a.m. After long, emotionally charged days, we came home to wash off the red dust of the camps in our dip showers and wash our clothes by hand, actually finding that using our feet was easier and cooler! Each evening we had dinner together as a team, discussing the news of our work and the things learned from other agencies and praying for various situations. Every evening we had to fill up our cars with fuel before the petrol stations closed at 6:00 p.m. We parked the cars facing outward in case of a quick evacuation. Each member of the team was allowed a small bag to grab on the run. Living and working in the stress and trauma of a war—having babies die in your arms and seeing people with their limbs blown off—was extremely difficult. We were learning how to care for our team, making sure they took a break from the border for a week every three months to reenergize and recuperate.

We faced dangers right in our own backyard as well. One day we heard shouts from the neighbors and learned that they had caught a boa constrictor in the ditch near our house. They had killed the snake and were inviting us to partake in the feast. Marie and I politely declined, giving our neighbors more to eat. We were shocked at how close we had been living to such a huge and dangerous snake.

During May and June a wave of malaria and dengue fever hit our team. Malaria comes from mosquitoes that bite at night, and dengue comes from mosquitoes that bite during the day. Because our pottery jars, full of water that we used for washing, were a place for mosquitoes to breed, we had covers made for them. During the outbreak, half the team was down with one or the other sickness. About the time one group revived, the other half went down. Dengue in particular is very hard to deal with. It gets into your bones and causes severe pain, along with fever and aches, and in some cases long-term depression. Thankfully Marie and I were spared from catching either illness. However, we all suffered from diarrhea. We ended up talking about it like we talked about the weather—it became normal for us. Our parents would have been shocked to hear our dinner table conversations.

Despite the conditions, we were all focused on KID and longing for the broken and hurting refugees to see the love of Christ through our practical service. At the camp we saw suffering every day. Refugees were still coming over the border from Cambodia, and the situation in many ways seemed hopeless. We realized that when you see such pain on a daily basis, the first thing shaken is your faith. We saw that if your trust and faith in God isn't grounded, you really don't have too much to keep you during the storm. If you can't lean into the character of God, even when you don't understand what is happening around you, the intense suffering and injustices can be fatal to your faith.

The teaching we had had in Switzerland on the nature and character of God helped us deal with seeming hopelessness, but we still had to press into Him for even more understanding of what that love meant in the midst of such pain and suffering. None of us had ever seen this kind of mass suffering caused by war and injustice. The Bible includes over two thousand verses on compassion, injustice, suffering, and poverty. Many of these verses came alive to us, as if we had never read them before. We encouraged the team to dig deep into them, to know God's heart, and to make these verses their own. We also urged them to listen to tapes and read books by people who were acquainted with suffering and pain, people like Mother Teresa and Francis and Edith Schaeffer. These servants and many others became mentors to us through their books on God, suffering, and our responsibility as followers of Jesus to the poor of our world.

As the months went by, so many YWAM short-term teams came to help out that it felt as if we were in a bus station with people constantly coming and going. Because of the high-stress war environment, it was difficult to cultivate a personal, family environment. The challenge of growth and long-term development that included communication, orientation, housing, logistics, financial accountability, and oversight was getting too much for us administratively. We had to process camp passes in Bangkok for each new visitor, which meant hours in traffic and hours waiting for the passes to come back. This job alone was taking up a lot of our energy and staff power. In the end we decided to accept volunteers for a minimum of one year only. This caused quite a challenge in our short-term operations within YWAM, but it turned out to be one of the best decisions we could have made. With longer-term commitments we were able to draw the multinational, multiskilled team closer together in a high-risk environment, with plurality of leadership. When we were operating in unity, service to the refugees flowed out of that bond of peace and strength. The opposite was also true: when the team was not working well together, even the simple things became difficult.

Back in January, one medical NGO had moved out of Khao-I-Dang, and the UN asked if YWAM had doctors and nurses who could take over the outpatient clinic in what was called Section 2. YWAM agreed, and our staff began to see three hundred to five hundred patients a day. These Khmer patients were present in the morning when our teams arrived and still there when the medical team left in the evening.

Inger Kristensen, a Danish nursing assistant, worked in one of the KID camp hospitals, where she met Man "Kal" Mabaskal and his pregnant wife, Senghuen, who were the only survivors from a family of twelve. Kal became Inger's translator, and the longer Inger worked with him, the more he told her about his life. His entire family had died under the Khmer Rouge, and Kal wanted revenge. One day he told Inger that he wanted to kill some former Khmer Rouge soldiers housed in KID camp.

"Do you want to be like the Khmer Rouge?" Inger asked him.

"No, I would never be like the Khmer Rouge. I hate them and will kill them," Kal replied vehemently.

"If you kill them, then you have become just like them," she explained.

This hit Kal deeply, and he knew she was right. "I don't want to be like them, but what can I do? They killed my family," he said.

"There is something that you can do, but it may be too hard for you," Inger said kindly as she cleaned wounds.

"What is it?" Kal asked, eager to find a way out. He was not expecting the answer she gave.

"You can forgive them."

Kal exploded. "I can't forgive them for what they have done!"

Gently putting down her sponge, Inger looked at him and replied, "I know, but when you cannot do it, Jesus can help you to forgive."

Inger then began to tell Kal who this Jesus was and what He came to earth to do. She also told him some of her own personal story of her journey of faith. Inger saw that her words were making Kal think. Kal asked more questions, and it was not long before he accepted Jesus into his life. He then asked Jesus to help him forgive the Khmer Rouge and those directly involved in killing his family. An amazing thing happened. Kal said it was as if a huge weight had been lifted off his shoulders.

The change in Kal's life was remarkable. When we met him and heard his story, we were amazed by how he had become a new man through forgiveness and reconciliation with God. The weight of hatred and bitterness had been replaced with a supernatural joy. One day I had UN business outside the camp and was able to take Kal along as my translator. Kal told me many times how wonderful it was to feel that moment of freedom outside the camp.

Later, Kal and Senghuen were sponsored by a US agency and relocated to California. Kal got a job as a serviceman at a local car dealership. He went on to have three children and work in a large computer firm. He continues to work through Khmer organizations to see those responsible for the deaths of his family brought to justice. In 2012, some perpetrators were being tried in Cambodia for the first time.

Also in the camp were a group of about twenty Khmer families who had miraculously survived Pol Pot's genocide and a trek through the jungle to Thailand. They were Christians, having come to the Lord through Cambodian missionaries before the Khmer Rouge came to power. They told miracle stories of how God had awakened them one night and told them to leave their village. They obeyed, hurrying out in the darkness. A couple of hours later, the Khmer Rouge attacked the village, leaving no survivors. This happened many times—God guided them and kept them safe. No one from their families had been killed, an astonishing occurrence under the Khmer Rouge. In the camp, the other Khmers began to notice something different about this group: they smiled a lot and seemed to have peace. People were attracted to them and wanted to know more about this God they followed.

As this little group of Christian refugees grew, they wanted a place to worship. They tithed the bamboo allotted to them for their homes and built a church building. Soon over twenty thousand people were worshiping in multiple services all day long. People sat on the church grounds, listening to sermons and worship transmitted by loudspeakers across the larger community. Small house groups sprang up, and at one time more than fifty house meetings were going on in the camp.

Going to these small-group meetings that were spread throughout the camp was easier for the refugees, and sometimes we were asked to teach. At one meeting I spoke at, about three hundred people sat on the floor, waiting to hear my message. I gave a simple talk, which was translated into Khmer, about sin, forgiveness, and who Jesus was. I asked how many people would like to know Jesus. Everyone raised their hand. Because I thought that the people had misunderstood the translation, I asked them again. This time I requested that they stand up if they wanted to know Jesus. All of them stood up. Not sure that these people were getting what I was saying, I asked them one more time. This time I said if they wanted to know Jesus, they should come to the front. All of them started moving forward until there was no more room. As they prayed to ask Jesus into their lives, they began to be discipled by the Khmer Christians living around them. This type of response occurred several times when others spoke during those days. Transformation was happening in the refugee camp!

Khmer people were hungry to know God, to be free from the power of spirits, and to find healing and wholeness. We will never know how many came to the Lord in the refugee camps, but these tens of thousands of new believers eventually planted new churches in Cambodia, Australasia, Europe, and America. Research done in Cambodia in 2012 showed that the Khmer who came to know the Lord in the border camps are playing a significant role in the church and in building up society in Cambodia.

Although we rejoiced at the decisions of many Khmer refugees to accept Christ, we were also concerned about people becoming "rice Christians"—people who thought that if they became Christians it would be easier for them to be sponsored for a new life in a new country. The UN required that we sign a contract that we would not proselytize. This meant we would not force people to become Christians, in any way or provide inducements to come to faith with things like rice, clothing, or money. We agreed with this requirement, as Jesus must be followed for who He is. He does not force, bribe, or threaten people to know Him. We also knew that the UN Universal Declaration of Human Rights, article 18, states: "Everyone has the right to freedom of thought, conscience and religion; . . . freedom . . . to manifest his religion or belief."

To comply with the UN we did not conduct weddings and funerals or give out literature unless it was asked for. Khmer Christians could fill these needs. The UN was generally happy with us, but we fell in and out of favor with individuals because we were a Christian group. Some did not like it when we took over the KID hospital ward from World Vision, the previous organization serving there. One UN official said to me, "You may have your foot in the door with World Vision's withdrawal and someone in Bangkok saying you can have this ward, but mark my word, I am going to slam that door shut."

I tried to be gracious and just prayed for God to somehow give us favor with this man who had authority to stop our work. We regularly checked in with God to see if we were doing what He wanted us to do. It seemed He wanted us to serve where we were most needed.

YWAM LEADER JIM Rogers arrived with Joe Portale just before a YWAM strategy conference in Chiang Mai, in northwestern Thailand.

He wanted to visit one of the border camps with me. The situation was dangerous. The Vietnamese were trying to control Cambodia and didn't like pockets of refugees gathered on the borders. Often soldiers—or at least people with arms—in these groups were part of the resistance. Because we had been told that an attack on the camp was expected before the monsoon season, we were on high alert. We made sure the team got home before the six o'clock curfew each evening.

As Jim, Joe, and I reached the camp, we realized we were witnessing an attack. Suddenly we heard machine-gun fire very close and saw water buffalo running in every direction. Refugees were rushing along a muddy track, fleeing in the rice paddies to escape the crossfire. As we turned our car around to get out of the situation, we saw a little boy carrying a baby in a sling on his back. We felt desperate knowing there was nothing else we could do but pray that lives would not be lost. Thankfully the battle did not last long, and as far as we could see, no refugees were injured.

We finally made it to the leadership strategy conference in Chiang Mai. The conference was packed, and we were so busy in training sessions we didn't have a chance to debrief with anyone. Don Stephens visited the border camps with us afterward. As we drove to the border in our Nissan pickup truck, we talked and talked, telling Don everything that had happened and all we had been learning. I guess it was an intense debrief while driving, since we were so full of so many experiences over the past few months.

Marie and I sensed God was speaking to us about our time in Thailand. There was much need, and we thought, *How can we leave?* But at the same time it seemed impossible to stay. We were committed to lead the January 1981 SOE in Lausanne, and we felt we needed to honor that. Some leaders at the Chiang Mai conference expected us to stay in Thailand, while other leaders were expecting us to return to Switzerland. We felt torn and needed to hear from God.

After patiently listening to everything we had to say about our experiences, Don was very enthusiastic. "That all sounds incredible! After being so stretched and challenged here, can you honestly go back and lead the Lausanne SOE and be as fulfilled?"

After a pregnant pause during which Marie and I took in what Don said, I stammered, "I, er . . . um. Well, I don't know!" We had never looked at it like that, and being asked to consider the option of staying in Thailand seemed to us a very big deal. Marie and I were much quieter during the second half of the journey as we thought about what Don had said, and we started to imagine life, longer term, in Thailand— whatever long-term meant.

The next day we were in the same vehicle with Joy Dawson, who had also come to visit the camps. We poured out our hearts to her. "I'm confused. We made a commitment to the SOE. People are depending on us," Marie said. She didn't know if it was even right to be asking the question about staying in Thailand.

"Honey," Joy said, turning to Marie with a smile, "your responsibility is to be obedient to God. That school is God's responsibility."

Later as we prayed about the direction we should take, we were reminded of what God had spoken to Marie after my second surgery in Memphis. Marie had been crying out for my healing. She hated seeing me go through the surgeries and was concerned that the reason she was not getting pregnant had something to do with my injuries. Marie felt God say that we had a choice: my healing, a pregnancy, and our longed-for baby, or His maximum for our lives. It was one of those sacred moments where we realized the choice was really ours to make, one that would set a direction for our lives. Tearfully we chose His maximum, knowing that whatever that would be, we could trust Him fully. Now at this point, we felt Him say we had a choice again: we could go back to Lausanne or choose His maximum, which seemed to be staying in Thailand. We chose to stay.

Expanding the Work

I know God will not give me anything I can't handle. I just wish He didn't trust me so much.

—MOTHER TERESA

IT JUST SO happened that David Boyd was in Thailand during this conference time. He and I laughed that he always seemed to pop up when Marie and I had major decisions to make. As we prayed together, David had two verses for us: 1 Corinthians 15:58, "You must stand firm, unshakable," and Luke 9:62, "No one who puts a hand on the plow and looks back is fit for God's kingdom." Marie and I knew it was right for us to stay, and the thought both excited and scared us.

That night under our mosquito net we counted the cost of all we were giving up by staying in Thailand. With deep sobs we released our European family and friends, important relationships to us. One by one we gave our precious friends back to the Lord. We realized we had come to know these dear ones by obeying God in the first place, and we could trust Him again to be faithful in new transitions. We also released our home—a corner room in the Lausanne chalet with a private bathroom and view of the mountains and forest in Switzerland—and our coveted Swiss *Permis B* visas, which we had struggled so long to obtain. By letting go of relationships and the security we had come to know, we would be fully available to God in Thailand. We wanted to let go, but it was much harder than we thought, as if our hearts were being wrenched from inside us. The poor women who lived with us must have been wondering what all was going on as we cried in our room that night.

The next day Cindy Albrecht sweetly said to Marie, "I knew something big was going on for you last night. I knew I needed to pray." Still raw with emotion, Marie tearfully hugged Cindy. God was leading us and our teams step-by-step. We had no idea of the far-reaching consequences of this decision, but we knew in our hearts it was the right one.

We were now working in many of the camps on the Thai-Cambodian border, but God was also speaking to us about our neighbors—those in the Thai villages—who had also been affected by the fighting along the border and the influx of refugees.

Paula, our dear friend from Trinidad, was a good bridge into the Thai community, since she picked up Thai very quickly with her gift for languages. She had come to know the Lord in Germany while she was dancing in the European production of *Hair* and had heard the gospel from a woman who had waited outside the theater to talk with the cast and crew about Jesus. Paula had an encounter with the truth and gave her life to the Lord.

God had then led Paula to join YWAM, and Paula was on staff with us in Lausanne before coming with the group from Athens. She was part of that first support team in Aran, working at our main house and looking after logistics and administration: going to the market, cooking, and cleaning. With her amazing linguistic gift, Paula was able to work with our medical teams as they served in more than thirty local Thai villages. These rural people, living in such poverty, had basic needs. The significant difference between them and the refugees was a barbed-wire fence that separated them.

Our medical staff shifted their work between refugees and affected Thai villages. At this time YWAM Thailand consisted of Joe and Colleen

Harbison and Art and Ellen Sanborn (and children) in Chiang Mai, and Judy Hayden, Mike Carey, and Julie Fitzgibbon, who were studying language in Bangkok and preparing for ministry among the Thais. They would take needed breaks from their ministry and language study and join our mobile medical teams as translators. Their ability to work with us was a good break and experience for them and a blessing for our medical staff. Often, these medical outreaches were held at Buddhist temples, which are the center of community life. Not only did we serve the health needs of the Thais, but also much good will occurred between YWAM and the Thai military and government.

This next phase of work involved my taking on the responsibility of leading YWAM Thailand's national relief effort. Marie and I planned to move to Bangkok after Christmas. We would miss our home in Aran. We had come to love rural Thailand—the daily interaction with refugees and our wooden home on stilts—but with the lack of electricity and communications, we knew it would be difficult to lead YWAM relief services in Thailand from where we were. Aran had only one public phone, which worked periodically, and we were still in the days of postal letters, telex, and telegraph. It would be five years before we were able to use a fax machine, and many more until cell phones, printers, computers, and the Internet would appear. Sometimes it was easier to drive the five hours to Aran from Bangkok than to get through on the telephone.

We decided to make our first Christmas in Thailand a special occasion. The Thai military cut us a tree that we decorated with costume jewelry. It was a challenge to think of Christmas in the tropics, with the occasional elephants lumbering past our team house. A retired ob-gyn, Charles "Chuck" Marshall, and his wife, Doris, a nurse, were serving with us. Seated in a big armchair by the Christmas tree, Dr. Chuck opened his Bible and, with his glasses propped on his nose, began to read the Christmas story. We realized it truly was Christmas, unlike any other we had ever known.

Another new experience took place sometime later. The same UN official who had earlier unsuccessfully tried to slam the door on YWAM once again called me and my assistant in for a meeting. We did not know what to expect, but when we sat down in front of him, we saw that his former hostility was gone.

"We are rebuilding the Nong Chan refugee camp, and we would like YWAM to oversee all of the medical work there. I've been watching you and see that you're willing to do the dirty jobs. You don't complain, and you are not out to make a name for yourselves," he said. In amazement, we said yes. And we praised God for the favor He was giving us in opening a door to serve at this camp.

By this time several additional refugee camps had opened nearby, and we had stretched ourselves to help meet their needs. Meanwhile, the work in KID was expanding, and we ended up running fifteen different projects there. This was encouraging confirmation that we were right where we were supposed to be.

One of those projects was, surprisingly, a bakery. Rebecca, a twenty-year-old from Canada, had come to volunteer because she had heard about the refugees and her heart had broken over the mothers left widowed after their husbands were brutally murdered by the Khmer Rouge. When she arrived, we weren't sure where to place her, since she wasn't a doctor, a nurse, a social worker, or even a teacher.

"What can you do?" I asked.

Rebecca thought for a moment and then replied, "I can bake!"

Rebecca had grown up with six brothers and sisters, the daughter of Mennonite missionaries from the far north of Ontario. She had learned to cook and bake at an early age. And, she added, she was good at it.

We decided that a baking project might work. Since the camp had no ovens or kitchens, we would have to build a makeshift kitchen from bamboo and find a way to make an oven. We found a Khmer refugee who could make large ovens with clay and cement, framed by steel pillars that were built under thatched huts.

Rebecca had a vision for the bakery: she wanted to create a place of interest for the widows and single mothers, enabling them to think of something other than their loss and the pain of fleeing their homeland. It would also be a place where they could be trained in hygiene and to care for their families.

Rebecca was inspired and came up with thirty recipes—one for each day of the month. The recipes were user-friendly, with ingredients that could be found in the local camp markets. Rebecca created recipes such as rice-pineapple cookies, pumpkin cookies, red bean cookies, and coconut cake. Because there were no baking tins, Rebecca used recycled fish cans. Everything was both creative and delicious.

At one point 140 widows, single mothers, and orphans were attending the program each month. Rebecca, who learned the Khmer language very quickly, trained the women in dough making, helped by a young Khmer Christian translator named Sovaro. As the refugees began to trust Rebecca and Sovaro, they slowly started to talk, opening up about the grief, suffering, and pain they had gone through. We have always sought to find redemptive keys within the Cambodian culture that would unlock the door for an effective introduction of the gospel. Rebecca found a Cambodian legend that said: "A man is coming where four rivers meet (Phnom Penh), and he will bring peace with him. You will know him because of the scars on his hands and feet." With that legend she began to talk about Jesus, explaining that He is the man with the scarred hands and feet.

One extremely curious woman kept coming back to ask Rebecca questions about Jesus. When Rebecca found out the woman was one of the camp's fortune-tellers, we began to pray that the powers of darkness would not hold her back from knowing Jesus personally. Within two weeks the fortune-teller went to church and publicly gave her heart to the Lord, repenting of her sins. Rebecca was not so sure of the woman's understanding of the gospel, and later she went to the woman's house to talk with her. As she walked into the bamboo hut, she noticed that all the woman's fetishes used in fortune-telling were gone. The woman said she had destroyed them because Jesus was not pleased. Together with Rebecca she then prayed in the house, committing it to the Lord.

Mark Erickson, a young man from Montana who was working with us, was reading from Luke 14:12–14: "When you give a luncheon or dinner, do not invite your friends, your brothers or sisters, your relatives, or your rich neighbors; if you do, they may invite you back and so you will be repaid. . . . Invite the poor, the crippled, the lame, the blind, and you will be blessed." Mark decided to do just that. He invited three hundred of the poor, crippled, lame, and other disabled people to the church at KID for a feast. The people came by wheelchair, on crutches, or by vehicle. YWAM's farm provided the fatted calf (or pig, in this case) and fish from the fish ponds. Afterward the people watched the *Jesus* film. We know of at least ten amputees who accepted Christ, and all were touched by the love of God.

World Vision had started the KID camp fish farm, and they had asked us to take it over when they left. Fences and guards protected three large ponds, where we bred tilapia and Indian and Chinese carp by feeding them leftover rice from the food centers. We recycled just about everything in camp. At the fish farm we began integrating other farming practices and were able to acquire two large pigs, affectionately named Steve and Marie by our team. When we bought two water buffalo, they were given the honor of being named Loren and Darlene for YWAM's founders, Loren and Darlene Cunningham.

To control unwanted predatory fish, we drained our three fish ponds. We would put the fish from the drained pool into one of the other ponds—but one time we did something different. We had some of the church members go through camp to find the poorest of the poor and give them a slip of paper allowing each of them to receive a kilogram of fresh fish. One thousand refugees showed up with their papers. As we watched them receive fish, we saw a little of the excitement that must have been present when the five loaves and two fish were given to the multitudes.

One of our housemates, Dorothea Hoffmann, started working with the approximately three hundred people with leprosy (Hansen's disease) in the camp. Leprosy is transmitted through bacteria called *Mycobacterium leprae* and prolonged contact. It affects nerve endings, causing the afflicted to lose feeling in their extremities, and can lead to blindness. Leprosy patients were treated terribly by many of the other refugees, who often beat them with sticks or threw rocks at them. Because of the shame of their illness, victims would not look a person in the face, interact socially, or expect human touch. But God started speaking to us about the power of human contact—that we needed to touch and show our love to these rejected people. We knew we would not easily catch the disease by simple touch. At first the ill refugees would scrutinize us to see if we would really accept them. Eventually the love of God broke down barriers.

One day Dorothea was treating a refugee with leprosy. "Can a

Khmer be a Christian?" the man asked as Dorothea gently cleaned open sores on his fingerless hands.

"Of course," she said smiling, and then added, "Do you know anything about God?"

"No," he replied.

"Have you ever heard of Jesus?" she went on. Again, he answered no.

"Then why would you want to become a Christian?" Dorothea gently probed.

The man looked her deep in the eyes and slowly said, "If your God is anything like you, I want to know Him."

Dorothea couldn't stop her tears, so touched that the man had seen Jesus through her simple acts of love. Forty of these patients eventually became Christians and were baptized. A new church was born.

KID camp refugees were hungry for God. They had lost everything and were searching for hope and a future. One man had cried out to the "Owner of the Earth" while he was imprisoned by the Khmer Rouge. He did not know whether there was a God, but he knew there was a Someone. The first Christian he met at the camp told him the name of the "Owner of the Earth," and the man quickly submitted his life to this Owner. Another disabled patient said he wanted to know this God of love who would send foreigners thousands of miles from home to serve them.

God was working among the refugees, proving He was very present in the midst of their pain. We were often asked if it was difficult to communicate the gospel when we were not yet fluent in the language. A letter from a friend who was volunteering with Ethiopian refugees answered this question. My friend's letter tells the story of a father of one of her patients bending low and kissing her legs and feet and then getting his young son to do the same. The translator insisted that my friend would not be happy with this, as it was God, not her, who had healed and who should be worshiped. The father of her patient simply asked, "Is it not true that God makes His dwelling in her? If that is so, as I am kissing her feet, am I not also kissing His?"

My friend said in the letter, "Love is not the servant of words, but it is in a deed or action that God makes Himself known." We were making Him known through mercy and compassion.

Another program we started met the needs of thousands of children in the camp. Tove Pedersen began the first KID preschool, which quickly multiplied. By the end of the first year, we had four preschools, with almost eight hundred children attending and nine Khmer teachers whom we had trained. We knew that the first five years of a child's life are very significant, and these refugee children had been born into war. All they knew were the emotional scars and hurts they had experienced from the terror around them. The preschool vision was to provide a place of peace, safety, order, and love to help the children thrive and heal.

One person who helped us with this vision was Mary Los Banos. Mary ran a very successful school in Honolulu called The Children's House. She came to Thailand to look for the family of a Khmer refugee in Honolulu (who was later featured on the cover of *Time* magazine when he graduated from Stanford University). Years before, Mary had lived in Thailand with her husband, Domingo, and their family, and they had adopted a Thai daughter. Mary had a deep love for this country and was brokenhearted by the refugee situation. In fact, God set Mary on her lifework while she was consulting at KID. He showed her that when we serve the child (the least of all), we are serving Jesus.

One day I stuck my head through the KID preschool door and could not believe my eyes. The school had an atmosphere of peace and calm as two hundred children sat quietly drawing, their sandals neatly ordered in a line by the entrance. Mary told me of a Cambodian mother who had come to her and said, "What have you done to my child? The school has changed her—she talks to us with such respect!"

Mary smiled, and when she told me the story, I realized how significant the schools were in training up the next generation. The children's future did not have to be dictated by their past.

During fighting close to the camp, part of the hospital was destroyed. Because our preschool was next to the hospital, it was turned into a ward until the hospital could be rebuilt. Mary would teach parents how to care for and teach their children. Sitting on a straw mat, she would be surrounded by a crowd of adults, eager to learn. Whenever she left the camp at the end of the day, she would have children holding onto every inch of her. Her teaching and training had an incredible impact on the camp and preschools.

WHEN WE WERE challenged with a problem in the camps, we tried to find a solution. One such situation was the need for communication, which we addressed by opening a post office next to the Red Cross tracing office. Five thousand letters were coming in each day. Families had been separated in Cambodia, and many more had lost contact with friends or family when they escaped the country. The letters were a vital way for the refugees to connect and the only way they could hear news—no TVs or newspapers were available. Often people were sent money through the post office, and in response to that we started a bank. All of these projects were staffed by refugees and facilitated by YWAMers.

Our goal was to train the refugees to operate programs themselves, providing them with training and qualification certificates to use when they left the camp. We were able to pay refugees for their work but had to comply with a Thai government policy stating that Cambodian refugee workers could earn only ten baht (fifty cents) per day. The government did not want refugees to have more than their own people, who were also suffering. At the height of our time in the camps, we had about five thousand refugees working with us.

We had arrived in Thailand to work in emergency relief assistance, but the idea of development was in our minds from the beginning. We knew we could give people shirts to cover their nakedness and *also* teach them to sew, giving them skills to make shirts, sell them, and provide for a family. With this in mind, we started a sewing project using treadle (powered by foot pedal) sewing machines purchased in Bangkok's Chinatown. We established a three-month training program that produced 58,000 pieces of clothing, including school uniforms and *pakamas* (sarongs) that men and women wore.

Soon, we made plans to open a soap factory to combat the skin infections prevalent in the camp. I met with a UN official and told him of our plan. The UN agreed to finance the operation and then commissioned us to make enough soap for fourteen newly opened border camps.

A young Vietnamese man whose grandmother had taught him soap making helped us in this. He trained forty disabled refugees, giving them a job and purpose, and thus our soap factory was born. It cost seven cents to make one bar of soap, and we produced 150,000 bars a month. The refugees asked for pink soap, and that is what we made. We used palm and coconut oils from large tin containers, which were then recycled into buckets and bakery pans. Again, nothing was wasted.

As the Khmer Christian church grew, the Khmers began composing worship songs in their own language. We realized they should be using their own musical instruments, but there were not many in the camp. World Vision knew of a few refugees who could make instruments such as the *tro Khmer*, a three-string fiddle made of coconut shell and hardwood, and the *tro che*, a two-string wooden fiddle covered with snakeskin. We opened a small craft school to manufacture these instruments, and soon the beautiful voices of Khmer church worshipers were accompanied by the Khmer instruments from their own culture.

THE KHMER REFUGEE crisis forever changed the lives of those of us who served among the refugees. We have heard thousands of stories from the Khmer. One of them is about Saveth, a refugee with an extraordinary story. When Saveth was a young child, a missionary came to his village and gave him a tract. When Saveth took it home, his mother got angry and told him Christianity was a foreigner's religion. Cambodia had been ruled by a Buddhist monarchy for centuries and was set against Christianity. The French had colonized Cambodia, and Khmer leaders branded Christianity "white man's religion."

When Saveth was ten years old, he helped get income for his family by smuggling sugar into Thailand from his border village, Poipet. On one of his trips across the border, some people in Thailand told him that the communist Khmer Rouge were going to take over his nation, and they urged him to bring his family to live in Thailand. Saveth told his father what he was hearing.

"Don't worry, our nation is not going to be overthrown by the communists," his father told him.

That same year, the Khmer Rouge did overthrow the government troops in the nation's capital, Phnom Penh. They occupied Saveth's village, closing the border with Thailand. The Khmer Rouge tormented families, first taking fathers away to murder them, then coming back later to kill remaining family members.

The Khmer Rouge soldier who killed Saveth's father was someone Saveth knew well. The soldier had been a Buddhist monk in the local temple, and many times Saveth and his family had presented offerings of food and other things to him. Saveth made a vow that he would someday find a way to kill the monk and avenge his father's death.

Miraculously, the soldiers never came back for Saveth and his siblings. But as time went on, the entire village was torn apart. Families were separated and sent away, forced to work on Khmer Rouge projects around the country.

When the Vietnamese army invaded Cambodia in 1979, they began fierce battles with the Khmer Rouge around the country, including the area where Saveth was living. The day the battle hit his village, Saveth and the villagers took the opportunity to escape, running down the road and away from their Khmer Rouge captors. They couldn't traverse fields or forests because land mines were planted everywhere, so the group ran straight down the road, without cover.

Saveth had been separated from his mother and siblings and didn't know whether they were alive. He was terrified. He began to pray to Buddha, to Allah, to a Japanese Shinto god that he had heard about, and then suddenly he remembered hearing about the Creator God who had made the world. Still running for his life, he prayed, "God, if You are real, please protect me and I will follow You all the rest of my life!" As Saveth prayed those words, he saw a picture of a huge hand reaching down from above and completely covering him so that he was hidden. Filled with peace, he kept running. He ran until he was exhausted, sank to the ground, tears streaming from his eyes, and committed his life to the Creator God.

When Saveth finally reached the border of Thailand, he was not able to get across. For six months, he lived in this no-man's-land war zone, trapped between the murderous Khmer Rouge and the closed Thai border.

With no aid from the outside and no food to eat, many people were dying of starvation. It was during this time that Saveth was reunited with his mother. Saveth found out that sometime after his father had died, the Khmer Rouge had forced his mother to marry another man.

When Saveth found her, she was so weak from sickness and lack of food that very soon she died. These six months were the darkest time of his life. He did believe in the Creator God to whom he had prayed on the road that day, but he didn't know Him. He was losing all hope.

Just when Saveth thought he couldn't take any more, the Thai military opened the border. Saveth was able to get across to a refugee camp in Thailand, which at that time was nothing but a vast former rice paddy. There he found both food and some medical services. One day he saw a group of Christian Khmers in the middle of the field praying and worshiping God. They were thanking God for sending them rain, providing food, and protecting them. Saveth began attending their meetings, thinking that perhaps they were worshiping the Creator God who had saved his life on the road in Cambodia. It was confusing for him because they were talking about a God named Jesus, of whom he had never heard. They told him that Jesus had died on a cross, but Saveth was certain that his Creator God was too great to have ever died. Moreover, Jesus had to be alive because He had saved Saveth's life just six months before.

As time went on, Saveth became convinced that this Jesus really was the Creator God who had saved his life in Cambodia. Still, he was holding on to his Buddhist beliefs because he thought that if he was a faithful Buddhist, in his next reincarnation he would be reunited with his deceased parents. He would arrive early in the morning to the Buddhist temple to make merit, then go to the church later in the day to worship Jesus. He said that he really felt lucky, having the better of two worlds.

Saveth's thinking changed one day as a pastor gave an example showing how we must be totally committed to Jesus Christ. The pastor talked about how two trains run on two tracks alongside each other. He said that if those tracks were ever divided or went in two different directions, the trains would certainly crash. As he spoke, Saveth realized that he had been traveling two different directions, Buddhism and Christianity. After the service he talked with the pastor, wanting to follow Jesus. He experienced great joy and peace and knew for the first time in his life that all his sins were really forgiven.

As he walked out the door of the church and began to walk home, Saveth saw directly in front of him the man who had killed his father five years previously. The two men were just a few feet from each other. Their eyes locked, and instantly, all the hurt, bitterness, anger, and revenge from all those years erupted inside Saveth.

Saveth always carried a gun with him so he could be ready to kill this man. As he looked at the man's face, all the memories flashed in his mind, and at that moment, he wanted more than anything to kill the man. He prayed in his heart, "God, please just let me kill him right now, and then I will follow You forever. I really need to do this to avenge my father's death." He heard very clearly in his mind the voice of the Lord speaking to him, saying, "Son, killing this man will not bring your father back to you. What just happened to you five minutes ago inside that church? Did I not just forgive all your sins? You need to forgive this man, just as I forgave you."

Saveth knew that he could not kill his enemy. Instead he said to the man, "I am just as sinful as you are. God has forgiven me for my sins, and I must forgive you as well. The past is gone. I forgive you and will not hold my father's death against you any longer."

The man turned and fled. Instantly, Saveth was filled with incredible peace and joy, and all the bitterness, anger, and heaviness of those years disappeared forever. From that day onward, Saveth was never again afraid or ashamed to share with anyone he met the good news of his Creator God, Jesus Christ.

Sometime after this, Saveth was moved to Khao-I-Dang refugee camp, where we were working. For the next few years, he was a translator and had a leadership role in the work of YWAM in that camp. He and his siblings were eventually resettled in Australia in 1986. The following year, he began to travel around Australia sharing the gospel with Khmer people. He challenged them to pray for Cambodia to open up to the gospel, for missionaries to go in, and for Christian Khmers to return and share the good news with the people still living there.

Saveth prayed for God to send other Khmer believers, but not himself, back to Cambodia. The memories were painful, and he greatly feared the thought of returning. Finally one day he said to God, "If You want me to go back, I will." A few years later, in 1989, Hun Sen, the prime minister of Cambodia, wrote a letter to the former leader of the Christian and Missionary Alliance, who had led their work in

Cambodia prior to the war, and asked them to return and help rebuild the nation. The doors opened for many mission organizations, including YWAM, to begin long-term work there. The door was now open for Saveth to return for a visit. He was still very fearful but obedient. As he stepped off the plane for the first time in Phnom Penh, he burst into tears at the mercy of God to be back in his country as a follower of Jesus. Saveth is now a senior leader in a Cambodian church in Australia, which is doing regular outreach into Cambodia.

After hearing stories like this, we gave thanks to God and welcomed all that He was doing in our midst. As the work expanded, so did our hearts.

Life in the Camps

*I ask God to give you strength, and to make it possible for you
soon to find the peace and security of a stable home. And may
you experience God's love in your hearts.*
  —POPE JOHN PAUL II, Phanat Nikhom Refugee Camp, 1984

EVEN THOUGH MANY refugees were being reset-
tled in third countries, for the remaining refugees this was a time of
diminished hopes, of realization that there would be no quick path to
resettlement and that the prospects of returning to a free and peaceful
life in their own countries remained small and distant. (In addition to
those from Cambodia, large numbers of refugees were from Laos and
Vietnam.) Both refugees and those who worked with them faced a long
and painful period in which provision needed to be made not only for
the immediate needs of food, medicine, and shelter but also for education, spiritual support, and the encouragement of culture.

The refugee crisis had ceased to command the same media attention it had previously commanded. For this reason, events like the visit

of Pope John Paul II to the camps in May 1984 were most welcome. The pope spoke at the Phanat Nikhom transit center refugee camp near Bangkok:

> Dear Brothers and Sisters,
>
> I have greatly desired to meet you during my visit to Thailand. Although my stay here at Phanat Nikhom is very brief, it has a deep meaning for me. I want you to know that my words transcend all barriers of speech: they are spoken in the language of the heart. My heart goes out to you. It is the heart of a brother who comes to you in the name of Jesus Christ to bring a message of compassion, consolation and hope; it is a heart that embraces each and every one of you as friends and fellow human beings; a heart that reaches out to all those round the world who share your condition and experience life as refugees.

The refugees were amazed that such a global religious leader would come to be with them and pray for them. The pope's visit opened the door wider for us to share the gospel.

In the border camps we had contact with three leaders of the Free Khmer group. A YWAM nurse was able to pray with one of them who wanted to walk in the ways of the Lord Jesus. The Free Khmer leader requested that our teams share with his other leaders more about what the Bible has to say about issues like public health, community, and leadership development. This was encouraging because we had been praying for these opportunities since we'd arrived in Thailand.

Meanwhile, almost losing my leg as a teenager was still having an impact on me. I had no feeling on my upper right leg and had to keep it out of the sun. I also continued having surgeries to remove scar tissue from the urethra. The scar tissue, if allowed to build up, would cause a blockage and serious infection. My first surgery in Bangkok was in 1985, and I continued to have these operations every six to seven years. However, I realized, as it says in 2 Corinthians 1:4, that I was able to give to others the comfort and compassion I had received from God. The consequences of my accident had enabled me to relate to disabled refugees in a powerful way.

Mou was one of those with whom I felt a special bond. At age nineteen while fleeing Cambodia, he had stepped on a land mine, resulting in his left leg being blown off. Mou ended up in the KID hospital and was very depressed, thinking that his life was over. He hardly ate and was skin and bones, letting his nails and hair grow long and dirty. He didn't care about living.

Silke Bernstein, a German YWAM nurse, started to care for Mou. She was bright and bubbly and began to bring him out of himself, washing and cutting his hair and fingernails. Even though I had not lost my leg, I could identify with Mou's disability. I told Mou my story, translated by another refugee into Khmer.

"Mou, life is not over for you," I said again and again until I felt he had taken it in.

Slowly Mou started living again, and after a few months he was walking around on crutches with a huge smile on his face. His recovery touched me deeply, since it reminded me of myself. I also had thought my life was over, but God had stepped in and intervened in my crisis, and I would never be the same.

AS THE MONTHS at Aran turned into years, our long-term YWAM team working in the camps became very close—so close that special relationships formed. The first was with a couple who ended up marrying in KID in January 1984.

Canadian John Paddon had taken over the leadership of the border team along with American Jesse Ylauan after Marie and I moved to Bangkok. They were both eligible bachelors, and John was smitten with Norwegian Tove Pedersen, who headed up the preschools. Their romance was not altogether smooth sailing, though. Tove, a strong-willed Viking, was running away from the idea of commitment to John. She wasn't sure if John really cared for her.

It all came to a head when John and Tove were in Bangkok for a Cambodian language course. Tove left the course early, upset with something John had done. Marie and I arranged to meet with them at five o'clock to talk things through, but Tove decided to head straight back to Aran on the four o'clock bus. John was very dejected when we arrived back at the house.

"I guess that's that," he said bleakly.

"Are you kidding? Let's go get her!" I replied.

Always up for a good car chase, I drove like there was no tomorrow to catch up with the bus that had left an hour before we did. Just three stops before the bus arrived in Aran, we saw it on the road in front of us. By now it was dark. As the bus was letting passengers off, I swung our four-wheel-drive vehicle in front of it while John jumped out of the car and onto the bus to find Tove, who was shocked and amazed that John had come all that way to get her. John's actions spoke volumes. It wasn't long before a wedding was organized in the Khmer church in KID, a place they chose to celebrate with all their refugee friends.

Tove wore a simple and beautiful white peasant-style dress made for her in Bangkok. Purple orchids adorned her hair. Marie was Tove's matron of honor, and Tove had two bridesmaids. The church was decorated with palm leaves and orchids.

Most of the refugees had never seen a Western wedding, and in a culture where public displays of affection are frowned on, they all laughed and clapped when John kissed his bride. The couple walked away from the church with a crowd of refugees cheering and rejoicing with them.

Despite the successes and the weddings, we were still in a war zone. We realized this when some of our team came close to being kidnapped and murdered. In 1985 our medical team was departing Site Six, one of the new camps, at about 5:00 p.m. Four nurses and one doctor were traveling in a yellow Toyota van with a Thai driver, Khun Suwit. Just as they got outside the camp, the driver saw three men in black fatigues with scarves covering their faces jump out from behind the bushes onto the red clay road. They were in the middle of no-man's-land between Cambodia and Thailand.

The medical team gasped in shock as they saw the men raise their AK47s and start spraying the van, blowing out the front window. Thinking fast, the driver veered to the left side of the road, then quickly reversed, speeding the van backward away from the men. All of a sudden another gunman appeared on the other side of the road and started shooting. The side windows of the van were blown out by the bullets, spraying glass onto the team members, who by now had scrambled onto the floor. As one of the nurses fell to the floor, he looked up and saw a bullet lodge itself straight into the seat where he had just been sitting. He escaped death by a fraction of a second.

The team's van driver showed incredible courage, reversing and ducking as low as he could to avoid the bullets. When the van had traveled about three hundred meters away from the men, who were still shooting, the group saw a water truck coming toward them. Without hesitation the driver pulled up next to it, and the team scrambled out of the van and into the truck. The water-truck driver then turned his vehicle around and sped back with all of them to the army checkpoint at Site Six. Only the doctor was wounded, his forehead grazed by a bullet. The injury was superficial, but he still needed ten stitches.

Later the UN said it was miraculous that no one had been killed. The team members were all remarkably calm, each one knowing God's protection and having peace. It was a mystery to us why the team was attacked, but later we found out that a Khmer leader also traveled from camp to camp in a yellow Toyota van. The situation was likely a case of mistaken identity.

Our team was spending a lot of time on the road traveling to new refugee camps built up along the border. By 1985 we started a new base of operation in a town called Ta Phraya, an hour north of Aran. John and Tove headed up this team. Jesse Ylauan continued to lead the team in Aran, but he was not alone for long. In April 1985 he married a beautiful German nurse named Ute who had been working with us. It was another wedding for the YWAM team. Over the years about twenty couples met and married while serving in the camps.

Hundreds of water trucks were traveling daily in and out of the camps to provide the twelve liters of water now allotted to each refugee. Site Two grew to be one of the largest border camps, with over 220,000 inhabitants.

In the early morning hours of March 31, 1988, a water truck was heading to Site Two when the driver was stopped by a man in black clothes who stepped onto the road with an AK47. The gunman demanded the driver take him to Site Three, an empty camp being prepared for a new influx of refugees. At 8:30 a.m. the gunman then ordered the driver to get back on the road. It seemed he was looking for foreigners to kidnap or rob. The terrified water-truck driver obediently drove off as the gunman pointed an AK47 at his head.

As they drove, the first vehicle the two came across was from the American Refugee Committee (ARC), with a Thai driver and American nurse inside. The water truck came to a standstill, and the gunman got out, stopping the ARC vehicle. He pulled his gun out and tried to shoot the ARC driver, but his gun jammed and didn't go off. It was just enough time for the ARC driver to slam the jeep into gear and speed off, with the gunman's shot now hitting their mirror. When they arrived at the next checkpoint they reported the situation to volunteer soldiers.

As this was happening, YWAMer Sally Rymer, a midwife from Yorkshire, England, was on the road with a Thai driver named Khun Sutin. As they approached the same intersection where the ARC vehicle had been, they saw the gunman and the water truck. Sally quickly got out her radio to contact UNBRO security, but it was too late. The gunman was already pointing his gun at Sally and Sutin. He ordered them out of the front of their vehicle and into the backseat. He and the water-truck driver then got into the front. The gunman took Sally's radio and kept his AK47 pointed at her while shouting to the water-truck driver. They drove about three kilometers until they were in an open area a good distance from any village. The gunman took the keys and ordered Sutin to sit in the passenger side of the vehicle.

Sally had no idea what the gunman was about to do, but all of a sudden three *au saw* (volunteer soldiers from the village) came speeding up on motorcycles. The gunman panicked and started shooting out the window. In the flurry of bullets one of the volunteer soldiers was shot dead and the other two were badly injured. One later died and the other was paralyzed.

Meanwhile, Sutin and the water-truck driver had made a run for it into the bushes. Sally, her heart beating fast, quickly got out and crouched next to the vehicle's rear wheel. She found herself in the middle of the cross fire, with the bullets hitting the ground all around her. Sutin had grabbed one of the guns from the injured *au saw* volunteers and was shooting at the gunman, who was hiding at the other side of the vehicle. Suddenly there was silence. He had shot the gunman dead.

By 8:55 two truckloads of Thai soldiers arrived, shooting their bazookas straight at the vehicle where Sally was hiding. The UN security officer arrived on the scene and gasped as he took in what had happened. "It's a miracle you're alive, Sally," he said as he helped her to safety.

Shaken, Sally and Sutin were driven back to the team house in Ta Phraya. Marie and I were in Bangkok, and when we heard the news, we jumped into a truck to drive the five hours to Ta Phraya, not knowing the outcome of the kidnapping and shooting.

During the Ta Phraya 6:30 staff prayers that morning, Australian Dr. Bruce Wauchope had felt God give him Psalm 91: "Living in the Most High's shelter, camping in the Almighty's shade, I say to the Lord, 'You are my refuge, my stronghold! You are my God—the one I trust!' God will save you from the hunter's trap and from deadly sickness. God will protect you with his pinions; you'll find refuge under his wings. His faithfulness is a protective shield. Don't be afraid of terrors at night, arrows that fly in daylight, or sickness that prowls in the dark, destruction that ravages at noontime. Even if one thousand people fall dead next to you, ten thousand right beside you—it won't happen to you." Thus when Dr. Bruce heard of the kidnapping and ambush, he had peace that everything was going to be all right.

When we arrived in Ta Phraya, as soon as Sally saw Marie, she fell into her arms. Marie held Sally tight like a mother. We were amazed as we heard the story. Even though we rejoiced at the sparing of Sally's and Sutin's lives and were deeply grateful at the heroic actions of the volunteer soldiers, we were all distraught for the soldiers' families. The soldiers were very poor Thai villagers and had left behind wives and children.

Some of us attended the funeral of one soldier—Hanpasop Suriya, who was twenty-nine years old and had two young children. It was the first time we had been to a Buddhist funeral. The body of Hanpasop was placed in a rickety plywood coffin while people mourned to the sound of rockets and shelling in the distance. Hanpasop's brother walked around and around the coffin, crying out and hitting it hard with his hand, so hard that we wondered if the coffin would fall off its perch. We were told that the man was calling out to his brother, asking for forgiveness for something in the past, crying because it was too late to receive that forgiveness. There was such a heaviness at the funeral, with the family believing that the untimely death was their karma, or lot in life. Our hearts broke for them.

YWAM took an offering to help provide for the families of the soldiers, as did UNBRO and other volunteer agencies. Sally's parents later set up a trust so that money could be given out in regular allotments to pay for the education of the soldiers' children.

Sally had had amazing peace in a terrifying situation. She remembers being on the ground, crouched behind the wheel, hearing bullets whiz past her, and praying, "Lord, I don't know if I am coming to see You now, but I am ready."

This was the Thursday before Good Friday, and the experience led to an amazing Easter celebration for us all. The resurrection message of Jesus again spoke to us. Regardless of the difficult situation we had just faced, we needed always to be ready. God, as He promised, would always be with us and never leave us.

We knew we were not immune to the dangers of living in a war zone, and the team members were making a huge sacrifice to live and work there. Sometimes it was harder for their families back home, hearing of a situation like this on the news, with sporadic telephone communication with their son or daughter and letters that could take two weeks to arrive. Since Marie and I felt we could help ease the minds of family members, every time we traveled to a country where parents of our team members lived, we would call or visit, just to let them know how well their sons and daughters were doing. However, we learned very quickly that a phone call out of the blue from the leader of one's son or daughter's team could cause parents to immediately think the worst. We had to start the conversation by saying, "Hello, this is Steve Goode, your daughter is fine, your son is fine." We would have to repeat that until they realized that we were not calling to inform them that their child had been injured, or worse.

MANY OF OUR volunteers came initially to work with the refugees, but while working in Thailand, some of them, like Sam and Pat Sarvis, started to hear from God about long-term work among the Thai people. Sam and Pat met while on staff at the YWAM New Jersey base. In September 1981, as newlyweds they traveled across the United States to California to fly to Thailand to work with us in KID. At that time we had a "no children at the border" policy because of the war zone instability and possible danger. However, by the time they had reached California, Pat was pregnant. If we had known, we would not have accepted them, but they arrived and became pillars of this YWAM work. Luke, Rachel, and Joshua were all born in Thailand, and the Sarvis family was a great blessing to the team and the Khmer people. The Sarvises left at the end of 1986 for home leave and more training and returned to Thailand in June 1988, focusing on Thai language study. While serving the refugees, God gave them a love for the nation and spoke clearly to them that Thailand was their place of calling and destiny.

Our favorite memory of Sam is the night of the lunar eclipse in 1982 when we learned that according to Thai tradition, there is a frog spirit that will eat the moon. The villagers' job is to scare the spirit away, which they do by making a lot of noise and shooting in the air at the spirit. With so many weapons around at the time, when night fell, the noise of pistols, AK47s, and shouting filled the air. It was terrifying. Sam and the team—not yet knowing this tradition—thought the Vietnamese had finally invaded Thailand. They were all crawling along the floors so as not to be seen. Sam inched his way to the phone we had recently installed and called us in Bangkok.

"The Vietnamese are attacking," he whispered.

I could hear the shooting in the background, and my heart sank. I knew the very real danger the team was in now. Or so I thought.

We rallied the team in Bangkok and began to pray for the Aran team. It was not until the next morning that we got the full story. Since we had not heard from Sam, I decided to call.

"Ah, yes," Sam said sheepishly. "It wasn't the Vietnamese."

"Who was it? The Khmer Rouge?" I asked.

"No, not the Khmer Rouge," Sam said.

"Who then?" I went on, confused.

"Well, it was the frog spirit," Sam said with a hint of a smile coming across in his voice.

We all had a good laugh when we heard the whole story, but this experience only prepared Sam and Pat for their new home in Bangkok, since they felt called to minister in the slums. The Sarvises were living in a big white duplex close to the slums, and the landlord opened a casino on the other side. This didn't prove too problematic until one night they heard gunshots from the casino. The next morning Sam asked the landlord what happened.

"*Mai mii phanhaa! Pi Nong gan!*" he replied, laughing.

He was saying that there was no problem, it was only friends having a good time together, but the Sarvises decided it was time to move in another direction with their family. Sam became director of our Thai foundation, called Project L.I.F.E. (Love/Life in a Family Environment), before becoming YWAM Thailand national director. In 2009 Sam and Pat went on to pioneer a ministry to the urban poor in Bangkok. We always say every team needs a "Sam and Pat."

We could fill several chapters with stories about the many people who came to Thailand to minister to the poor and needy during the refugee crisis. As we worked together, God was also opening our eyes to the plight of refugees in other countries. We began to ask Him how and what we should do, and step-by-step He began to open doors.

TEN

Mercy Ministries

History belongs to the intercessors who believe the future into
being. —WALTER WINK

NEARLY 100,000 KHMER refugees had left Thailand to be resettled in third countries. This was only the tip of the iceberg. Refugees would continue to flee until 1990, long after Vietnam had overthrown the Khmer Rouge.

The decade of the 1980s was a significant emphasis on and expansion of Mercy Ministries (MM) internationally as a mission—to bring hope to the hopeless, love to the vulnerable, and care to the orphan, elderly, and homeless. I was appointed MM director by YWAM's Asia Pacific leadership council in August 1985. That role would involve visiting refugee crisis locations and situations of poverty around the region.

I increased my travel to Asian countries to see the needs of the poor and look for opportunities and ways to serve. This meant an increased level of faith and financial support to meet additional costs. In a visit to Calcutta (Kolkata), two other leaders and I met with Mother Teresa at the Home for the Dying. At this home, the Missionaries of Charity had cared for more than 400,000 people, with half of them dying at this center. Mother Teresa had said, "There is much suffering in the world—very much. And the physical suffering is suffering from hunger, suffering from homelessness, from all kinds of diseases . . . but I still think no one should ever die alone."

Mother Teresa had just returned from visiting Bhopal in India, the site of the worst industrial catastrophe in the world at that time. Approximately fifteen thousand people had been killed by leaked methyl isocyanate. Mother Teresa was not stopping long in Calcutta but was going on to Ethiopia, where a famine was destroying the country. The team I was with had only a few minutes with her. Somehow she knew that this year would be YWAM's twenty-fifth anniversary, and she simply took our hands and said, "Thank you for what you are doing for the poor."

We really felt the presence of Jesus in the Home for the Dying and knew that He was the One we had to look to, to bring hope and comfort to the broken and hopeless. Mother Teresa prayed with us that God would use our hands even more to show the love of Jesus to the poor. The Missionaries of Charity wrote a book called *We Do It for Jesus* about why they serve the poor. It reads: "Our priority is Jesus, not social work. We meet daily for prayer and worship and then minister to Jesus among the diseased and dying."

Spearheading this crisis expression of mercy ministry among the poor meant serving at yearly YWAM International leaders meetings (now called the Global Leadership Forum) and participating with the Asia Pacific leadership team. Marie and I had come to know many of the European leaders while we were working in Switzerland and Europe, and as new initiatives were occurring, God was sending out more and more leaders around the world. It was an incredible privilege to work with these leaders and staff in pioneering new efforts in Asia.

Gary and Helen Stephens had pioneered outreach to the Vietnamese boat people in Hong Kong and then established Mother's Choice, a place offering young pregnant women alternatives to going to China for abortions, assistance in parenting skills, and adoption resources. God was strengthening us through deep, open relationships, prayer, and going through crises together.

One of my first challenges as part of the Asian leadership team took place in Nepal. In 1985 an outreach team of thirteen people was wrongly arrested in a rural area there. Because the case had been filed with the court, it had to go through the legal system, and the fact that it involved non-Nepalese made the process that much longer. I went to Kathmandu, where we were able to post bail for the team. They were freed but had to report to the court every four months until the trial was complete. Sometimes the wheels of justice turn slowly in this part of the world, and it took four years for the team to be exonerated. During this time I spoke at a GO (Global Outreach) festival of young people in Denmark about the arrests in Nepal. These young people took an offering, and what they gave covered travel and legal costs for the team members.

The case was closed in 1990, while at the same time democracy was birthed in Nepal and the Nepali church began incredible growth. From only a handful of local believers, estimates of up to one million Christians are now in the country.

THE MERCY MINISTRY work continued in Thailand, expanding to new parts of the country. YWAMers Harold Huang and John and Jill Bills had been part of the first team working in the Rangsit transit camp on the outskirts of Bangkok. They later moved to establish additional refugee work two hours away, in Phanat Nikhom, the last camp where refugees stayed before being resettled to a third country. The team lived in the town of Phanat and entered the refugee camp daily, providing the same care and assistance, except for health care, as at the border camps.

New Zealander Roslyn Jackson took up the leadership in Phanat Nikhom. She was a very practical leader who started out with sewing and knitting programs and developed the clothing distribution for refugees going to third countries. Also under her leadership, the Vietnamese preschools and primary schools began.

In 1988 Roslyn moved to Bangkok to coordinate YWAM Relief Services until the camps were closed in 1995. During this time God spoke to her about long-term work in Vietnam. Roslyn moved to Vietnam to begin her language study while our YWAM Mercy Ministry office in Thailand registered our first NGO in Hanoi in 1997. (Roslyn continues to lead that NGO, serving with community development programs through microfinance, business training, preschool training, waste management, renewable energies [biogas], cow banks, and small enterprise development projects.)

Yvonne Dos Santos from South Africa came to work with refugees in late 1980. She had been a friend since our training school in Lausanne in 1974, and we were very pleased to have her with us again. One day while at the Rangsit transit camp, she was introduced to a young Cambodian girl named Solina.

Solina was very depressed because although she and her father had been scheduled to leave for a third country, her father had contracted tuberculosis and their application was put on medical hold. As Yvonne spent time with Solina, trying to encourage her, she shared the gospel, telling her about the God who loved her.

Solina was from a Buddhist background and had been captured by the Khmer Rouge before escaping with her father and finding her way to the border. After hearing the gospel, Solina simply said, "I want to give my life to God."

"Really?" Yvonne said, taken aback by how quickly Solina had decided to be a follower of Jesus. Yvonne prayed with her then and there and, together with another YWAMer, received permission to take Solina out of the camp for a couple of hours. The two YWAMers took her back to the base and spent some time praying and talking with her.

Solina was a new person. Her depression lifted, and she had a smile on her face. When the Phanat Nikhom camp was ready, the refugees from Rangsit were moved there, and Solina began working for YWAM. She did not want to accept any payment for what she did because her service was part of her worship to God. Solina ended up keeping all the payment envelopes, not even opening them and actually stamping them "Return to Sender." When she was in need, she trusted God to provide for her in a different way, and He was faithful to provide through letters she received containing small amounts of money. Someone even sent Solina a suitcase of used clothing that fit her father perfectly, coming at a time when he was in real need.

After six months Solina and her father were relocated to Canada. Before Solina left the camp, she put all of her pay envelopes into one big envelope and gave it to a YWAMer, instructing that the envelope be taken to the base and not be opened before evening. By then Solina and her father would be in Bangkok, en route to Canada.

Solina spent seven years in Canada. She found a good church with a former Thai missionary to support her, attended a DTS, and traveled on outreach. When she returned to Bangkok, Solina spoke at a YWAM meeting. She said that in the years she lived in Cambodia, God had put a hunger in her heart to find out if He existed. She remembered looking at a grain of rice during the Khmer Rouge time and thinking of creation, wondering who it was that created the first grain of rice and who created the world. Solina now lives in Cambodia, where she is involved in recording and broadcasting Christian programs.

WHILE WORKING IN Bangkok and at the camps along the Cambodian border, we saw the need to assist the Vietnamese boat people who were streaming into southern Thailand, escaping their communist country after the Vietnam War. When they arrived in Thailand, barely alive from the harrowing journey, they were held at a refugee camp called Songkla.

A small team of women moved to Songkla to teach English in the camp. It was important for the refugees to learn English, since they had to know a certain amount of the language before resettlement. The team was heartbroken to hear refugee stories of women being brutally raped as they came over in rickety boats, often attacked by Thai pirates. Most of the refugee group were part of a Saigon middle class who sold everything for a place on a boat. The journey across the South China Sea and Gulf of Thailand was treacherous, and many came without food or water.

THE NEEDS OF the refugees were huge, but we had to be careful not to spread ourselves too thin. Our main strategy was to bring the needs we knew before the Lord and ask Him where we should go and what we should do. God was speaking to us from His Word as we loved and served the refugees. Matthew 25:34–40 was particularly poignant:

Then the king will say to those on his right, ". . . I was hungry and you gave me food to eat. I was thirsty and you gave me a drink. I was a stranger and you welcomed me. I was naked and you gave me clothes to wear. I was sick and you took care of me. I was in prison and you visited me." Then those who are righteous will reply to him, "Lord, when did we see you hungry and feed you, or thirsty and give you a drink? When did we see you as a stranger and welcome you, or naked and give you clothes to wear? When did we see you sick or in prison and visit you?" Then the king will reply to them, "I assure you that when you have done it for one of the least of these brothers and sisters of mine, you have done it for me."

Our 1989 year-end Thailand report spoke of our scope of service: we clothed 80,000 refugees and aided Thais along the border, served an average of 3,100 Khmer refugees who visited our health clinics daily, administered 13,000 vaccinations to children under the age of five, and fed 220 malnourished children daily. In that year, YWAM-trained traditional midwives oversaw 4,000 births, and our schools and libraries enabled over 11,000 refugees to receive development training. Through YWAM post office and banking services, 90,000 letters or transactions were averaged each month. Thousands of refugees saw and heard the gospel presented through acts of mercy, personal sharing, Bible studies, and practical support to churches. In everything we heard the words of Jesus: "When you have done it for one of the least of these brothers and sisters of mine, you have done it for me."

During this time we had been trying to get into Cambodia to help the poor living there and particularly those who had yet to see or hear the gospel. Many were living in terrible conditions because of the Khmer Rouge genocide and the Vietnamese invasion. Three times we tried to get permission, and each time our visa request was denied. In 1990 we were allowed to visit the country. There was huge excitement when we found out, and plans were made for my first trip with a doctor and an agriculturist who had previously served with us. I took a second trip with Philip Scott and Pierre Tami. Philip, from the UK, was a leader of YWAM work at one of the border camps, and Pierre, a Swiss Italian, worked with YWAM in Japan and Singapore. We flew into Cambodia from Vietnam. At that time the Red Cross flew in three times a week from Ho Chi Minh City.

Immediately upon arrival in Phnom Penh, we were placed under close watch and were not permitted to travel anywhere without a government escort. The civil war was still raging in many areas, and what immediately caught our attention was the abject poverty. We made an appointment to visit the Ministry of Foreign Affairs to see where we could serve the people.

We knew we wanted to go to the place of greatest need, areas where the UN and other NGOs were least likely to go because of challenge or remoteness and where people had not yet seen or heard the gospel.

As we entered an old French colonial-style building that housed the Ministry of Foreign Affairs, two men in uniform greeted us. In French, we explained that we wanted to learn about the poorest provinces of Cambodia with the greatest need, places that would most likely be overlooked. "Please meet with the Committee for the Development of the Northeast," we were told.

One of the officials told us, "There are five provinces like that in the northeast, including Ratanakiri and Stung Treng, but they are difficult places. That is where Pol Pot started the Khmer Rouge in 1972. There are still many Khmer Rouge there, plus they have no electricity or running water."

"Can we go there?" I asked.

The man nearly fell off his chair. "Why would you want to go *there*?"

I told him we were serious about working with the most poor and needy.

"Okay," the official said, shrugging his shoulders. "When can you leave?"

"Tomorrow," Philip replied.

The man nodded and left the room. A Khmer official was able to get us seats on an old Russian Antonov 24 plane with Russian pilots. The plane was overbooked, with rows of plastic stools placed down the aisles and armrests lifted to fit three people in two seats. As we squeezed into our seats, it felt as if we were in a sauna. The plane had been parked in the tropical sun, but the air conditioning could not be turned on until after takeoff. When it was eventually turned on, clouds of condensation poured out of the vents, making it impossible to see the row in front of us through the fog.

Because Cambodia was still a communist country, a government minder traveled with us to keep close watch. Poor Ms. T, who was assigned to mind us, was terrified to travel to the northeast because of the Khmer Rouge and the prevalence of malaria. We flew to Stung Treng and visited the main hospital to begin our need assessment there. The hospital was an old building with no electricity, running water, or medicines. It had large holes in the roof and pools of water on the sunken ward floors. The atmosphere was sad, and the hospital was simply a place for people to go and die.

We then drove in two army jeeps to the neighboring province of Ratanakiri with armed soldiers to protect us along the roads. Bridges were washed out, and we had to drive down the embankments, through the streams, and back up the other side. The landscape was beautiful, with dense jungle, wild animals, lakes, and hill tribes. A bombed-out building next to a beautiful crater lake called Bung Yeak Laom had once been the winter residence of Norodom Sihanouk, king of Cambodia. We enjoyed a cool swim there, and a stone we picked up from the lake is now cemented into the Plaza of the Nations at the University of the Nations in Kona, Hawaii.

Even though the scenery was breathtaking, the area had very few people, since it had been bombed heavily during the Vietnam War. We passed many soldiers along the road who warned us to stay on the beaten path to avoid land mines. We were able to visit a tribal village and were told that one of the young tribal girls had just died of malaria. The village was eerily silent except for the piercing wails of the mother mourning her child. While in this village, incongruously, a tribal man showed us a photo of one of his relatives in Paris and asked us to contact the relative for him. Our reception was not very welcoming in Ratanakiri, and I heard one of the Khmers complain to his friend in French that they did not need us there.

"We don't want to be where we are not needed," I replied, and we headed back to Stung Treng. We felt God was making it clear to us, through the reception of the officials in the different provinces, where we should serve.

Stung Treng was where Pol Pot had strengthened the Khmer Rouge in the late 1960s and early 1970s, and there were no known Christians in this province of eighty thousand people. It was reported that a Khmer evangelist had traveled through the province in the late 1960s, but we could see no visible response. We realized this was the place where the poorest lived, where disease was widespread, and where the gospel had not yet been seen or heard. We prayed, asking God if Stung Treng was where YWAM should start a work. God spoke to us through Psalm 24, confirming this location by reminding us that "the earth is the LORD's and everything in it, the world, and all who live in it." This ancient place was included: "Lift up your heads, you gates; be lifted up you ancient doors, that the King of glory may come in."

While we were in the town, Pierre and I asked our communist minder for permission to take a walk after dinner to look around. She seemed disinterested, not concerned at all that we would be out alone in the town.

We stayed in a small guesthouse on the Mekong River, forty kilometers from the Lao border. Our room was quickly infested with bats because the guards were trying to catch them in nets and they were flooding into our room to hide. In the morning the guards offered us a meal of deep-fried bats, which we decided to generously leave for them to enjoy.

As we were strolling along the bank of the river, we saw a man by his bicycle repair cart, repairing a wheel. The cart was filled with wheels, rubber tubes, and other tools for fixing bikes. Pierre walked over and started talking to the man, who immediately greeted us with a welcoming smile. We were able to communicate in French, and the man told us he was called Ly Soun. He was married with five young daughters and invited us to come back for dinner that night at his home. We eagerly accepted his offer and a little later waded into the family's small house that was flooded from the afternoon monsoon rain. Despite having very little, Ly Soun and his family were generous, offering us each a bowl of rice and soup.

Ly Soun told us more of his story over dinner. His father had died when he was young, and his grieving mother abandoned him on the streets of Phnom Penh when he was six years old. To survive, Ly Soun joined a gang and started to rob and steal. It was while he was living on the streets that he met a Catholic priest who had started a home for boys. Ly Soun realized this was a chance to escape life on the streets and so asked the priest if he could live there.

At first the priest refused the boy because he was a troublemaker, but after Ly Soun begged and begged, the priest relented and allowed him to come to the home. The home had a lot of rules, including mandatory chapel every morning. Over the years the only prayer that Ly Soun remembered praying was "Dear God, please have mercy on me and my poor family." He had prayed this every day, even through the Khmer Rouge times.

As Ly Soun told me his childhood prayer, I realized it was not a coincidence that we happened to meet him on the banks of the Mekong River. God was answering the prayer Ly Soun had first prayed as a very small boy. Ly Soun was now in his forties. We saw how God had kept him and his family through the Khmer Rouge. Ly Soun had to act crazy at times to survive being murdered. As I told him that God had heard those prayers, he got very excited.

"Do you want to know more about the God who answers the prayers of a little boy?" I asked.

"Yes!" he said immediately and began to ask us lots of questions about this God.

While with the family, I noticed Ly Soun's girls had terrible skin infections. I knew a simple bar of soap would help, and I went back to the guesthouse to get the bar I had brought with me. Then with the whole family, we went to the Mekong to wash in its muddy waters. With water buffalo lazily watching us from a distance upstream, I gave the family the soap, and the little girls washed their hair and infected skin. Later we found out the girls' skin conditions had cleared up within days.

From then on every time we returned to Stung Treng, we met with Ly Soun and his family. We were able to give him a Bible in Khmer and French on our next visit to the province. His business was blessed, and each time we saw him he had upgraded, going from bicycle repair to motorbike repair to repairing radios and stereos. Ly Soun asked us many questions—something that had been forbidden during the reign of the Khmer Rouge—and within six months he decided that he and his household would serve the Lord. He was baptized in the Mekong River along with eighteen other new believers.

Despite the success of our trip, we nearly had a fatality. After Pierre returned to Singapore, he was diagnosed with a rare strain of cerebral malaria, leaving him with less than 50 percent chance of survival. The doctors at one point told YWAM leader Don Gilman that he did not know if Pierre would make it through the night. Don told Pierre's wife, Simonetta, the next day how serious it had been. While in the hospital, Pierre was in much pain, going in and out of delirium, but through it all he felt God laying Cambodia on his heart and that he needed to return there.

After his near miss with death, Pierre made several trips back into Cambodia in 1991. His first donation to the country was four new microscopes to be used in the Stung Treng hospital to help diagnose malaria. In 1992 he brought not only his wife but also his three very young daughters. During that time, Cambodia was like the old American Wild West. UNTAC (United Nations Transitional Authority in Cambodia) had been created in 1992–93 to oversee the election in each province. However, the organization had its hands full with robberies, drive-by shootings, carjackings, and hostage takings, not to mention the isolated groups of Khmer Rouge that still existed in various parts of the country.

At the same time Philip and his wife, Wendy, and three nurses became the pioneers of the first YWAM base in Stung Treng, which was officially started in 1992.

After Ly Soun's decision to follow Jesus, we saw a real change in him. One day he came to Philip with a troubled expression on his face. "I think God is asking me to help Khmer children who are abandoned or orphaned. Do you think that could be God?" he asked.

"Could be," Philip said, smiling.

Ly Soun obeyed what he felt the Lord was saying, and he and his family moved to Phnom Penh to work with our newly established Hagar Project, started by Pierre and Simonetta, serving women and children at risk on the streets and those sold into prostitution.

ELEVEN

Project L.I.F.E.

*The greatest suffering is being lonely, feeling unloved, just
having no one. I have come more and more to realize that it
is being unwanted that is the worst disease that any human
being can ever experience.*

—MOTHER TERESA

A PATTERN WAS emerging. While we simply obeyed
God in whatever He showed us to do, He then showed us the next steps
to take. We were so encouraged by Ly Soun's story. God had not forgot-
ten the prayer of this young boy and was now using him to bless Cambodia. We saw how Thailand welcomed in refugees, even though it was
a developing country itself. We felt that as Thailand blessed the poor
and the needy, God would bless the land.

YWAM was working in over thirty Thai villages along the border, setting up mobile clinics on the grounds of Buddhist temples, the
center of life in any village. We did public health outreaches, provided

vaccinations, showed women how to better care for their children, gave out mosquito nets to prevent malaria, and helped with basic first aid.

Meanwhile, ten people from our staff moved to Vietnam, fourteen went to Cambodia, three left to work among the Afghan refugees in Pakistan, and a nurse went to serve among refugees in Sudan. Five staff members returned to Europe to begin other YWAM Mercy Ministry operations.

The longer we were in Thailand, the more we saw the brokenness of the country—rural and urban poverty that creates vulnerability and gives opportunity for exploitation. Thailand today is a center for a multibillion-dollar sex industry that includes sex tourism and trafficking. In the early days we were mostly unaware of the extent of this industry, but before long our eyes were opened.

The first time we were touched closely by the issue of trafficking was back in 1984, when the cousin of YWAM Thailand staff member Gampon Kumdee was sold to a brothel. It was a sizzling hot day in Bangkok, and the air conditioning in my tiny office was not working as it should. Just as I was about to go for lunch, Marie came in saying Gampon was outside and wanted to see us.

"I think it's important," Marie said, letting me know that lunch would have to be postponed for a little bit.

In his early twenties, Gampon had been working with our DTS for the past year. He wasn't from Bangkok but was of Thai Lu ethnicity from northern Thailand. He was one of the first Thais to join us after he became a Christian through his father. His whole family had been Buddhist until his father, Pho Sila, became very sick with a mystery illness. Pho Sila was on his deathbed, but he cried out to Jesus and prayed for God to heal him. Miraculously he got better, becoming a believer at the same time. Pho Sila was so impacted by the experience that he told his children about it. His children in turn were amazed at the change in their father. Gampon and his brother and sister became Christians, although an older brother did not.

As Gampon arrived at the door, I offered him a seat. "What can we help you with?" I asked.

"I just found out that my cousin has been sold to a brothel . . . she's only fourteen," Gampon blurted out, distressed.

As Marie and I asked more questions, Gampon filled us in on what had happened to his young cousin. She had been born to his relative's fourth wife. Major and minor wives are common in Thailand if one has the money. For some reason the wife did not want this daughter, nor was the poor girl loved by her father. The wife needed money and so offered her daughter to a brothel in Bangkok, selling her for $1,200.

After Gampon told us all he knew and answered our questions, we prayed together. This was new territory for us, and we prayed for God's wisdom to know what to do.

A ministry in Bangkok called Baan Sukniran (House of Everlasting Joy) worked with child prostitutes under the age of fifteen, either buying them out of brothels or seeing them rescued and referred to shelters. We contacted them and explained the situation. They were able to find Gampon's cousin and rescue her from the brothel, and not long afterward the girl returned to her village. However, now that she was no longer a virgin, she was considered "broken" in Thai culture. Her mother rejected her again, and the girl was resold to another brothel. We were all heartbroken when we heard the news, even more so when we found out her story was not so unusual.

We had to do something. Despite the sad outcome for Gampon's cousin, we had hope that YWAM could make a difference in this area and save other girls from the same fate. A righteous anger rose up in us as a team, and we began to pray about the sex industry, asking God to use us to help those innocent children stolen or sold for sex.

God began to answer these prayers when two YWAMers moved to Bangkok to research the issue and find the place of greatest need. Christina Overeem was Dutch, and Heidi Rau, who had served at the border camps, was German. For one year they studied Thai and carried out a needs assessment on children at risk. They set up Baan Phak Phing, "House of Refuge," as a small home in Bangkok. The home, based on a family model, was for at-risk girls who had been sexually abused by a family member. Christina and Heidi worked closely with the Thai government, and the Ministry of Social Welfare referred girls to them.

After about a year Christina and Heidi realized that the province with the largest number of children at risk was Chiang Rai, eight hundred kilometers (five hundred miles) north of Bangkok toward the borders of Myanmar and Laos. In one year alone in Thailand an esti-mated 800,000 children under the age of sixteen were in prostitution or at risk of being trafficked. After much prayer Christina and Heidi felt that they should move to Chiang Rai, the center of the "Golden Tri-angle," where arms, drugs, and people were trafficked under warlords in Thailand, Myanmar, and Laos.

In the first year they had one house with eight girls. This grew to a second and then a third house. Eventually Baan Phak Phing was asked by the Thai government to build a fourth house just for girls between six and twelve years of age who had been rescued by the Thai police after being trafficked. They now have the capacity for thirty girls to be loved and cared for in a family environment.

One of the girls, called Wan, had been sold to be a human sacrifice to a village seeking gold. Condemned to die, her life had been one of pain and sadness. Her sister had been forced into a marriage, and when Wan was eight years old, her brother-in-law had forced her to look after their children. Wan knew he was not a nice man, and it was not very long before he raped her. After he had finished with her, he sold her to a village who believed a human sacrifice would help them find gold.

One brave man, however, took pity on Wan. He was able to rescue her, and she ended up, broken and afraid, on the doorstep of Baan Phak Phing, where she was welcomed and loved. But healing does not come right away to one who has been so deeply wounded.

After days, weeks, and months of love, prayer, and tender care at Baan Phak Phing, Wan began to trust her new friends and started to blossom. She had hardly spoken a word over those months, the trauma having caused her to remain silent, but slowly she started to speak again. Her life was transformed.

AS YWAMERS IN Thailand began to get a vision for crisis, relief, and development projects like these, I realized we needed a Mercy Min-istry arm for YWAM Thailand. The only way to do this was to set up a foundation. I knew it could be a long and complicated process, taking a minimum of two years.

At this time, Marie and I were attending Christ Church, an Angli-can church in the center of Bangkok. At the morning service on Sunday,

I bumped into a friend who was the acting executive director of the Project L.I.F.E. Foundation.

"We have to close the foundation. We have no one to take over the leadership," my friend informed me.

I told him how sorry I was to hear that, but as we talked, an idea popped into my head. "Would it be possible for YWAM to take over the foundation?" I asked, going on to explain our need for a mercy ministry arm, a legal entity governed by a board that allowed us to operate long-term projects in Thailand, raise funds, buy land, provide audited financial statements, and give tax-deductible receipts. My friend was open to the idea and invited me to come to the board meeting the following week to speak about YWAM and our vision.

Excitedly I told the team the following Monday what had transpired at church. We asked the Lord that, if this was from Him, He would give us favor at the board meeting. I went with Jesse Ylauan and Anita Horton.

Anita had come to Thailand with her daughter, Sara, who was then five, and worked in the Phanat Nikhom refugee camp. Anita had come from a very poor background in Alabama. Someone had believed in her, and she had been able to graduate with honors from MIT, one of the most prestigious universities in America. Her heart was for Thailand and to help those from the poorest backgrounds to be given a chance in life. I felt that Anita should lead Project L.I.F.E. if the board agreed to let us take it over. We met with the board. They heard our hearts and agreed that we could take over the foundation. Instead of changing the board, Jesse, Anita, and I simply joined it, and Anita took over as executive director.

Right away we began to work with what had been started. The first project was helping in a government orphanage for fourteen hundred autistic, disabled, and other special-needs children from Bangkok. Over the five years we worked in the orphanage, it grew to almost five thousand children. However, our heart was never to see a large institution created, because we believed that God put children in families and wanted to encourage this model, especially for disabled and other special-needs children.

At the time we took over the Project L.I.F.E. foundation, which raised educational sponsorship funds, it was down to supporting only three children. Pontip Tamma, who came to the Lord through our YWAM refugee team in Phanat Nikhom, provided new leadership for the program. It was amazing to see how God used many of our relationships in Europe and Asia to mobilize support for hundreds of vulnerable Thai children.

HELP International, a German organization, invited me to speak at their training school. They had a heart for Asia and had experience with the rehabilitation of drug addicts. I asked them to prayerfully consider work with Project L.I.F.E. in creating a shelter for men coming out of drug addiction. Amphetamines, called *yaa baa* (crazy medicine), had flooded into Thailand, destroying families and ruining lives. Baan Op Un Jai, "The Shelter," in Bangkok was subsequently founded. A program that helps men out of addictions and into healing and wholeness in Christ continues to this day.

Vern and Audrey McCauley had a burden to start Eden House, a live-in facility with three homes for thirty-three girls. The girls, between five and twenty years of age, are from hill tribes and are at risk of being sold by a parent or village member into prostitution or slave labor to help support their alcohol and other drug addictions. Orphans in each village are particularly vulnerable. Girls in situations like these cannot fight for themselves and are offered little chance of hope or escape. Each girl resides at Eden House until adulthood so that she can finish school, develop a vocational skill, and have opportunity to prepare for life.

Chiang Rai—where the House of Refuge is located—is also the region where Thailand's AIDS epidemic is at its worst. An estimated 580,000 people are living with HIV—16,000 are under fourteen years of age. To meet this need, Penny and Paul Wilcox of Project L.I.F.E. opened Home of the Open Heart in 1999. Home of the Open Heart looks after orphans and raises awareness about HIV/AIDS in the local community.

We met Suphit (Noo) Sompharn while she was working with Cambodian refugees in Aranyaprathet. She became the coordinator of Rural Women's Development of Project L.I.F.E., providing small loans to poor farmers on the Thai-Cambodian border. While the refugee team was living in Ta Phraya, they would see poor Thai families plant a few vegetables, raise a few chickens, plant rice, and hope for the best. But when the rice harvest failed and drought came, often the husband would travel to Bangkok to work as a day laborer. Many times the men did not return, leaving the women to care for their families with little source of income.

Noo traveled to the villages to talk with the women about how they could generate an income so their husbands did not have to go to Bangkok looking for work. Every village was different. Some women began planting flowers to sell at the market; others began weaving and making sarongs. The women were empowered to know they had the ability to make money when it was needed.

While all these projects were going on, Marie and I felt there was another area where we needed to see God move in Thailand. Very little Christian music was available, and we started thinking about introducing Thailand, and in particular young Thais, to Christian artists to show how they write and create music. Ted Bleymaier, who was working with Word Music, helped us secure the rights to begin producing and selling Christian music tapes in Thailand.

Our vision expanded, and with Ted's contacts we invited Sheila Walsh, a well-known Christian singer, to present two concerts in Bangkok. There had never been a large worship concert in Thailand, and we believed that with these concerts something would break loose in the spiritual realm. Little did we know what we were stirring up in the heavenlies.

We planned for the concerts to be held at two major universities in Bangkok—Thammasat and Ramkhamhaeng. We knew we were doing something right when everything started to go wrong! Knowing the spiritual significance of what we were doing, we told the team to keep praying. We had rented the most high-tech equipment, including a huge thirty-foot-tall light tower and smoke machines. Ten minutes before the first concert was to start, with about fifteen hundred people in the audience, the electric curtain started to close, but it wasn't supposed to. Someone must have thought we wanted the curtain closed before the concert started. We all watched in horror as the curtain slid into one of the light towers, which came crashing to the floor, smashing many of the lights.

At the second concert, with about twenty-five hundred in atten-
dance, Sheila sang one song, and then suddenly the electricity blew out
on the entire campus. For twenty minutes the auditorium was pitch-
black, and we desperately tried to figure out what to do as the crowd
started leaving. Eventually the lights came back on, and we were able to
finish the show. Fifteen hundred people filled out forms to know more
about God—an incredible and encouraging response.

Sheila's concerts marked the beginning of YWAM Music, which
went on to become distributors for Word, Maranatha, and Hillsong
Christian music in the country, with the profits going to Project L.I.F.E.
God had opened yet another income stream for us to help serve the
poor and needy of Thailand.

TWELVE

First Point of Call

Never be afraid to trust an unknown future to a known God.
—CORRIE TEN BOOM

OUR BASE IN BANGKOK became the first point of call for many mission teams. In 1982 alone the hospitality staff welcomed more than fourteen hundred visitors—averaging about four a day. Our team continued to expand to meet the needs we saw around us. This soon became a challenge because we were outgrowing our base in Bangkok and needed to find somewhere to house everybody.

From 1979 to 1984 YWAM Bangkok was housed in a subdivision close to Don Mueang, the old airport. We needed an office downtown, where most of the meetings were held with the UN, Thai government, embassies, and other NGOs that served what was going on in the camps. As Bangkok traffic became more and more congested, we spent up to four to five hours per day in traffic just getting across the city to various meetings.

We had been praying about where we were to move. I felt God prompt me to call my friend Khun Lanjul, who was from a Christian family and whose father had been the first to translate the Bible into the Thai language. I called him to ask if he could help in any way.

"But Khun Steve, I work with the YMCA—I am not in real estate!" he said laughing. I told him I realized that and apologized. I was baffled, having been quite certain that God had asked me to call him.

The next day Khun Lanjul phoned back very excited. "I think I have found a place for you!" he exclaimed. He said they, too, had been looking for a location for their preschool, but the building they had found was too big for their needs. He told me to come look at it with him.

We met later that day at an old Thai-style house on Soi Pipat (Pipat Street) in central Bangkok, a two-minute walk around the corner from Christ Church, the Anglican church we were attending. The YMCA would use the ground floor for their preschool, and we could rent the second floor for offices. Behind the old house was a small apartment complex with five two- and three-bedroom apartments for us and the growing Bangkok staff of YWAM Relief Services. The apartments had been rented to the embassy of Belgium, since the embassy office was right around the corner, but the embassy no longer needed the facility. It seemed perfect for us and was reasonably priced.

When we moved into the new office and apartments in 1984, we were told they were being put up for sale and that we would be able to stay only for about a year. However, the months passed, and the owners sold the property six times, almost doubling their profits each time. This worked well for us, as our low rent was not changed at all during all the transitions.

Christ Church became a real oasis in the city and a home church for several of us. Over the years we developed deep relationships with several of the vicars and their wives and other members of the church. When we outgrew our existing meeting space for YWAM meetings, Christ Church allowed us to use the chapel for three years every Sunday evening and to host our annual Christmas gathering.

In the same area we were introduced to a tennis club within walking distance. The club boasted tennis courts, a swimming pool, and a fitness center. It gave free memberships to volunteers from commonwealth nations who were working with refugees. I applied, and YWAM was accepted for membership. It was a wonderful provision for the staff who were from those nations.

At one point we were told that it would be better if the head of the organization was a paying member. We certainly did not have a tennis club allotment in our budget, but as in everything else, we simply asked God to provide the exact amount. Shortly afterward a British family who attended Christ Church gave us an unexpected gift in the exact amount of the membership. As is customary for us, we asked if the family had a special designation for the donation. They replied that it was a personal gift, and we told them this story. They were thrilled that this gift was an answer to prayer and that it would go toward the membership. We have enjoyed this club, played tennis, and exercised there regularly. Through the years we have made some very special friends, many of whom think and believe differently from us. It has been good for us to learn to listen, hear a diversity of viewpoints, and be able to express ourselves in terms they understand. On many points we have had to agree to disagree, but a continuing respect and appreciation exists for one another. There is seldom a time we enter this club without remembering with gratefulness God's provision for us through our friends.

YWAM WAS GROWING globally as we hit our twenty-ninth year in 1989. We had tripled in size since 1980, with seven thousand full-time staff in four hundred locations. We had subdivided the world into twenty-six regions geographically with regional leadership teams and global initiatives and ministries like Frontier Missions, Mercy Ministries, and Training. We as leaders met annually for prayer and worship, hearing from God and each other and strategizing for the future. God was leading us as a mission step-by-step.

After five years, in April 1989 we were told we had to be out of our Bangkok office and apartments by August. Since Marie and I were going to the United States for three months in June, we prayed that we could find somewhere to move everyone before we left or, if not, that everyone could stay until after we returned.

In the end, the date for vacating the property kept being pushed back. We had a bit more time, but still we felt a lot of pressure. We were working with refugees and carrying the ministries of YWAM Thailand and Mercy Ministries International in addition to being deeply concerned about the possibility of thirty homeless YWAMers in a couple of months.

A company from Taiwan had purchased the office and the apartments. After inspection, the building was not deemed sound enough to remodel, and the new owners decided to demolish it and build a new hotel on the land. It was now October 1989, and we were told that we would need to be out by January 31, 1990. There would be no extension of this date.

We had been expecting this news and weren't shaken by it. We were full of faith that God had a place for us and would reveal it in due time. We prayed as a team and were encouraged by God that He would look after us. However, this faith was sorely tested over the coming weeks.

October, November, and December flew by. Although all of us were pounding the streets, contacting realtors, looking at possibilities, and spreading the word of our need locally and internationally—doing everything humanly possible to find a place—all our efforts seemed fruitless.

On January 4 I met with our landlord and the new owner's lawyer. I could tell the lawyer was nervous, wondering if we would indeed vacate the premises in twenty-seven days or become squatters and never leave. "Where will you go?" he asked, hoping I could give him some new piece of information to calm his fears.

"I don't know, but God will provide for us as He has in the past," I replied with a smile, trying to exude an air of confidence while having no idea how God was going to do it.

"I hope so!" the lawyer replied, raising his eyebrows.

Every day brought fresh disappointment as our continued search failed. It seemed as though nothing in the whole city of Bangkok would meet our needs and budget requirements.

On January 16 Marie was scheduled to speak at the Christian Women's Club luncheon. The club had booked her a few months in advance, and she had been so excited at the testimony of God's faithfulness that she was sure she was going to have by that time.

"Lord, how can I tell these women about Your faithfulness when we have nowhere to move?" she asked, confused.

"Even if you don't know where you will live, you can still speak on My faithfulness, can't you?" the Lord seemed to say to her.

Marie knew she could. We had seen God's faithfulness throughout our lives, and He would come through again. Marie stood before the group of women and told them that in two weeks we were moving but did not have a clue where to.

"We trust in our Heavenly Father, who has never failed us or forsaken us," she declared.

The women were touched by her words, and they all rose up to pray for Marie and ask God to reveal the house or property He had chosen for us. Several also offered their guest rooms for our staff if needed.

In the final days of our faith adventure, my brother Ron and his wife, Sheila, came to Bangkok on business. We were daily fasting and praying during lunchtime, and Sheila joined us while Ron, who was working for a pharmaceutical company, was at his business meetings.

"It's like watching a friend have a baby. You know something is coming but not exactly sure what or when!" Sheila said with an encouraging smile.

We had let the wider YWAM family know our needs, and people around the world were standing with us for God's provision. A group from YWAM in Hawaii called and told us they prayed that God would sovereignly lead us as we drove around Bangkok. They believed that He had a quiet, secure dwelling place for us. After receiving the phone call, Marie and I were driving home in the middle of Bangkok rush-hour traffic with hundreds of taxis and motorcycles screaming past us. We had a flat tire. Our faith at being "sovereignly led" was at an all-time low.

What made our search difficult was that we wanted our office and housing in one facility, or at least in the same area. Bangkok traffic being what it was, we didn't want to spend hours in transit each day. On January 23 we had found a three-story office building but still no housing. We felt we had no choice but to rent the building even though it needed a lot of work—installing flooring, air-conditioning, and telephones. Adding to the pressure was that Chinese New Year, January 26–28, was a major holiday in Bangkok and the only time of year that the whole city shut down.

January 28 was our lowest point. We had two days to find somewhere to live, and everyone was looking to Marie and me to lead them. As dawn broke in Bangkok, we got out of bed with heavy hearts.

"What are we going to do?" Marie asked.

"I do not know!" was my only response.

I am known as an action-oriented, positive person, but at this point I was completely without inspiration. All I could do, I decided, was to get in the car and drive around until I found something. I felt I had to continue to do the possible and wait for God to do the impossible. Without an appetite for breakfast, I headed off, praying for God to guide me as I drove.

Marie continued with the packing, tears streaming down her cheeks as she filled our last boxes. Our friend Yvonne, who at that time was living in one of the apartments, came in to see Marie crying.

"What's wrong?" she asked with concern.

Marie looked up, and a fresh flood of tears spilled from her eyes: "Steve has left, and he said he's not coming back until he finds something. I'm scared I won't ever see him again!" Her tears turned to laughter as she realized how ridiculous that sounded. Yvonne comforted Marie, and the two women assured each other that I would find something.

From where I was sitting, it wasn't looking too hopeful. I had been driving and driving and ended up on the elevated expressway with the Chao Phraya River on the right and one of the financial districts of Bangkok on the left. From that height I suddenly noticed a subdivision to my left that I hadn't even known existed. The green of the trees around the houses caught my attention—lots of trees in one place is quite unusual in Bangkok. Getting off at the next exit, I circled back around to the entrance of the area and drove in. It was perfect, located next to two expressways for easy access but also quiet and secure, with mango trees growing in some of the small gardens surrounding the houses. Now we just had to find a big house or houses to rent there. I drove past a house with a sign outside, but the writing was in Thai and, though I did not read Thai, I was sure the sign must mean the house was for rent. I somehow knew this was an area that God had prepared for us. I went back to Marie and the team, full of faith.

I had been away for three hours by the time I got back. "I think I've found something!" I declared as I walked through the door.

Encouraged by my news, Marie, Yvonne, and our administrator Dave Swann and his wife, Ali, all came with me back to Moobaan Nakhorn Thai to have another look.

The Swanns were a young British couple who had plans to travel around the world and had contacted us about volunteering for one to three months. We encouraged them to stay for a year, which they did! Then they completed a DTS before returning to work with us for another eight years in Thailand, followed by almost two decades in Mercy Ministries International in Switzerland and then in South Africa.

We drove around the narrow streets and found the house in the Thai-Chinese subdivision with the sign out front. Marie could read enough Thai at this time to tell us, "The sign says, 'Bill collectors need to call this number.'"

Marie and I looked at each other, and no one said a word.

We carried on driving down each street looking for houses to rent, but there didn't seem to be anything. Despite the disappointment, I still felt we were onto something and didn't want to give up. As we were driving up one street, I noticed an older man sitting at the end of the street and pulled up next to him to ask for help.

"Excuse me," I said, rolling down the car window. "Do you know of any houses to rent in the area?"

The man inhaled deeply and shook his head. "No idea. No one rents here. Everyone owns his house, but if anyone knows of houses here, it would be the lady on the corner," he said, pointing down the road.

Off we went and asked the woman the same question.

"I know of one house that is empty. I can ask the owner," she said helpfully, telling us her name was Khun Meh (mother). I breathed a sigh of relief that there seemed to be a bit of hope. We thanked her and drove on after giving her our telephone number so she could let us know if the house was available.

Driving around the corner, we stopped outside a building and noticed a Thai woman in a tennis outfit getting something out of the trunk of her car.

"May I help you?" she asked.

Marie told her we were looking for a place to rent in the area and asked if she knew of anything.

"Actually, my neighbors rent out their house, and the people who were in it have just moved out. I can ask if they would rent again," she said. Taking our details, she told us she would call with the answer in a few hours.

That night we talked with the woman's neighbors and told them all about YWAM and who we were. We visited the house the next day with the landlord and his wife. The house was a lovely three-bedroom house with four mango trees in the small front yard. When we asked if they would rent it to YWAM, the landlord replied, "Well, we won't rent it to your mission, but my wife likes your wife, so we will rent it to you!"

This had not been the plan, and we told the landlord we would get back to him. After praying about the house, Marie and I felt it was right to accept. We had not lived on our own since joining YWAM nineteen years before and had arrived in Thailand with only one suitcase of belongings between us. We couldn't actually believe we would have a whole house to ourselves, and the idea took some getting used to.

Khun Meh's contacts had come up with a good response, and by the end of the week we had rented four houses in the area. Khun Meh shook her head in surprise as she told us, "Khun Steve, you are very lucky getting so many houses—it is most unusual."

We told our landlord at Soi Pipat we were leaving. He was visibly relieved and gave us another week extension so we had time to clean and paint our new homes in Moobaan Nakorn Thai.

Moving was a huge ordeal, and YWAMers from all over the city came to help us paint the houses and move in. The new owners of Soi Pipat told us to take whatever we wanted from the old buildings, which were going to be demolished. We were able to furnish our new homes with tables, cupboards, stoves, refrigerators, cabinets, and even sinks and light fixtures.

The first morning we woke in our new home, we were amazed. We could hear birds chirping in the trees outside our window, a first in Bangkok for us. This was significant, since a YWAM training school had told us they were praying. Someone had had a picture of God having a place for us but covering it with His hand until the time was right to reveal it. The person had said it would be a peaceful place with trees and the sound of birds singing.

When we first heard this, we smiled at each other saying, "Bless their hearts. They've obviously never been to Bangkok!" As far as we knew, there was no peaceful, quiet place with trees and birds singing in this busy, bustling city. How wrong we were! God knew, and He kept it for us.

Our new homes were a twenty-minute drive to the office, which was great for Bangkok. We had one community house where everyone ate together, plus guest rooms for the refugee staff coming into Bangkok for business and R&R. Our remaining staff members occupied the other houses.

We had no time to rest after the move. Marie had to organize three YWAM international conferences out of the new office, which was filled with boxes and workers. Despite the circumstances, all three ran smoothly. These gatherings on frontier missions became annual strategic meetings for us in YWAM. Because Thailand is such a beautiful, centrally located, inexpensive place with wonderful people, hospitality, and great food, it gave us an opportunity to serve our brothers and sisters in Asia and from across the world. We were able to see the growth in Asia firsthand.

Marie and I both turned forty that year. It was bittersweet for us, because we were still childless despite the many prayers and words given by those we loved and respected. We decided we needed to go back to the Lord with all the words and input that we had received and more intentionally give them back to God. We still trusted God. Even though we did not understand why these words about the blessing of having our own children had not come to pass, it was too painful to continue recording and reading these words as well as stories of the miracles others had experienced and passed on to us. We closed that part of our journal and gave these promises back to God. We told Him that we were not mad and that, though dealing with the disappointment, we would continue to trust Him with our present and future, believing that He had the best for our lives. It was helpful that we could put a word to it— *disappointment*—a major life disappointment. We realized that having children was huge, but it was not the most important thing in our lives, and we were not going to let it define who we were as people.

Often people would ask about our openness to adoption. Psalm 68:6 says, "God settles the lonely in their homes." Vulnerable children or children at risk should be in families, not in children's homes or institutions. The family environment is the place where one is prepared for life, and it is the building block or a primary sphere of influence in society.

We were very open to adoption, but somehow it seemed that we were never in the right place at the right time for that to come together. We often looked back over the years, wondering if we had missed an opportunity. We tried to imagine what we would have changed to be in that right place, but we believe that we have been where God called us and have been doing what He called us to do.

We were asked numerous times by refugee families to take their babies. From their perspective, we could have taken better care of them, but we could not take these lovely babies and children. Our good friends Gary and Helen Stephens and David and Carol Boyd also caused us to pause and ask God when they adopted their special-needs children, Jakob Lok Chi and Fuxia Taylor, into their lives and families. We asked God but once again did not believe that He was leading us in this way (though He had said that these two were to become our godchildren).

At one point we were contacted about a baby, born to a teenage mother, who needed a home. As we prayed, we were surprised when we both felt this was not to be our child and had to refuse. We did not understand until we later found out the teenage mother had given the child up for adoption but had then taken the baby back. God had spared us the pain and heartache of having our expectations raised about opening up our family, only to be dashed by rejection. The important thing we continued to learn was simply to ask God regarding these decisions and trust Him to speak and to guide, and then for us to obey what He said.

Marie and I were never angry at God. We had to walk through brokenness and pain at times, particularly in Thailand, since the first thing people ask you after your name and how old you are is, "How many children do you have?" It is a grief that hits when one least expects it. We used to say that *why* would be the first question we would ask God when we got to meet Him, but now we believe that once in His presence, it will not be the most important thing.

We both prayed for grace to not become bitter or resentful, and we are neither. Even though we have never had children of our own, the children of our family and friends have always held special places in our hearts, as have the children whom we serve. We love children and are privileged to have ten nieces and nephews and seventeen godchildren on whom we can lavish our love. Seventeen official ones, that is. It has been interesting and encouraging to hear from many of these now-grown children and to know that they appreciated a sense of security and covering, knowing that if something happened to their parents, they could come and live with us!

People often observe that we love children and do not hold back from them. Also, we seem to have found some keys for not being bitter from childlessness. Psalm 145:17 became a life verse for us in our YWAM training school: "The LORD is righteous in all his ways, faithful in all his deeds." We will always be grateful for how we were continually led to focus on and study the attributes of God and had leaders and staff who lived in an awareness of who God is.

We have said at various times that in this world we find ourselves in situations where we do not see or experience justice or kindness. But the truth is that God is just and kind, and we hold onto that.

Tom and Cynthia Bloomer became special friends from our time together as students in our YWAM training school in 1974. In April 2012 Cynthia was diagnosed with a rare disease that took her life in a matter of weeks. After Cynthia's death, Tom was sharing with a group of YWAM leaders and said it this way: "Psalm 145:17 has to be our starting point. That is not where we try to end up after we figure things out. . . . If we go about it that way, we will never get there. We have to start with the bedrock certainty that in anything that happens to us, the Lord is just and kind."

Because we are older now, the grief comes in different forms. At the wedding of our first goddaughter, we had a revelation that we had proven God to be enough through the years of our friends' childbearing and raising their children, but now we would need to prove God to be enough when our friends began to have *grandchildren* . . . and that can be even more challenging than their having children of their own!

We realized that God has brought many people into our lives

to whom we have been a father and a mother. One of those, a dear coworker named Kathy, wrote Marie a letter, grateful for how God had used her as a mother when Kathy needed it most:

Dear Marie,

About six months ago I went to a Christian Women's Club meeting with you and while we were there, someone at our table asked you how many children you have. Your response was, "Well, none . . . or a hundred—it depends how you look at it." You might not realize how fitting that response was. Wendy and Elaine joke and call you "Mom and Dad." I could never bring myself to do that, and yet subconsciously I think that is the role you fill in most of our lives. It has much more to do with position than age.

Marie, I've lived with many families, but none of them were as gifted as you at being a mother. I've never experienced such love, affirmation and encouragement from an authority figure before. It brought real security to my life at a time when I was very insecure. I appreciated the correction too. Marie, don't ever think that because you don't have children of your own flesh and blood that you're not a mother. I am sure you don't need to be reminded of the awesome responsibility He's given you for the physical, emotional and spiritual welfare of these spiritual children. . . . As a mother nurtures a child and receives joy at each new revelation of growth, I want you to know that any growth you've seen in me since I've been here can directly or indirectly be linked to your influence. And next time we meet, if I've grown to be a little more like the Lord, you can know that you've had a part in leading up to that too.

Lots of Love,
Kathy

We were both deeply touched by the letter, as God was opening our eyes to the "children" He was bringing to us in the form of young YWAM staff who would benefit from our affirmation, love, and attention.

One "daughter" whom we like to claim as one of ours is Lem, the Khmer refugee adopted by our good friends Bruno and Margret

Cavassini, when we lived in Lausanne. Lem had been able to reconnect with her mother and sisters in Cambodia through mail and the assistance of the International Red Cross. Some of Lem's biological family members were found to be living in a rural area still controlled by the Khmer Rouge outside of Phnom Penh that was unsafe for foreigners to visit. Nevertheless Marie and I really wanted to connect with Lem's Khmer family.

On her first visit into Cambodia, as the plane circled Phnom Penh, Marie wept as she recalled how the refugees spoke with love and the strong memories of their beautiful nation before the Khmer Rouge took power. "Oh, when you go, you must eat the fish from the Tonle Sap River," they would say, and speak wistfully of the home they had once had. Marie could hardly believe she was about to plant her feet on Cambodian soil.

Lem had given us some money to give to her mother, and when we arrived in Phnom Penh, we went to the guesthouse where I had stayed on previous visits and asked for the manager's help. I spoke French with Mr. Sok, since he and I had become good friends during our earlier visits. Mr. Sok helped me write a letter in Khmer to be posted to Lem's mother's village in hopes that the postal services were indeed working well enough out in the countryside. I cut my business card in half, putting one half in the envelope with the Khmer letter. I had written to Lem's mother that there was money for her in Phnom Penh, giving her the address of the guesthouse and telling her to take the cut business card to Mr. Sok. Then, giving him the other half, I instructed Mr. Sok to give the money only to the woman who had the card.

The last day of our two-week trip, after having visited Stung Treng up near the Lao border, when we came down to breakfast, Mr. Sok had a surprise for us.

"She's here!" he declared

"Who?" I asked, somewhat confused.

"Lem's mother!" Mr. Sok explained, by now very excited that our plan had worked and so quickly.

We looked over to where Mr. Sok was pointing and saw a little old woman with a brown weathered face and an old sarong wrapped around her waist. Marie went over to speak to her, not sure if it really was Lem's mother. But as she got closer, the woman reached out her hand, and in it was the other half of my business card.

Marie turned to me with tears in her eyes: "It really is Lem's mother!"

We gave the woman a photo of Lem, and in French translated into Khmer by Mr. Sok, we were able to tell her that her daughter was alive, well, and happy. Lem's mother looked at her daughter's photo without expression: it was as if the years of pain and hardship had robbed her of her emotions. She asked where Lem was living but had no concept of different countries and flying in airplanes—she was a simple, rural woman who had spent most of her life working in the rice fields.

"Lem is many mountains away, but she will come soon," I told her.

For the first time in almost twelve years, Lem did return to her homeland, and to her mother, who received her. Lem and her mother continued to enjoy visits every few years until her mother's death in 2013. What a privilege it was to come to our point of first call and meet the mother of Lem, through whom God had opened our eyes and led us to work in Southeast Asia all those years ago.

THIRTEEN

Refugees: Heading Back Home

Only now and then, on rare occasions, when some clear voice is heard giving more articulate utterance to the miseries of the miserable, do we pause from our daily duties and shudder for one brief moment at what life means to the poor.
—GENERAL WILLIAM BOOTH, *In Darkest England and the Way Out*

HOSTILITIES IN CAMBODIA were slowly coming to an end. Vietnam removed its troops in 1989, even though the Khmer Rouge was still active in certain parts of the country. The Cambodian Peace Agreement was signed in Paris in October 1991, and the UN-backed elections for a new government were to be held in 1993. All refugees who had not been sent to a third country had to be repatriated a year before the elections were held so that they could be legally registered to vote.

Khao-I-Dang, the once teeming refugee camp and one of the largest Khmer communities outside Cambodia, was slowly disbanded until

Site Two camp was the only border location we were working in. The camp held about 220,000 people and was divided into four sections— San Ro, Dong Rek, Ban Sangae, and Nong Chan, all names of the Thai villages where the refugees had first arrived.

Pressure was building in the camp as the refugees prepared to leave. In the final few months the atmosphere was increasingly tense, and life in the camp became more and more dangerous. In the middle of the hottest month of the year, when the camp was like an oven, tensions exploded when someone threw a hand grenade into a crowded hut, killing 13 people and injuring 125. People reacted by fleeing the scene, causing a stampede of hundreds of refugees running in fear.

A YWAM leader, Dean Sherman, visited us and reminded us of the need to increase our prayer and intercession for the camp and for our staff during this phase. We prayed for God to bring His peace and for no more violence. By April 1991 orderly repatriation started, and every week ten thousand Khmer refugees were bussed peacefully back to Cambodia.

Going "home" was not a joyful event for most of the refugees, who had escaped Cambodia in horrific circumstances and did not know to what they were returning. The refugees were scared. The buses were full not of celebration and singing but of sober and fearful Cambodians, praying that the home they once knew would be there to welcome them.

United Nations statistics showed that by April 1992, 80 percent of the 350,000 people waiting to return to Cambodia were under the age of forty-four. Of that number 45 percent were under the age of fifteen. The reality was that many of the refugees were children, many of whom had been born in the border camps and had no idea whether they had any family left in Cambodia when the bus dropped them off in their home province.

One friend of ours, a Khmer named Heng, was very concerned when he heard that he and his mother were being sent back to Cambodia after seven years in Khao-I-Dang. He didn't know whether any members of his family were alive, since he had not been able to trace them through the Red Cross. Without family, Heng and his mother would have no one to help them settle back into life in Cambodia. They would have to begin with nothing but the clothes on their backs.

To meet this new need, we began distributing repatriation kits to aid the refugees starting new lives. These kits, funded by the UN, included a sheet of plastic and rope for shelter, mosquito nets, rice and oil, and tools to cut wood and shovel dirt. The UN also provided each returnee with fifty US dollars.

Even though the camps were being disbanded, our medical teams were as busy as ever because TB was reaching epidemic numbers. In the Nong Chan section of Site Two, 780 new cases were admitted in 1991. TB treatment lasted for nine months, but if the medicine was not taken religiously every day, the patient would develop a resistance to the drug, and then there was no cure. Because of this we told those who were sick to come to the clinic every day to make sure they took their drugs. Since many of them were being sent back to Cambodia in the middle of treatment, we had to make sure that they had the full amount of medication and understood the importance of completing the course.

Our medical training program for refugees to become TB medics was paying off. With the influx of patients, these medics could diagnose and treat the illness, freeing up our doctors to deal with severe cases.

Since many of the refugees still had an incredible hunger to know God, ongoing discipleship was important. Many became Christians after hearing about Jesus from our health-care teams and the local Khmer church. Some refugees wanted to be baptized as the last thing they did before heading back to Cambodia. One day Khmer Christian leaders at the local reservoir baptized twenty-three new believers before boarding the bus. It was amazing to watch men and women who had been broken by war and hardship coming up out of the water with their faces radiating with joy. We prayed for God's protection over them as they went back and for God's provision for all their needs.

The Khmer church in Site Two was growing stronger. Barnabas, one of the Khmer Christian leaders, wrote more than three hundred new Khmer worship songs. The sound of the refugees worshiping Jesus in their native language was beautiful. Barnabas later told me that when these newly converted refugees returned to their homes throughout Cambodia, they planted at least fifty-seven churches and many more overseas.

As Khao-I-Dang was closing, most of our staff had left Aran and moved to the village of Ta Phraya, which was closer to Site Two. With new Thai believers in Ta Phraya, we were able to plant a church that grew from twenty to sixty people in a matter of months. We found out that some of these new Christians had first heard the gospel from our mobile medical teams ten years previously. These were the teams we had sent out to the thirty affected Thai villages along the border, Ta Phraya being one of them. We were encouraged because when the teams had gone out all those years before, they had seen very little fruit. However, we realized that the seeds of the gospel had been planted, God had watered them over the years, and now, ten years later, we were seeing the answers to our prayers with many people coming to follow Jesus. We had simply served the people, meeting people where they were, and God had taken care of the rest.

During this time Ros and Peter Davis, a doctor and midwife from Australia who had worked with us at the border, returned home to work with the Khmer and Vietnamese refugees who had been resettled in Australia. They started the first refugee DTS in September 1993 and then came on outreach back to Cambodia with a team of Khmer Christians. It was powerful to see Khmer missionaries being raised up to go back to their own people with a message of hope. I visited Ros and Peter in Sydney and met refugees who had become Christians through YWAM in the border camps. It was encouraging to see them flourishing in their new homes in Australia.

A few years earlier, I had been in Australia for a YWAM Asia and Pacific leaders meeting. While there, I met with former refugees from Khao-I-Dang. The highlight of my trip was speaking at a Khmer church of seventy former refugees, ten of whom had accepted Christ through the YWAM programs in Thailand. One couple, Seng and Paychin, had supervised the fish farm for us and now sent money to support YWAM missionaries still in Thailand. Another refugee had become a vibrant Christian. She learned that her mother, brother, and sister were not dead, as she had thought, but had escaped to Vietnam. She was now working two jobs to be able to sponsor them to come to Australia.

In 1993 I happened to be in Stung Treng with Philip Scott when two boatloads of refugees returned from the border camps to Cambodia, having gone first to Phnom Penh and then by boat up the Mekong River to within forty kilometers of the Lao border. The refugees had to wait until the floodwaters were high enough to allow the boats to maneuver through the shallower parts of the river to avoid the rocks. The refugees were scared at what was waiting for them, but seeing foreigners gave many of them the peace of mind to know they would be safe. The deputy governor, who was there on this occasion, was moved to tears to see the boats come up the river because this meant a new chapter of reunification of the country after the civil war.

For several years YWAM was the only NGO in Stung Treng, and we focused on health care and the hospital, helping to rebuild it and provide medical assistance. The situation was dire. One day a boy was carried in after having stepped on a mine. He had traveled for eight hours on the back of a cart drawn by ponies. The doctor would have to amputate the boy's leg, since there was no penicillin to fight the infection. We realized the boy would probably die. Even though the hospital did not have penicillin, the drug was available for purchase in the Stung Treng market—but at fifteen dollars, it was a tenth of a year's salary for the rural farmer and beyond his ability to buy. In this situation we were able to buy the medicine for the boy, but it underlined the fact that we were going to have to do a lot more to provide basic health care in the province.

Through our needs assessment and research we found that 40 percent of children were dying before the age of five in the five districts of Stung Treng province, and they were dying from preventable diseases. On our first visit to the hospital we saw a young man with a case of anthrax. Primary health care, malaria prevention, vaccinations, and prenatal care for mothers and children were desperately needed. We sent teams out to the various districts and ended up training the staff in the health centers and more than four hundred traditional birth attendants (TBAs), who were mostly grandmothers who had delivered children in the home. Our health-care team ran refresher courses every three months for TBAs being trained and equipped. We also worked with the World Health Organization (WHO) and the provincial department of health to provide mosquito nets for all in the province.

Philip, who oversaw all the YWAM projects and was discipling many of the new believers and church leaders in Stung Treng, also visited inmates several times a week at a local prison. While there, he found out that many inmates could not read or write, and he provided materials and supplies for them to learn.

One prisoner named Song returned to his village in the district of Siempang when he was released. Siempang was about five hours' boat journey from Stung Treng, and YWAM had two midwives living and working there. In prison Song had begun to read and write under Philip's instruction. Since the only Khmer literature available at the time was Christian tracts, Song started to read and soon became a follower of Jesus. He told his wife that he was able to read and write because of this Christian God. His wife was so impressed by the change in her husband that she asked to know the God of the Christians as well.

Philip traveled to the village and explained the gospel to many of Song's family and friends. He gave out literature in the Khmer language and copies of the *Jesus* film so that they could watch it on TV, powered by one of our generators. There had been no known believers in this province of about eighty thousand people, but today there are seven churches. In 2010 a provincial survey was taken, and Siempang District, where YWAM now does the malaria control project, had the lowest incidence rate for malaria in the province of Stung Treng instead of one of the highest. It also had the lowest maternal and child death rates for the whole country. The gospel is indeed life-giving.

The town of Stung Treng also had an antiquated water system that had been neglected for some twenty years. The water source was the Mekong River, but because it was no longer getting to people's homes, the people had to go to the river to wash their clothes and themselves. They then returned carrying two buckets of water, balanced on one shoulder and hanging from a flexible piece of split bamboo, that provided water for cooking. Since the hospital had no running water, it was very hard to maintain sanitary conditions.

We knew this was a critical need to meet in order to help the town and enable us to assist the hospital in providing better service. Two Australian engineers came out to survey and study the system that had been put in place many years before. They felt that with a bit of reconstruction it could easily provide water for about nine thousand families. With funding from Australian Baptist World Aid, we partnered with the government department to purchase and install pumps, pipes, and generators to get running water to the town for the first time in more than twenty years.

We had planned to install the new water system a few days before the elections in Cambodia, between May 23 and 28, 1993, but decided it would be best to delay the installation until after the elections. We used the Baptist grant for a loan to the city water department. After the water system was up and running and people had started paying their water bills, the loan was repaid over five years and the income used for another project.

A week before the elections, the church in Stung Treng had the first baptisms of four Khmer. It was very encouraging after twelve months of presenting the gospel in word and deed. But tension was building in Phnom Penh, and we all wondered what the outcome of the elections would be. The day before the elections, Khmer Rouge forces fired rockets into Stung Treng town. The rockets fell close to Philip and Wendy's home, but no one was injured. The church in Cambodia had prayed and fasted for three days before the election, launching a prayer vigil that went throughout the country. The result was a tangible change in the atmosphere in the capital city from fearful to calm, and 95 percent of Cambodians voted.

EVEN THOUGH MANY refugees were returning to their homeland and the border camps were closing down, Phanat Nikhom, just outside Bangkok, still held refugees who were on the list to be sent to a third country. It was the last camp to close, finishing operations in 1995. YWAM was privileged to have been in Phanat Nikhom when it started and when it closed.

Elaine Holwell, the Phanat Nikhom team leader from New Zealand, served in Thailand for twelve years. She headed up the last phase of the work there with the Khmer, the Lao from the lowlands of Laos, the Vietnamese, and the Hmong. The Hmong are mountain people from Laos, but there were also Hmong living in Vietnam, Myanmar, and Thailand. The Hmong of Laos had helped the American government fight against the Vietnamese during the Vietnam War. As a result, because they had a well-grounded fear of persecution in Laos, tens of thousands had fled to the Thai borders for refuge.

Elaine had the privilege to teach in a Hmong leadership training program in camp. During one of the sessions, Elaine emphasized the importance of forgiveness. One youth leader came to her after the teaching to ask for prayer. She knew she needed to forgive her father, but she could not do it by herself. She told Elaine how her father was responsible for the death of her sister and how on the journey to Thailand, he abandoned her young nephews in the jungle because they were hindering the progress of the group. When the family reached Thailand, her father became involved with another woman. He was eventually resettled with the woman in a new country, leaving his family to fend for themselves in the camps in Thailand.

This young woman's anger toward her father was great, but as Elaine counseled her, the young leader was able to forgive him and was set free from the hatred and bitterness that had taken control of her life. This newfound freedom would be a key in her leadership development and modeling to those she would lead.

All the work in the camps was finished in April 1996, sixteen years after we first arrived. It was a privilege to be around to see the end of the work that we had helped start, and we marveled at the six hundred YWAM staff who over the years had made it happen, coming to serve for anywhere from two weeks up to sixteen years. These wonderful people were educated and skilled and could have lived comfortable lifestyles with good incomes, but in obedience to God they had come. They gave of themselves in expertise, health, and separation from their families. They lived in the tension and sometimes fear of being in a war zone, worked in the stifling heat and red dust, or served in areas of support, communication, and logistics. We honor them. Together we learned, struggled, prayed, strategized, tried to do the next thing we felt God ask. We wept together and oh, how we laughed!

A few years after the camps were emptied, Marie and I took a trip back to the area where Khao-I-Dang and Site Two had been. These former camps were now open rice paddies. The only sign of the hundreds of thousands of displaced people who had once called it home were the blue water towers that had never worked while we were there.

While the camps were closing down, Sheila Walsh, a cohost on CBN's *700 Club*, asked me to come on the show to be interviewed about the refugees. As I walked into the CBN offices in Virginia Beach, I smiled to myself at how different my life would have been had I taken the job behind the camera that CBN had offered me all those years before. Choosing the life of faith was an adventure, and now here I was in front of the camera being able to tell about the miracles that God had done among refugees in Thailand. I would not have changed those last sixteen years for anything. Working with the refugees has changed our lives forever and taught us about the depth of God's love and compassion for those suffering from injustice. We would never be the same and were now looking farther afield to the plight of refugees in other countries, asking God how we could help them.

PART THREE

Central and South Asia and Africa

FOURTEEN

New Partnerships

The temptation is to see God only at work in values, but he also works to transform structures to promote the values of the Kingdom. —CONFERENCE PROCEEDINGS, 1983
The Church in Response to Human Need

BACK IN THE early 1980s, we still had our hands full with the refugee crisis in Thailand, but with new information about yet another crisis, we knew that God was continuing to expand our work.

Afghanistan is a nation composed of seventy-eight ethnic groups who have survived decades of war, poverty, and oppression. Since the overthrow of the Taliban in 2001, the people of Afghanistan have stepped closer to freedom and development. Women again have the opportunity to receive an education and to own companies, but insecurity still affects 30 percent of the provinces.

We had first heard of Afghanistan in our school in 1974. At that time, young people from the West were traveling the hippie trail in search of cheap drugs and truth in Eastern religions. Marie and I again heard of Afghanistan a few months later at the Lausanne Congress. Afghanistan and Nepal were mentioned as the two poorest countries with the least freedom of religion. We were challenged to pray regularly for both nations.

In 1979, the world was in the throes of the Cold War between the United States and the Soviet Union. Relations between communist China and the two superpowers further complicated the world geopolitical scene. The struggle was between democracy and two opposing communist structures: Marxist-Leninist and Maoist. Although the three major nations were not fighting each other directly, proxy wars in various parts of the world caused millions of people to be caught in the middle, with many of them becoming either internally displaced or refugees.

This conflict was widespread and complicated. The end of the Vietnam War in 1975 was not the end of the struggle between these opposing ideologies in Asia. The Vietnamese government, supported by the Soviet Union, invaded neighboring Cambodia on Christmas Day 1978 to oust the Khmer Rouge, who were supported by China. Within two weeks, Vietnam controlled Phnom Penh, and the remnants of the Khmer Rouge were being pushed toward the Thai border. The Vietnamese occupied Cambodia for almost a decade. China invaded Vietnam in February 1979 in a brief but bloody war over the Vietnamese invasion of Cambodia, keeping troops on alert on the Sino-Vietnamese border after the war ended. China succeeded in another objective: letting the Soviet Union know that they could not protect Vietnam.

On Christmas Eve 1979, another invasion occurred, this one in Central Asia, and it caused one of the largest refugee movements in history. The Soviets invaded Afghanistan to stamp out anticommunist Muslim guerrilla fighters known as the Mujahideen. The Soviet Union never completely occupied Afghanistan, but that war forced almost five million refugees to flood across the borders to Pakistan and Iran. It was in these refugee camps that more Mujahideen were recruited and out of which a fundamentalist political group arose: the Taliban.

With nearly five million Afghan refugees, we had to ask, "Lord, is there anything that You want us to do in Pakistan and Afghanistan?" Marie and I prayed and felt that I should go, take a look, and assess what was going on and see which organizations were working with the refugees, what the needs and gaps of service were, and whether we could respond to this refugee crisis in any way.

I had an opportunity to visit Lahore, Pakistan, in 1987 and then travel on to the Northwest Frontier Province, where the refugee camps were located in and around Peshawar, Pakistan. In Peshawar, we saw firsthand the Muslim refugee exodus, with thousands of displaced Afghans crammed together and living in mud huts inside the Pakistan border. These refugees had fled across the snowy mountains of the Hindu Kush over the Khyber Pass and were in makeshift camps surrounding the city. It became evident that we would be too stretched from Bangkok to service a refugee operation as we were doing in Thailand. Instead we decided to support the work of other partner organizations that were already established there. YWAM Relief and Development began partnerships with organizations working with the refugees. We would second (transfer to another organization) staff, as we had done in the early days of the refugee work in Thailand, support them in prayer, and assist with fundraising, technical support, visits, and other member care.

The situation in Peshawar was volatile and chaotic. Arms were being sold openly in markets alongside shops selling marijuana, heroin, and other illicit drugs in an intense environment of conservative Islam. It felt as if we were in a powder keg that was getting ready to explode at any moment.

At first short-term volunteers came to serve in Peshawar, and in 1987 we coordinated efforts from Thailand and sent longer-term staff to work inside Afghanistan through various partnerships. In 1988, our first two volunteers moved to Afghanistan to work long-term.

From Thailand, we would trumpet the call for volunteers worldwide, speaking about the incredible need in Afghanistan. But it was a challenge to get longer-term staff to serve. I started making yearly visits and then two visits a year to Afghanistan so I could meet with and listen to staff, visit projects, and communicate to supporters and other YWAM locations for prayer, recruitment of staff, technical support, and raising funds for specific health or environmental projects.

A young couple was considering work in Afghanistan and came to Bangkok to meet us. Because we had to realistically describe the context in which they would be living and working, we challenged them to seek God to find if this was His will for them. They went away and prayed, and He spoke very clearly, in a way that left no doubts about where they should be. Years later they wrote to us saying, "We are so glad for how you challenged us to hear His call. In these nineteen years of war, danger, hardship, and, of course, a lot of joy living in Afghanistan, we have never doubted that we were supposed to be here. It has been a foundation for us. Thank you for being open about the challenges."

In 1988, Jesse Ylauan took over leadership of Thai Ministries, and Roslyn Jackson took over Relief Services, which was a tremendous support to me. Their leadership also helped me to fulfill my new appointment for five years as YWAM's South Asia Regional leader, serving our workers in Afghanistan, Pakistan, Bangladesh, India, Nepal, and Sri Lanka.

The war-zone situation in Afghanistan spread from the rural areas to the major towns and then to Kabul. The Mujahideen first fought against the Russians and then, when the Soviets left, fought a civil war against the Afghan government, turning Kabul into a bombed-out city. Our people worked in health-care situations that were so volatile that outsiders were unable to enter the country. Between 1992 and 1996 we held our partnership meetings in either Peshawar or New Delhi because it was next to impossible to have them in Afghanistan. We had five people in country working with partnering organizations. These people are our true heroes. They met the needs of the Afghan people in the most challenging environment we had ever witnessed. On our trips we advised them on leadership decisions, listened, prayed, and tried to give encouragement.

Afghanistan's resistance groups were born in confusion, and at first regional warlords waged virtually all of the country's war. As warfare became more sophisticated, outside support and regional coordination grew. Even so, the basic units of organization and actions continued to reflect the segmented nature of Afghan society. Eventually, the seven main parties allied themselves into the political bloc called Islamic Unity of Afghanistan.

In 1991, I flew into Kabul on the same small plane as Dr. Christy Wilson. I remembered hearing about Dr. Christy from Floyd McClung during my SOE. Floyd was the founder of Dilaram (Peaceful Heart) in Kabul, an outreach to Western young people on drugs and exploring Eastern religions in the late sixties and early seventies. Kabul was one of the meccas on the hippie trail. This romantic route was a magical mystery tour that extended from Europe through Morocco, Turkey, Iran, Afghanistan, Pakistan, and India to Nepal—and then back. Christy served as the pastor of the international church in Kabul for eleven years during that time while his wife, Betty, founded a school for the blind in Kabul.

On this plane ride, Christy recounted many stories about Dilaram and about his life in Afghanistan. He was returning for the first time since the church building had been bulldozed in 1973. At that time, police had ordered the bulldozers to dig deep into the foundations of the building. They had heard there was an underground church, which they understood literally.

As we came closer to Kabul, Christy could not believe the damage of decades of fighting. He pointed out landmarks along the way, like the infamous Pul-e-Charkhi, a prison for political prisoners built by East Germans. As we flew over the city, our plane let out heat flares so that if any heat-seeking missiles were aimed at us, they would be diverted by the flares—*inshallah*, God willing.

Sadly, the worst impact on the beautiful, rugged country of Afghanistan and its people was yet to come through the Taliban. The Taliban, whose name comes from the Arabic word for *student*, were conservative Sunni Muslims. They dominated large swaths of Afghanistan and the Federally Administered Tribal Areas (FATA) in Pakistan. The Taliban were fundamentalists, young men trained in madrassas—Muslim religious schools that focused primarily on the study of the Qur'an—who persecuted anyone whose form of Islam diverged from their own. Democracy was scorned as an offense against Islam.

Beginning in 1994, the Taliban rose to power and established their brutal totalitarian rule over 90 percent of the country, in part by leading a genocidal campaign against Afghanistan's Hazara people, who were Shiite Muslims and one of the largest ethnic groups. Schools for girls were closed, and women were forbidden to work or leave their homes without male permission. Wearing non-Islamic dress—makeup and Western products such as purses and hard-soled shoes—was also forbidden. One of our foreign female teachers was actually physically struck by a member of the "vice and virtue" squad because the tennis shoes she was wearing made noise when she walked and because she laughed in a class she was teaching. Enforcing humiliating laws became commonplace.

This kind of intimidation was not limited to the Afghan population. On August 7, 2001, Shelter Now, an international NGO, had twenty-four of its workers arrested for "propagating Christianity." This became an international media event. In August and September 2001, the Taliban expelled all aid groups from Afghanistan.

On September 9, 2001, Ahmad Shah Massoud, a national hero from the northern part of Afghanistan, was assassinated by two al-Qaeda suicide bombers posing as journalists. Two days later, on September 11, 2001, the world changed as terrorists made a murderous attack on New York City in the United States that was traced back to Afghanistan.

My first trip back into Kabul was in May 2002. Our landing slot was dictated by US military based in Oman. If a plane came in without authorization, it would have been blown out of the sky. The airport was like no other I had ever seen. It had limited electricity, and destroyed fighter planes lay abandoned along the runway. Even the main airport clock was stuck in time, after having been hit by a Russian missile in 1989.

As I exited the airport, I was taken aback by the huge photo of the people's hero, Ahmad Shah Massoud. Massoud had been a Kabul University engineering student turned military leader who had played a leading role in driving the Soviet army out of Afghanistan, earning him the name "the Lion of Panjshir."

The danger was very real traveling in and out of Afghanistan, but Marie was given special grace to cope with my twice-yearly visits. She realized this when someone asked her when I was coming home. She calmly replied, "It depends on whether the airport is being bombed. If it is, he'll have to go overland through the Khyber Pass with an armed guard."

Her friend replied in shock, "Do you hear what you are saying? This is not a normal conversation!"

Many people had warned us and said it was too dangerous to enter Afghanistan, but we knew that if we would not go into a country where we were recruiting people to serve, we had no right to recruit them. We were not living where we were living or doing what we were doing because it was the safest place to be, but because the God of the universe loves all people and He wants to demonstrate that love to all people by serving them, meeting their needs.

When the time came that Marie could come with me on the trips, every day was filled from early morning to evening. The November weather was so cold that Marie was glad for the headscarf she had to wear, and we huddled around the potbellied kerosene-fueled stoves in our friends' houses. Many times we were in the country during Ramadan, the Islamic month of fasting. During this month we watched the women working hard, getting up in the middle of the night and preparing a meal for their families to eat before sunrise, having to make lunch for the children, and then preparing a meal to serve just as the sun set and the *muezzin* would sing the call to prayer. At the end of the month, Eid al-Fitr, "Festival of Breaking the Fast," is celebrated. Food is donated to the poor, everyone puts on his or her best (usually new) clothes, and communal prayers are held in the early morning, followed by feasting, visiting relatives and friends, and giving gifts to children.

During *Eid*, Marie went with our team member Joy to visit with a family in a village about an hour and a half from Kabul. They traveled in an eight-passenger van with over fourteen people, and it was a tight squeeze. Thankfully, because Joy had mentioned that Marie was prone to motion sickness, Marie was given the place of honor in the front seat. She was sitting alone next to the male driver, which could have been scandalous, but because of her grey (or ash blonde!) head of hair visible under the edge of her scarf, she was allowed that honor.

Joy had previously lived in this village, and when she and Marie arrived, everyone honored her. Even the patriarch of the family came to tea and thanked her for all she had done for his son's family. She had saved his son's infant twin girls from death and had watched the girls' mother die just two days after the birth of the twins. After complications arose, the mother had been taken from hospital to hospital. She died not long after being admitted to a hospital that tried to help her.

Joy had been troubled as she watched several of the woman's seven children (including a two-year-old) and relatives say their goodbyes. When the body was taken home, the relatives were so distraught that they left the twin babies in a dark room with a bottle between them and no one to care for them. Neither baby was able to suck. The twins were premature and needed to be in intensive care, but no neonatal intensive care was available.

Joy and her husband, after quickly praying, decided to care for the girls. After they were given permission by the men in the family, they bundled up the babies and took them to their home to care for them along with their own four children. One girl weighed nine hundred grams, and the other twelve hundred grams (about two pounds and two and a half pounds, respectively). Joy and her husband contacted all their friends to ask for help, and that night a pediatric nurse they knew came from across town to feed the twins milk with a small spoon. The next day a doctor and nurse came to insert stomach tubes and start tube feedings every two hours around the clock until the babies could suck on their own. These twins were prayed for every day by many people around the globe because their chances of survival were very poor and the risk of infection was high.

All sorts of volunteers who lived in Kabul came to help. Joy's own children, the youngest of whom was three, all contributed. The babies gained weight every day and eventually had their feeding tubes removed. After four weeks the healthiest baby was ready to be adopted by her maternal uncle. She had been named Hope (in their language), and the family kept that name. After six weeks the weaker baby, who was named Beloved, was adopted by a paternal uncle. It was sad that the twins were separated, but this was Afghanistan. Joy's family was grateful that both girls had gone to loving homes. The girls continue to thrive.

Marie was deeply moved as she sat Afghan-style in the sun-baked-brick home on beautifully woven carpets from the region and witnessed the amazing honoring of her friend by the Afghan patriarch.

After visiting the grave of the girls' mother, Marie and Joy made their way back to Kabul. They were taken to a large village intersection to wait for a public "taxi" that would go to Kabul. Because they would have to share the taxi with anyone else who was waiting, one of the family members went with them for protection, a demonstration of the Afghans' incredible, lavish hospitality.

When the taxi came trundling along the road, Marie and Joy ended up sharing it with a burka-clad woman. Three men sat in the front seat, and Marie and Joy quickly started up a conversation with the woman, who turned out to be a young bride in her twenties. They talked non-stop with the woman (via Joy's translation), who told them she'd been married only a few months. In her father's family she was not required to wear the burka, but her in-laws now required it. Joy asked her if they could see her under her burka, which covered her whole face. She hesitated, but while her husband was busy in conversation she lifted the burka to reveal a beautiful young woman with lovely makeup and sparkling jewelry. She gave them a quick grin and then in one swift movement covered her face again. The effect of seeing her was powerful to Marie because the woman instantly became alive and more of a real person. This underlined for Marie the dehumanizing effects of the burka.

As they came into the outskirts of Kabul, Marie and Joy were being dropped off to take another taxi back to where they were staying. They hugged the bride goodbye, and the woman quickly invited them to have dinner with her family that evening—another display of Afghan hospitality. The woman was 100 percent serious about their joining them.

"I am so sorry, but we are leaving tonight," Joy translated for Marie.

As they walked away from the taxi, both women prayed for the young bride, asking God to bless her marriage and reveal Himself to her.

Marie and I returned to Bangkok, but I had only a few days in the city before I was scheduled to go on another trip. While I was traveling so much, Marie was not home alone. Our friend Yvonne Dos Santos had come to live with us. With the camps closing and structures changing, several of our Bangkok staff left in 1995, and Yvonne needed a place to live after serving in two transit camps. Yvonne, a woman of prayer, was also Marie's right hand in all the conferences and a very active partner in their affectionately named "Parties R Us" for all the various celebrations through the years. Yvonne prayed, laughed, and cried with us, encouraging us with her strong faith in her Father God.

We were blessed to have Yvonne with us, especially in situations where we realized we could not do things alone. For example, in 1999 Marie started having pain in her right shoulder that would not go away. When she reached out to hold something, throbbing seared up and down her arm. A visit to the doctors showed that she had a shoulder impingement, and if she did not have surgery, very soon she would not be able to move her arm. We opted for surgery in Thailand in January 2000, grateful that we had good insurance to cover the costs.

The operation and pain were new for Marie, who, unlike me, had always been healthy and had never had to deal with pain or spend time in hospitals. I was very used to being prepped for one operation or another.

The surgery was a success, but as Marie came round from the anesthetic, she started to feel an intense amount of pain. She was also a bit afraid, since she had never experienced anything like it before. I called the nurse, who gave her an injection for the pain. Concerned, I watched Marie's face—which had been tense as she tried to deal with the pain—slowly relax into a gentle, serene smile. It was as though the sun had burst through the clouds, and her whole body relaxed.

"I am numb from my nose to my toes—I love drugs!" she said groggily with a smile.

Even though she was joking, she later said the effect of the medicine really made her think. She said it was like a warm feeling starting from her middle and easing all through her body until she was pain-free. The drugs enabled her to escape the pain, and she understood for the first time why people become addicted to drugs: not having to face the pain of the life they are leading or of the past that hurt them. A deeper compassion and understanding came out of that experience.

When Marie came home from the hospital, she decided not to allow herself to take the pills given to ease the pain for fear of getting addicted. It took Pat Sarvis, wearing her nurse's hat, to convince her that it was okay to take them, since pain management was part of rehab and recovery and she would not become addicted.

Marie had physical therapy for nine months. The progress was slow and a battle of her will, since every movement was painful, but slowly the daily sessions turned to three times a week and then two times a week. We were told she would get back as much mobility as she was willing to work for. Thankfully it all came back.

At a weekly checkup Marie asked the doctor if he could assure her she would have a strong tennis serve after this.

"Absolutely!" he said, confident that she would get full movement back.

"Great, because I didn't have one before!" Marie quipped, laughing.

While Marie was unable to work, Yvonne picked up the slack in hospitality and in the office, allowing Marie to focus on her rehab and physical therapy. We had more work ahead of us, and we were thankful that Marie would be healthy enough to do it.

FIFTEEN

Light over Darkness

*I prefer a church which is bruised, hurting and dirty because it
has been out on the streets.* —POPE FRANCIS

THE LIGHTS OF the strip clubs and go-go bars twin-
kled brightly in the evening light. Since 1980 YWAM had held yearly
staff and Frontier Missions meetings in Pattaya, a seaside town about
two hours south of Bangkok. Pattaya was virtually unknown until 1961,
when a shipload of American servicemen fighting in the Vietnam War
arrived for some rest and relaxation. The soldiers were looking for one
thing, and Pattaya soon became a regular destination for soldiers and
other travelers who were seeking sexual adventures.

Each year we booked the Baptist retreat center for the staff conference, descending upon what was once a sleepy Thai fishing village. Each
year, our hearts broke to see the increase of open prostitution, tourists flocking to the now bustling town to participate in the booming
sex industry. Yet at every conference we prayed intensely for the town

and the many women and men who were trafficked—or at the very least forced or defrauded to prostitute themselves. We would often walk around the town in small groups, talking with these hurting souls and praying for God's love to break into their lives.

We began to see prayer answers in 1999, when Nella Davidse, a Dutch social worker, was called to serve Pattaya's sex worker population. For the first year Nella and her small team simply walked the streets and prayed every day. The Lord gave them a strategy. He said to not focus on the darkness but focus on Him through worship and prayer: light always conquers the darkness. Soon, Nella saw God work as churches and Christian organizations came together to pray and worship. Nella continued to walk up and down every *soi* (street or lane) proclaiming Jesus's lordship and asking for His kingdom to come and His will to be done. She contacted every pastor and Christian organization in the city, asking them to join a weekly prayer meeting. Most of them agreed, and the group grew.

Next, Nella's team began befriending the open-bar girls and letting them know of God's love for them. (Pattaya has many open, outside bars where women offer men a drink and then their services.) Out of that, the Tamar Center was born, meeting the needs of the women and training them in alternative jobs so that they could leave the sex industry behind.

The Tamar Center began classes in cooking, hairdressing, and computers. With the training came discipleship, often before conversion, as many of the women were drawn by the love of Jesus but did not make a decision to follow Him until months after living at the Tamar Center and experiencing the safety, grace, and love there.

As the women grew in their understanding of the love of God, they wanted to spread that love among their families and their villages back in Isan, the northeast region of Thailand. Outreach teams were formed, and the women traveled back to their villages to give their testimonies and help others who were at risk of being trafficked. The girls and women at risk would come from poor families and were vulnerable to someone offering their parents money in advance for giving their daughter a job in a restaurant in a town. The offer would be made to sound very attractive, and pressure was put on the girl to leave home right away. The girl would often be raped the first night, making her *sia*, meaning broken or ruined. When a girl is no longer a virgin, she believes she has become worthless and no one will want her, making it easier to push her into working as a prostitute. Also, many men walk out on these women, leaving them alone or divorced, with few legal rights and no way to support their children. Many feel that selling their bodies is the only option. The women stand outside the bars luring customers inside, and when they go off into the night, the client must pay the bar as well as the woman a sum of money. It is a very small amount, and thus the slavery has begun.

From the Wednesday prayer meetings an annual "Pattaya Praise" event started, and one year a team from a church in Northern Ireland came to be part of it. Some of the members were in a band called Bluetree. They were allowed to play a two-hour set in one of the open bars called The Climax Bar, the prerequisite being that everyone on the team had to buy a Coca Cola! It seemed incongruous to hear songs worshiping Jesus in such an environment. English-speaking tourists began to stop at the bar, not quite believing what they were hearing. It turned into one of the most powerful times of music and worship, and the lead singer started speaking out words over Pattaya that were coming into his thoughts. The words he sang out turned into the song "God of This City."

> You're the God of this city.
> You're the King of these people.
> You're the Lord of this nation,
> You are.
>
> You're the light in this darkness.
> You're the hope to the hopeless.
> You're the peace to the restless,
> You are.
>
> There is no one like our God.
> There is no one like You, God.

Greater things have yet to come
And greater things are still to be
Done in this city.
Greater things have yet to come
And greater things are still to be
Done here.

Ms. Oh was one of the women who were helped by Tamar. She was born into a poor household with fifteen children. Oh's elder sister was unable to have children and therefore adopted her. When Oh was six years old, her brother-in-law began sexually abusing her. At the age of twelve, Oh started working in construction to help the family. However, their financial problems continued, and they decided to send Oh to Japan to work as a prostitute. Luckily, visa regulations were changed and Oh could not go.

Oh moved to Bangkok and got married. Her husband abused her, and her life was very difficult. Oh had a daughter with her husband, but because of the circumstances, it was difficult for her to love and care for her child. She divorced her husband and remarried. She gave birth to a son and life started to go better, but when her son was four years old, her second husband died of AIDS.

Oh had to find a job to support herself and her family. She felt her only option was to move to Pattaya and work as a prostitute, leaving her children with her family. Oh hated it but thought it was her only option. Eventually she met a foreign man, who she believed was the answer to her problems and the way to happiness. However, after she had introduced him to her family, he left her and found another wife. Oh was devastated.

Oh heard about the Tamar Center but could not believe something like that could really be free in a city like Pattaya. However, she decided to give the training program a chance, and during one of the lessons on the father heart of God, she finally let out all the pain and sorrow caused by her past. At last she had found love and forgiveness, and the road to healing had begun.

When Marie spoke at Oh's training program graduation, she gave each woman a small bottle of perfume as a reminder that through each of them, God would spread everywhere the "fragrance of the knowledge of him" (2 Corinthians 2:14), and that God would lead them step-by-step.

Oh eventually reconciled with her children, and for the first time in twelve years her children came to live with her. She could now love them and care for them. Oh attended a YWAM DTS and went on to work for Tamar Center. She led the training program for several years before becoming a counselor at the crisis pregnancy center.

RANDY AND EDIE Nelson, leaders of the True Friend Church, had a vision to go out into all the bars and invite every working girl to a banquet held in the girls' honor. The Nelsons had been inspired after reading Luke 14:23: "Go out to the roads and country lanes and compel them to come in, so that my house will be full."

The first banquet was quite a success, and Tamar had a heart to continue them, but the cost of such a venture was far above Tamar's budget. Each girl who was invited would need income for the work she missed at the bar, and booking a hotel and providing the meal were not cheap. Nella started to pray about this idea, asking God to make a way if it was from Him. A church in Florida heard about it and began to sponsor Tamar to hold many more of these banquets—quite an answer to prayer.

Marie and I traveled down to Pattaya for one of these events. Before the women came to the hotel, the team prayed in this beautifully arranged banquet hall, asking for God's presence to come and fill the room with His love. Nella and her team had invited the women a few days earlier, and on the evening of the dinner, they collected them at the bar and paid for their night out. Over two hundred women came to the hotel, most dressed for their normal night of work.

The evening started with door prizes and lighthearted games, and then a youth pastor from Bangkok opened by singing well-known Thai pop songs, getting the women to sing along. He would see whether they knew some Thai worship songs, which, unsurprisingly, they didn't, and so would teach them simple songs about the God of the universe. He was very funny and had a great rapport with the women.

At the buffet that followed, Marie and I sat at a table with ten women. Most were scantily clad, and at first they tried to hit on all the men. They soon stopped when they realized the men were not potential clients. After the meal a pastor from the church in Florida spoke. The talk was short and simple and kept the women's attention. Through an interpreter, the pastor spoke about his daughter. He told the women how precious she was to him and how much he loved and wanted to protect her. He explained that God is our Heavenly Father and He sees us in the same way. The pastor ended with an offer to pray for anyone with needs. A few of the women stood up right away, visibly moved, and in the end everyone was standing. We took the time to pray for each woman, and as the women left, they were given a bag of beauty supplies and a long-stem red rose. They gave us a *wai,* a Thai greeting for coming or going and a sign of respect, with a slight bow of the head and the palms pressed together in prayerlike fashion.

Many asked, "Do you have another meeting?" They knew they were loved and accepted by us and wanted to keep up the contact.

We told them that there would be a meeting on Sunday afternoon and that they could bring their friends or boyfriends. The True Friend Church was a good place for them to learn more about loving God, loving their neighbor, and loving themselves. God was answering the prayers of many, many people who had come to Pattaya over the years.

The success and fruit from Tamar's work was such an encouragement to us in what turned out to be a long season of grief for Marie and me. It started in March 2002 when my father, Thomas Howard Goode Jr., died. I had been traveling in the United States the week before he died and had been able to stop in Memphis to see him. By this time he was eighty-three and had moved from assisted living to the Alzheimer's ward. All four of his sons were in town that week, and we each had time individually with him. It was a precious time, and I was able to tell him how much I loved him. The last words I heard from my dad were "I love you, son."

It seemed like he was doing better, and I was surprised when I landed in Bangkok after a thirty-hour flight to receive a call from my brother David saying that the doctors thought our dad had less than twenty-four hours to live. Only two hours later I received another message that Dad had gone to be with the Lord. Marie and I headed back to the States.

My brothers asked me to give the sermon at our dad's memorial service, and I put together some notes on the plane. We brought only carry-on luggage, and as we landed in Minneapolis before catching the flight south to Memphis, Ron called and said we would be taken straight to the funeral home from the airport. Once on board, we dug through our suitcases trying to get our dress clothes out for the funeral home while others were trying to board. The flight attendants were frustrated by our behavior. As I headed to the small airplane toilet to change, Marie explained to the flight attendant, "His dad has just died, and we are being taken directly to the funeral home when we land." The flight attendant understood, apologized, and, when we landed, helped us to get off the plane quickly.

The funeral was full, as Dad had been a pillar of the church and was much loved. He had been a welcomer at the church, giving everyone a "Tom Goode handshake," particularly noticing the lonelier people or people from other countries and taking them under his wing. Ron gave the eulogy, David read the scripture, and our brother John sang our dad's favorite hymn, "The Love of God." We laughed and cried as we celebrated a life well lived.

Ron mentioned in the eulogy that Dad never finished high school but left early to work and help support his parents, who were hardworking, God-fearing, honest sharecroppers. The youngest of eight brothers and sisters, three of Dad's sisters had died before reaching the age of two. The legacy of Thomas Howard Goode Jr. was that he first and foremost gave his life to God; second, he lived his life with integrity and honesty; and third, he taught his children to love and serve the Lord.

After the service we followed the hearse for the painfully slow procession to the grave site, about an hour away. A few of us were in one car, talking about how much Dad would have loved the service.

"I think Papaw [Dad's nickname] would have been honored by today, except for this ride—it would have driven him crazy!" Marie said with a smile, and everyone burst out laughing. Dad had been an ambulance driver and was famous for his speedy driving.

Nine months after my dad died, Marie received the somber call that her mother needed to be moved to a nursing home. I was in the US on a ministry trip and ready to board a plane to return to Thailand when Marie called asking me to meet with Thomas, her older brother in Tennessee, to help with the arrangements. Though there is an eight-year age difference between Marie and Thomas, the two of them have always been close. Thomas often introduced Marie as his twin sister, saying they were only eight years apart!

Marie joined us in the US. Once when Marie was checking in to see how her brother felt about her living on the other side of the world, leaving the responsibility of their aging mother to him, Thomas said, "I cannot do what you are doing. But if my doing this keeps you doing that, then everything will be okay."

Marie's mother had developed senile dementia and could no longer live by herself. This brought up a lot of grief and guilt in Marie, who knew that living in a nursing home was something her mother never wanted. The cost and sacrifice of Marie's calling weighed heavily on her heart, and Marie asked God how she could honor her mother while living halfway around the world.

Marie had lived far away from her mother for most of her adult life, and for a daughter, that was a particularly difficult part of being obedient to the call of God. Marie didn't question the call, but she felt the pain of sacrifice—separation from family and friends—very deeply. When their mom had been moved to the nursing home, Marie and Thomas returned to empty the apartment. They saw the several obvious signs that their mother truly needed additional care. Marie saw this as the kindness of the Lord to allow her to see for herself that this move was necessary and the right decision.

After a month settling her mother into the home, Marie returned to Bangkok. Nine months later we were at a staff conference in Thailand and had planned to return to the States the following Monday for my nephew's wedding. On the next to last day of the conference, Marie's brother called and told us her mom was in the hospital and it did not look like she had long to live. Her mom's heart was failing.

"Tell her I'm coming. Tell her to hold on until I get there," Marie told her brother, weeping.

We tried to change our flights to leave earlier, but it was impossible. We would be leaving home to get to the airport at 3:30 a.m. on Monday, but at 2:30 a.m. we got a call from Marie's brother. Marge had died. She was gone.

Marie cried tears of grief because she hadn't been able to say good-bye. Her pain was deep, and she questioned God. "Why couldn't You wait to take her until I got there? Did she know I was coming? Did she know I cared?" she asked.

On the plane, Marie's grief overflowed in silent tears. Marie realized she had a choice—to be angry, upset, and bitter, full of self-pity, or to choose thankfulness that her brother and sister-in-law had been with their mother so that she was not alone and that after eighty-eight years her mother had lived a good life and died fairly peacefully. Marie realized she could harbor bitterness for small things—like the fact that she would not be able to choose the burial dress for her mother. She felt that as the daughter she should have been there to do that. But instead of resentment, she chose to be grateful that Frances, her sister-in-law, loved and cared for her mother and that she could trust her to do a good job. And Frances did choose the perfect dress for Marge.

Marie's grief was heartfelt. "I feel like an orphan," she told me as we were flying on the plane. Even though Marie was fifty-three, was married, and had a large group of friends and a great support system, she still felt the loss of her last surviving parent very deeply. "If this is how I feel, just imagine how an orphaned child must feel," she said.

We talked with a renewed compassion about the orphaned refugee children we had worked with. For the first time, Marie fully understood the feeling of abandonment, and it fueled her prayers and action in a new way.

After Marge's funeral, we visited my mother, who had known and loved Marie's mom. My mother was in a wheelchair, but she laid hands on Marie and comforted her, praying that the Lord would be near to her. We felt pummeled by grief, but it was not over. Six months later, in April 2004, my own mother went to be with the Lord. She had lost her will to live when my father died a few days before their sixtieth wedding anniversary and had been living in a nursing home for the past two years, refusing to walk and eating very little. Her funeral was held in the chapel at First Assembly, and I could hardly keep it together as I stood to say a few words.

Burying our parents within only a few years was painful, and we saw again that God's original design and purpose had never been death and the terrible separation and loss one feels. However, we had the peace of knowing that they knew and loved God and had lived full and happy lives and that we would see them again.

We were soon to know another kind of grief, that of losing a dear friend. Nancy Ross and her husband, Dana, were coworkers, both from America, and they had become close friends, our family in Thailand. As we were going back and forth between Thailand and the US, burying our parents, Nancy was diagnosed with stage four ovarian cancer. Marie was overwhelmed by Nancy's diagnosis. She asked God for some encouragement and comfort and was directed to the simple words in Psalm 46:10 (NIV): "Be still, and know that I am God." That word brought peace to Marie, to know that even with everything going on, God was present with us.

In June of 2004 we attended the Asia Pacific Staff Conference in Pattaya. Nancy and Dana were with us, but Nancy was very weak. The day before the conference, Nancy had gone to her doctor in Bangkok, who said she needed treatment immediately, recommending that she not delay a week by going to the conference. After praying with Dana, she simply said, "What I need more than anything is to be with my family and worship Jesus." Worship kept her going, enabling her to have peace in the midst of horrible pain.

Along with Bangkok leaders Phil and Cindy Porter, Dana and Nancy led us in worship at the conference. Nancy sat in a chair so that she would have the strength to sing. Her sacrifice of praise caused many tears to fall in the room as we once again heard her incredibly beautiful voice proclaiming the faithfulness of God in song. Nancy had to be admitted to the hospital in Bangkok straight after the conference, but she slowly gained strength after receiving several blood transfusions.

In the midst of Nancy's illness, Marie was asked to speak at the Tamar training in Pattaya. Feeling it was right to go, she took the bus for the two-hour journey and was met by Nella.

The women who attended the Tamar training were hungry to know God, and Marie returned feeling as if something had come alive in her again. She loved teaching the women and was reminded afresh of her call to provide hope to those without hope.

Nancy's wish was to record a CD of worship songs, several of which she, Dana, Phil, and Cindy had written. The two couples worked around Nancy's treatments and bouts of weakness, but they finished the project. There was much rejoicing when we held their CD *In His Presence* in our hands. Marie and I and the Porters had a special worship time in Nancy's hospital room. Cindy and Marie were sitting at the end of Nancy's hospital bed. Nancy looked at them with compassion. "What is sad is that if I die, it will not seem long when I see you again, but for you two it will seem like a long time!"

Nancy's faith was never shaken by her illness. "He said He will heal all our diseases!" she said, believing for complete healing despite the doctor's prognosis. Even though she knew God could heal her, she was also longing for heaven. Death held no fear for her.

In August of 2004 Nancy's doctor allowed her to travel to the US to visit family, but soon after arriving, Nancy again became critically ill and needed treatment. She never returned to Thailand.

In November Marie had the choice of going to the US to help care for Nancy or traveling to Afghanistan with me. She had been asking the Lord what His highest was and was very torn as to what to do. Marie called Nancy and told her that if she wanted her to come, she would.

"Marie, I can't do what you are doing—go to Afghanistan!" Nancy replied adamantly. "I will pray for you and look forward to hearing the report when you get back."

We felt we were walking with Nancy through the valley of the shadow of death. But we also learned, sensed, heard, longed for, needed, and received more of the Lord than at any other time in our lives.

As soon as we returned from Afghanistan, Marie called Nancy to tell her we were back. Phil, who had been spending hours with his keyboard in the Rosses' living room, answered the phone. Worshiping Jesus had been Nancy's only wish. Nancy was weak but wanted to speak to Marie. As Nancy was passed the phone, Marie said, "Nancy, I don't know if I will see you again on this earth, but I will see you again—I know that to be true."

We prayed for Nancy and then said goodbye, putting the phone down. Nancy died later that night. We were told that she was determined to hold on until we were safely out of Afghanistan. Nancy was with Jesus, and we celebrated that, but Marie and I felt hollow with grief.

After a few weeks, Dana returned to Thailand, and we conducted a memorial service in Bangkok for the YWAM family in early December. Nancy had asked that we scatter her ashes on her favorite beach in Phuket at sunset, since she had so many wonderful memories of being there. Marie and I, the Porter family, Yvonne, and Dana decided to travel down to Phuket the day after Christmas. Little did we know that early in the morning of that day, Phuket would be ravaged by a natural disaster that stole hundreds of thousands of lives and destroyed the homes and livelihoods of even more.

SIXTEEN

Tsunami

God is against, not behind, all the evil in the world.
—GREGORY BOYD, *Is God to Blame?*

WE WOKE EARLY on December 26, 2004, to make the 800-kilometer (500-mile) journey south to Phuket. Our two vehicles left Bangkok about 5:30 a.m. to avoid the busy traffic. On the journey Dana filled us in on all that had happened since he and Nancy had left for America. It was cathartic for him to tell and for us to hear all the details of her last months.

The hours of travel went by fast, and by two o'clock we were nearing Phuket. We had been communicating by cell phone with the Porter family in our respective cars and were about to call them again when suddenly the phones went dead and Marie couldn't get a signal.

"This is Thailand!" Marie smiled, shrugging her shoulders. We had become used to things not always working the way we expected. But a few moments later Marie jumped as her phone started ringing on her lap. It was a staff member from Bangkok.

"Hello. Are you all okay? Where are you?" he asked in a panic when Marie picked up the phone.

A little surprised by the concern in his voice, Marie assured him that we were fine and were nearly at Phuket for this special time.

"There has been a terrible earthquake in Indonesia, and a tsunami has hit Phuket," he said. Before Marie could reply, the line went dead as the signal faded out, and he could not ask any more questions.

"There's been a tsunami," Marie said.

We all looked at each other but couldn't quite take in what that meant. Because we had never experienced a tsunami before, we had little idea of the scale of the devastation and destruction that one could create.

"Look at all those cars," Marie exclaimed suddenly as we arrived at the Sarasin Bridge, which connects the mainland of Thailand to the island of Phuket. The bridge was backed up with vehicles, and crowds of people were looking out to the ocean. At this point we were still so much in our own world of grief that we didn't quite connect the crowds with what we had just heard about the tsunami.

"Maybe someone is making a movie?" I suggested, as it was common for large crowds to be drawn to watch film stars. I also wondered if there had been an accident and a car had driven off the bridge. A massive wave hitting the beaches was the last thing we would have imagined.

Later we realized that in grief people are often surprised that the world is still carrying on normally around them, since it feels like their world has stopped. Time was standing still for us. We were going to Phuket to fulfill a task and to grieve and heal together. What was going on around us was like watching a movie, and we weren't part of it—yet.

In the weeks coming up to our planned time in Phuket, we had tried to get a hotel on the beach, but the hotels were all full. In the end the only way we could confirm somewhere to stay was through a friend pulling some strings for us. Our friend found us a hotel on a golf course on the other side of the mountain from the beaches.

Phuket was in the middle of the "the mother of all high seasons." Tourists were returning to Thailand in droves after the end of SARS, the economic crisis, and the avian flu. Even though we were sad not to have an ocean view, we were just relieved we had found a place to stay.

Eventually our two cars made it across the bridge, and after stopping to discuss what to do, we decided to drive down to the beach before we went to the hotel.

"I want to see the ocean," Dana said. The reality of the tsunami was still so far from all our minds.

As we drove down the narrow roads, there was a feeling of eerie quiet.

"Something is not right here," Marie said. We had all stopped talking and were just looking out the windows. As we got closer to the beach, the police stopped us. The roads were blocked off, and we were directed to the road up the mountain.

"What's going on?" I asked one policeman.

"Big wave, big wave," he said, before directing us on.

We realized we would just have to go to the hotel. On our way, Marie's phone came to life again, and we got a call from the friend who had secured our accommodation. "The hotel called, and they were wondering whether you're still coming to take the rooms because they have people from the beaches who need a new place to stay."

"We're coming. We're nearly there!" Marie replied quickly.

When we pulled into the driveway of the hotel, tourists were wandering around in their bikinis and shorts, many bleeding from scratches and cuts. All looked dazed and confused.

"Which beach are you coming from?" the receptionist asked as we checked in.

"We're not coming from a beach—we just arrived from Bangkok," I replied.

We heard then that another, bigger wave was on its way, but no one knew when and where it would hit. Everyone who had seen or been in the first wave was terrified.

Trying to take in what was happening, we walked to the restaurant, where a group of people were huddled in silence, watching the CNN news updates of the tsunami. We could not believe our eyes as the screen showed image after image of devastation and loss less than a mile from where we were staying. Even though the TV footage was shocking, it was still early in the day. The extent of the death and destruction would continue to unfold over the next days and weeks.

We realized that if we had come before Christmas to spread Nancy's ashes, we would have been on the beach that morning and most likely would have been among those lost or seriously affected by the tsunami. The epicenter had been off the west coast of Sumatra, Indonesia, and with a magnitude of between 9.1 and 9.3, it was the third-largest earthquake ever recorded on a seismograph. Over 230,000 people were killed in fourteen countries. We suspected the number was much higher but will never really know the actual number of deaths, and we had missed the tsunami by a matter of hours. The fraction of time between life and death is so small, and the enormity of what we had been saved from was starting to sink in.

Exhausted and in shock by what was happening, we had an early night. The next morning Dana and I hired motorcycles from the hotel to inspect the damage from the tsunami. We could see devastation everywhere. Tears poured down my cheeks as I took in destroyed buildings, boats lodged in trees, and cars crushed on top of other cars. The only words that came out of my mouth were a desperate moan: "Jesus, Jesus, Jesus!"

A thick covering of sand and debris was over everything. There was also a fine dust in the air, and although I tried to keep my mouth closed, the air was causing me to cough.

Marie stayed at the hotel, spending much of her time in prayer, asking the Lord for grace to cope with what was happening. This was a mind-boggling shock on top of our grief.

We were a pitiful group, burned out from the past two years of a lost battle with Nancy's cancer, overwhelmed with grief, empty physically, spiritually, and emotionally. We thought we didn't have anything else to give, but here was a crisis on our doorstep in the country that God had called us to bring His compassion and mercy to. We could not turn away.

We were finally able to get through by telephone to our friends and coworkers in Bangkok, John and Kim Quinley. The Quinleys had worked for several years as church planters in the province of Phang Nga, an hour north of Phuket, and were now working with us in Bangkok, pioneering the microenterprise project Step Ahead.

"We're coming down," John said on the phone. He and Kim had been unable to just sit and watch the devastation of the places where they had once lived. Knowing their friends were in need, they dropped everything to come as soon as they could. John had gathered a small team, and he and Kim were going to Phang Nga Province, where they still had many friends. It was one of the worst affected parts of Thailand. Phang Nga includes Khao Lak, one of the most beautiful spots on the coast. Over the past few years it had grown, through Scandinavian investment, from a small fishing village to a tourist resort.

Marie and I decided to drive north to Phang Nga the next day to see where we could help. Derek Porter, who was fourteen at the time, asked to come with us.

Having driven through the night, John and Kim and their team were there when we arrived. The group went straight to Phang Nga General Hospital and asked how they could help. The doctors and nurses nearly wept with joy at seeing them.

The hospital director said, "Foreign patients are coming out of surgery and saying things like, 'Where are my wife and children?' Please set up something to deal with this."

From that request they set up the International Crisis Coordination Center. It started very simply with paper lists of people missing and a bulletin board set up with enlarged photos of people and telephone numbers to contact if the person was found. The boards would truly rip your heart out—they showed people of all ages. Photos with scribbled details about the missing were posted everywhere possible: hotels, stores, telephone poles, makeshift boards, and so on. Eventually some YWAMers from Chiang Mai helped us put the documentation on a computer database, and we set up an office in Phuket.

This provincial hospital had treated very few foreigners in the hospital over the years, but now over six hundred tourists needed medical help. Most of the hospital staff members were unable to communicate with them.

We had prayed with Derek as we drove that God would help us to help others and to be able to serve where we were most needed. God responded immediately. We joined John and Kim and their children, Carter Kae and John-John, who were all fluent in Thai. Derek also spoke Thai, and we were put to work as translators helping the foreigners in any way we could.

People were desperate to find family members. A board was already up in the hospital with photos of dead people who had been found and taken to the morgue. Marie had to lead many people to the board to see if their loved one was posted there. In one instance, two German men in their late thirties came in looking for their mother, who had paid for the whole family to enjoy a once-in-a-lifetime holiday. When the tsunami hit, they had been separated from her, and they were now hoping she was at a hospital or clinic. Marie took them to the death board. She knew the hospital had two older women who had been brought in, both swollen and dead from drowning in the powerful wave. She tried to prepare the brothers, but there was little she could say. When they got to the board, the brothers were relieved that their mother's picture was not posted there. We never found out if she survived.

The different crises we had known over the past twenty-five years while working with the refugees in a war zone in Thailand and helping the Afghan refugees could never have prepared us for the amount of suffering, death, and destruction brought by the tsunami. We were very impressed with our YWAM kids—Derek, Carter, and John-John—who were only teenagers. We would never have wished for them to experience what they did, but they dealt with the situation heroically and with great love and sensitivity, throwing themselves fully into meeting and serving those in need.

While Kim led the organization of the center and made a plan of action in Phang Nga Hospital, John and I gathered a group of volunteers already at the hospital to travel north. We headed for the hospital in Takua Pa to coordinate the situation there and continue to assess the impact in coastal villages. As we arrived, I met a Swiss couple who were desperately trying to communicate with the Thai doctors. They were very grateful when I was able to step in and translate from Thai to French.

All this time Marie and I were trying to contact our close friends Erik and Jeltje Spruyt, who founded Le Rucher Ministries in France near the Swiss border. The ministries provided counseling and debriefing for people who had come out of traumatic crises. The Spruyts had

come to Thailand for a holiday with their adult son and daughter. We
had had a good evening of fellowship with them in our home before
Christmas, and then they headed to Koh Tao (Turtle Island) for their
holiday. We had been trying to get hold of them, but the lines were so
jammed with thousands of people trying to contact their loved ones
that it was impossible to get through.

"Lord, please let them be okay," Marie and I prayed again and again.

Over the next few days in Phuket and Phang Nga, we felt the heaviness of an almost overwhelming spirit of death and destruction. But
when we were at our weakest, we felt God's strength and grace rise up
from within us and were able to take each moment as it came.

After a few days helping in Phuket in practical ways, we realized
we would be of more use back in Bangkok helping to coordinate disaster response. I spoke with an outreach team about this, who, though
they were scheduled to work in Chiang Mai, asked if we needed any
volunteers.

"Is your team able to handle dead bodies?" I asked, wanting to be
clear and direct.

The greatest need at that time was to collect the dead bodies that
were washed up on the beaches and inland. Something had to be done
before they decomposed in the tropical heat and added to the issue of
disease. The team bravely got back to us saying yes and headed down by
train to Phuket. The twelve of them ended up helping transport bodies
to three Buddhist temples.

The temples had been converted into morgues, and the corpses
were put on dry ice until they could be identified. Large refrigerated
trucks were brought to store the bodies. The estimated death toll of
Phang Nga Province alone was over ten thousand Thais, European and
American tourists, and migrant workers from Myanmar.

On the drive back into Bangkok my mind raced with more ideas of
how to meet the need on the ground. I thought perhaps the best solution
would be to have the equivalent of CCSDPT (Coordinating Committee for Services for Displaced People in Thailand), which had worked
so well previously with the Indo-Chinese refugee crisis. Through the
years of helping a million refugees, this committee had met monthly to
coordinate the work of all the NGOs, international agencies, embassies,

and the Thai government. I realized that to maximize our potential for relief we needed to coordinate a Christian response to the tsunami and started praying for God to show the way.

A few hours later, when I was able to sit down in my office, I received a call from Randall Hoag, International Director of Food for the Hungry. Randall had the same idea about coordinating efforts and was already in contact with some of the major Thai churches. Together we called all the Christian organizations, arranging to meet at Christ Church in the center of Bangkok. From that first meeting, We Love Thailand (WLT) was born—a consortium of more than sixteen hundred Thai and international churches and more than twenty-five Christian NGOs, including World Vision, Operation Blessing, World Concern, Habitat for Humanity, Food for the Hungry, and YWAM, partnering in tsunami relief.

Peter Mawditt, an Englishman who had taken early retirement from Standard Chartered Bank in Bangkok, headed up WLT with his Thai wife, Jip. Peter and Jip were on their way to Boston for Jip to pursue a master's degree at Harvard, but they put this plan on hold. We discussed a three-phase strategy to serve the Thai communities affected by the tsunami. First, we would provide immediate emergency aid for the aftermath of the tragedy. Second, we would bring in short-term recovery assistance to rebuild lives and livelihoods through community projects. Third, we planned to identify needs and help communities develop a long-term plan that would take into consideration each unique situation. This last phase embraced social and economic development such as children's education, microenterprise, and ongoing counseling and care. We decided the best thing was to coordinate with the government, finding the gaps and seeing how we could serve.

In the midst of this we heard good news about our friends Erik and Jeltje, who had not been affected by the tsunami, having been on the Gulf of Thailand when it struck. Erik and Jeltje told us they were shocked when they arrived at Bangkok International Airport from their internal flight to see it full of shaken and dazed tourists. Erik had seen the look of trauma and devastation on people's faces. Many of these people had lost entire families. Jeltje reported that on the plane home she had spoken with the couple next to her and learned a bit of their story and pain. Realizing that it could have been her story, she thanked the Lord for the protection of their family.

Ten days after the tsunami, Southeast Asia was reeling from the aftereffects. It felt as if the tidal wave would never end. Marie and I flew back down to Phuket to meet with the governor's representative for Phang Nga Province.

"How can We Love Thailand help you?" I asked him.

The governor was still overwhelmed by the tsunami, and even though his immediate family was safe, he had lost many friends. His phone was ringing constantly during our meeting, but between calls he told us of whole areas north and south of Phang Nga that had not been visited. He asked us to travel north to assess the damage, providing us with a letter from his office to help us gain permission from the military to enter restricted areas.

Our team set out right away, driving from village to village along the coastline. Most of the villages had been completely destroyed. The people who were able to move to higher ground in time lived, but they lost almost everything else. The locals made their livelihood from fishing, but all their boats, nets, and gear were destroyed. There would be a great need in the months ahead to rebuild many houses. To begin to rebuild lives, we had to start by building fishing boats. Peter, Jip, John, Kim, Marie, and I would hold community meetings at each village, asking how many people had died or were injured, what the survivors had lost, and how many boats had been destroyed. When we asked them how best we could help, they typically replied, "We are simple fishing folk. If you just help us to rebuild our boats so we can get back to sea and fish, we can take care of the rest and fix our homes."

Being a teacher, Kim was quickly drawn to the urgent need to protect children through providing child safe zones and support to educators and rebuilding of schools.

We recorded all we heard and saw, giving our findings to the governor, who was grateful for our report and gave us free rein to work where we could.

Because donations were coming in fast, we were able to mobilize communities to help each other, agree on priorities, and work together purchasing building materials. Even in those early days with such tragic loss and devastation, it brought us joy to see how quickly these Muslim and Buddhist communities went from a sense of utter despair and helplessness—many just sitting silently and staring through you with empty eyes into the distance, reliving those tragic minutes when their lives were ripped apart—to noise and movement and even laughter as they busied themselves making decisions and working together.

The sense of community spirit inspired us. One village decided to put all the fishermen's names in a bowl and draw one name at a time. That draw decided the order of who would get their boats built first. Another village decided they would work on all the boats together, and only when they were all finished would they launch them into the ocean together and begin fishing again.

Marie and Jip led fishermen and boatbuilders in the search everywhere for materials to make shrimp cages and nets along with other supplies needed for the boats. We had thrown ourselves totally into the situation, yet despite how weak we had been personally when the tsunami hit, we were amazed at the strength and grace God was giving us.

Even though we were focusing 100 percent on WLT, none of our other work and ministry stopped. As YWAM's international leader for Mercy Ministries, I had responsibilities for other teams around the world. YWAM was already working on the ground in India and Sri Lanka in response to the tsunami, but the city of Banda Aceh, Indonesia, had also been badly hit, and we had not heard from our partners working there.

Aceh is the northernmost tip of the island of Sumatra and was closest to the epicenter of the earthquake and resulting tsunami. With a population of four million people, it is thought to have been the place where Islam first entered Southeast Asia.

Before the tsunami Aceh had been nearly impossible for foreigners to get into. Because of a civil war that had killed up to thirty thousand people, only a handful of individuals were allowed yearly visas, and both syariat (Indonesia's sharia law) and emergency law were in effect. After the tragedy the borders opened for international assistance. One hundred seventy thousand people had been killed in Aceh, and 60 percent of Banda Aceh, the capital, was completely destroyed.

Even without the tsunami, Aceh was in need of an incredible outpouring of tangible love and care. The civil war had raged intensely for the past seven years, with the rebels, or freedom fighters, trying to gain independence from the Indonesian government. However, the central government in Jakarta was not willing to let go of resource-rich Aceh, with its gas and oil. Sixty members of the previous provincial government had been arrested and were in prison in the city awaiting trial when the tsunami hit, destroyed the prison, and killed them all.

On January 20 I was able to get a visa from the Indonesian embassy. I planned to fly into Banda Aceh from Jakarta, but before departure I started to feel very ill. My doctor ordered bed rest in Bangkok for three days, and I obeyed. I knew if she had not ordered me to rest, I would have gone to Aceh, since I felt every moment was precious. By February 2 I was able to fly to Sumatra.

The scenes that met me in Aceh were like nightmares. It was as if with every step I took, the spirit of death was invading my being. Because Banda Aceh is flat, the tsunami had traveled up to five kilometers inland in some places until it hit the mountains and then returned this ugly, black water back to the sea, leaving complete devastation and destruction in its wake. Piles of dead bodies were everywhere, and red flags in the ground blowing in the wind showed where bodies were still under the rubble. According to Muslim custom, these bodies would normally have been buried within twenty-four hours, but bodies were still being found up to six months later. In the end two giant graves, holding over eighty thousand bodies, were made like landfill sites inside Banda Aceh. Many smaller mass grave sites were also constructed. This was the only possible way to prevent the massive spread of disease from those bodies lying in the tropical sun. When I arrived over a month after the tsunami hit, I couldn't help but notice that there was still a large number of red flags. Destruction was everywhere. Tile floors, where homes had once stood, stretched as far as the eye could see.

In the midst of such devastation I began to hear amazing stories of survival. Our partner team leaders, a married couple, had awakened at 6:00 a.m. feeling refreshed after their sleep, even though it had been only a few hours because the man had been on neighborhood security watch for much of the night because of the civil war. The man had wanted to take his wife and their two daughters to the beach, but the children did not want to go. Instead they all decided to take their final

Christmas presents—some cakes the wife had baked—to their team with whom they worked.

They family had not been able to deliver the cakes on December 25. On the morning of December 26, five minutes after they left the house, the earthquake hit. It was about eight o'clock. The couple and their two young daughters were in their car and had to stop because of the power of the moving, shaking ground. They made it to a friend's house, at this point knowing nothing of the terrifying tsunami that was headed their way. They then began driving to another friend's house when two of their team members came speeding up on a motorcycle.

"Don't go down there. The ocean is coming. Get out of here now!" their friend yelled.

They quickly turned their car around and, along with thousands of others, headed back up the mountain, making it to safety just in time. Everyone from both their teams survived. Our friends marveled that if they had left their house any later, they would have been killed since the house had collapsed under the power of the earthquake. If they had left the first friend's house any earlier, they would have been swept away by the wave.

One of their friends had a different story. He was engaged and was to be married in a few months, after he and his fiancée graduated from university. On that fateful day he had tried to escape the tsunami by driving his aunt and two nieces in his uncle's car to higher ground. His uncle followed with another niece on his motorcycle, but they were slowed down by all the other cars, motorcycles, and pedestrians fleeing the rising water. Frantically, the couple's friend got out of the car to climb a building and see if he could find a way ahead. Looking back, all he could see was the wave of black water rising on the horizon, coming his way. In seconds the forces of the water hit the car and swept it away with his aunt and nieces inside. That was the last he saw of them. He found out later his fiancée had not survived either. Family after family suffered a similar fate.

This wasn't like any of the war zones we had ever seen. This was a killing field of a different kind. My body was still weak from my previous infections, and while in Aceh I developed bronchitis. I tried to ignore my symptoms; I just did not have time to be ill.

In Jakarta we were able to meet with Muslim and Christian groups available to work together and to help in this response. I explained what we had done through We Love Thailand and suggested we start something similar. There was unanimous agreement, and Cinta Aceh (Love Aceh) was born. However, because of the civil war and other factors, including the loss of most of the government in Aceh, the coordinated response did not take off as it had in southern Thailand.

I ended up traveling to Aceh every four to six weeks to help coordinate the relief work and long-term development. Marie came with me in March 2005. One of the villages we visited used to have twelve thousand inhabitants; now it had only one hundred. We wept over the tragedy and with those who were suffering. One poor woman told us how she had lost everything. Ata was with her eleven-member family in their home near the sea when they saw the oncoming wave.

"We can't outrun this. We can only gather around mother and die together," Ata's older brother had said.

The siblings put their mother in the middle of a circle and stood with their arms around each other, bracing themselves for the force of the wave to hit their building. The thundering water gushed through the windows and pushed their bodies along with the bricks, razor sharp corrugated tin roofing, and tables and chairs. Unable to swim, Ata was carried almost three kilometers away. Amazingly, she survived. She woke up alone, unaware of how long she had been unconscious. Her clothes for the most part had been ripped from her body. She suffered cuts and minor injuries, but nothing serious. Although she searched for months, she never found the bodies of her family members. She was the only one who survived. All the homes in her community were destroyed. Ata gathered a few pieces of wood for a makeshift shack that she placed on the top of five concrete steps—all that remained of her family home. When we arrived, Ata was on her hands and knees, cleaning those five steps. Marie and one of our partner leaders sat with her and asked her what she was doing.

"My mother and I used to clean these steps every day. We would talk together and watch the sunset. Cleaning them helps me feel close to her," Ata said with a sad smile.

In meeting the needs of the province, our partners in Aceh were rebuilding six businesses and starting a business producing windows and doors for the 110,000 new houses needing to be built. They also started a microfinance program that provided loans for capital, helping to restart over one thousand destroyed small businesses.

We held a meeting at the beach on that first Easter after the tsunami, trying to provide a way for Christian team members to gather and remember the resurrection of Jesus and the power He has to heal, restore, and save. Some Muslim friends joined us. I asked the friend who had seen his aunt and nieces drown in the car he had been driving if he would like to go a few feet away and go into the sea with me.

"No, I hate the water and I hate God. I have not prayed since the tsunami," he said in anger. (He was not unlike many others. Even several months after the tsunami, thousands of people in internally displaced camps had yet to take a bath or shower because they were too afraid of the water.) The man told me that he hated God because He had brought judgment on the people of Aceh through the tsunami, killing so many, including his fiancée and his aunt and nieces. He was speaking about what many were thinking—that the tsunami was God's judgment on Aceh.

"God is not like that. If He judged us like that, we would all be dead," I told him. I went on to talk about the history of Adam and Eve and what happened to the earth when people sinned against God. "This earth is not functioning the way that it was designed to function—God is a God of compassion, love, and mercy. Even in His judgment He remembers mercy."

For more than an hour we talked. As we were leaving, the man said, "Pak [older brother] Steve, I am still mad at God, and I don't believe like you, not today . . . maybe someday, but not today."

WHILE IN BANDA Aceh the house where Marie and I were staying was suddenly shaken by an earthquake. We tried to stay calm as we felt the walls become like gravy and the floors shudder under the force of the shock.

Our friends did not seem as concerned as we were. "Oh, that was only about 6.8," someone said, as if it wasn't a big deal. They had become so used to the aftershocks, many over 7.0 on the Richter scale, that their reaction was no longer fear.

We flew to Java that evening to spend time with some other partner families. Arriving late, we went straight to bed but were awakened after only a few hours by a telephone call from a partner in Aceh saying that there had been another huge earthquake. The team was okay, but they had left their house and were spending the night in the open to avoid being crushed under falling buildings. Many of the Acehnese had been sleeping out in the streets for months.

We prayed for their safety and then tried to get back to sleep, but it wasn't long before the calls started coming from Bangkok. Friends knew that we had gone to Aceh, and now they were hearing about the earthquake. After reassuring them that we were okay, Marie and I again went back to bed. However, our sleep was interrupted again when at 3:00 a.m. I woke with a high fever. By four o'clock my temperature was 39 degrees centigrade (102.2° F), and Marie was getting worried. She talked to our hosts, who drove us to the nearest medical clinic. By this time my temperature was 40 degrees (104° F). I was sweating profusely and almost lost consciousness. A local doctor at a little pharmacy seemed quite panicked by my condition, which in turn made Marie more nervous. He said the nearest international hospital was a good six hours away, but there was a reputable local hospital only an hour and a half away.

After I was admitted into the closer hospital, in Semarang, we met the doctor, who greeted us with a smile and asked if I was ready for surgery.

"He isn't here for surgery!" Marie exclaimed.

It turned out that the doctor had the wrong records. From that point on, Marie would not leave my side—she didn't want any more mistakes made. The medicine I had been given by the first doctor had brought my fever down, but I was still feeling so weak and sick that I could hardly move. They tested me for typhoid, malaria, dengue fever, and a urinary tract infection. The results showed I had typhoid and a possible urinary tract infection.

After a few days in the hospital, I regained my strength and was able to get to the next set of tsunami meetings in Jakarta. When I returned to Bangkok, I was immediately heading for the Netherlands for important meetings regarding Afghanistan. Marie encouraged me to cancel the trip, but I was adamant about going. The truth is that I was in denial as to how ill I actually was.

After the trip I was still not well, and the doctor recommended more surgery to clear my urethra of scar tissue that was building up again. My urologist thought this might have been the cause of the urinary tract infection, which was not responding to antibiotics. While I was in the hospital in Bangkok, Marie also had a checkup and found she had a cancerous growth on her face. It was dealt with quickly with no permanent damage or treatment needed, but the large bandage on her face made visitors wonder who actually had had the surgery.

By May we were due to go to Afghanistan, while activities in both Thailand and Aceh were going full steam ahead. I felt like we were on a high-speed train going from one disaster to another. It was a crazy time, but through it all God provided help and encouragement when we needed it. I was able to attend the annual YWAM Global Leadership Team meetings in Brazil. After I filled our senior leaders in on all we were doing and facing, my fellow leaders prayed with great compassion and tears for me, Marie, and our YWAM Mercy Ministries staff and partners. I felt surrounded and supported by love, and it gave me an injection of strength that helped carry me through the days ahead.

The YWAM Global Leadership Team had been led into fifty days of prayer and fasting as we felt God had spoken about a release of new apostolic, pioneering anointing on our mission. There was to be a new thrust for global prayer, evangelism, and mercy in YWAM at every location. The picture was of YWAM as a three-legged stool, with evangelism, training, and mercy ministry being the legs. Our mercy ministry leg was stretched and growing as we met the needs in Asia, Africa, and South America—the ends of the earth.

SEVENTEEN

Times of Crisis

God has commissioned us as agents of intervention in the midst of a hostile and broken world.
　　　—PHILIP YANCEY, *The Question That Never Goes Away*

IN THE MIDDLE of meeting the needs in Aceh, we experienced another tragedy, closer to home. A beautiful, young Thai YWAMer named Jeeranun Sangpunta, "Tuy" for short, was in a car accident and died from her injuries. Twenty-seven years old, she was engaged to be married, worked with the Project L.I.F.E. Child Sponsorship team in Bangkok, and had just completed a DTS in Chiang Mai. She had been planning to join the team working with tsunami relief in southern Thailand.

Tuy was raised in a Buddhist home and had moved to Bangkok at eighteen to attend Ramkhamhaeng University. While there, she heard about Jesus from a Christian student and gave her life to the Lord. After she had gone home to tell her family, her three sisters followed her into a relationship with Jesus.

Marie and I drove with a group of YWAMers several hours to Tuy's home province to attend her funeral, which the family had arranged in the local Buddhist temple according to the wishes of Tuy's parents. It was amazing to see Tuy's fellow DTS students sitting around in various groups on the floor of the temple, telling her friends and family how they had loved her and how her life had impacted them. All the YWAMers then knelt before Tuy's parents, showing love and respect to them with hands folded in a Thai *wai*. We thanked her parents for releasing their daughter to work with us and told them of the blessing she had been to the poor of Thailand. Tuy's mother, who had been in the accident with her daughter, was still in a wheelchair from her injuries. We were able to pray for her, and in the midst of pain, she was deeply moved by our show of love and respect. Tuy's motto was "Never give up." Even in death her words spoke to us. It was a solemn occasion, but the love of God was present in that temple. Many of Tuy's friends heard that day for the first time in their lives about the God that Tuy served.

At the funeral I asked if I could say a few words about Tuy and about her God and His comfort in the midst of suffering and death. I told this mostly Buddhist gathering that God was preparing a place for those who trusted in Him. I ended with the words of Jesus: "Jesus said to her, 'I am the resurrection and the life. Whoever believes in me will live, even though they die'" (John 11:25). This temple was a holy place where the love of God was expressed in so many ways. Tuy's death was a devastating loss for YWAM Thailand, but the shock waves continued.

IN 2001 KENNY Franciscus, who with his wife Vickie and their children worked in Chiang Rai, had found out he had a chronic liver disease, which had been discovered during a routine visit to a doctor in Bangkok for another complaint. Kenny had no pain or obvious symptoms, but the doctor said if he did not have a liver transplant, he would die. The Franciscuses had moved back to America for treatment, and someone from their home church offered his liver for a live transplant. The liver is such an amazing organ that even if you give 90 percent of it away, it regenerates almost immediately. The surgery was a success, and Kenny began his road to recovery.

We quickly learned, however, about the difference between a living donor transplant and a deceased donor transplant. In a living donor transplant, Kenny would get a part of the liver, and with a deceased donor transplant, which also has a longer waiting list, the recipient gets the whole liver, including all of the necessary liver "plumbing and connections." With this partial liver, the doctors had to craft new connections which were susceptible to infections and blockages. We had prayed continuously for this special family during the four years since Kenny had been diagnosed, but at this point, for some reason, Kenny's health was in serious decline.

Marie and I knelt on the floor of our room and cried out to God for mercy. "God, You have to heal Kenny. We cannot take another loss. Spare his life, heal his body, send the family back to Thailand and to our mission and to us. I bow to You. You are God, but this is my plea," Marie prayed in tears.

Although Kenny came close to death many times during the subsequent years, we continued to call out to the Lord on his behalf. In 2010 he had a second successful liver transplant from a deceased organ donor, and Kenny received new life and health. We gave thanks to God for this donor, and this incident has caused us to rethink and change our ideas about organ donations upon our death.

BECAUSE OF THE emotional roller coaster that our lives had become, we did not scatter Nancy's ashes until almost eight months after the tsunami. We were able to reconvene in Phuket in August 2005. Dana had returned to Thailand for a YWAM staff conference in Chiang Mai. At the conference we stayed close to Dana, who was still grieving. On the last night Dana joined Phil and Cindy on stage to lead worship. As he played his guitar, leading us in "Blessed Be the Name of the Lord," we wept through the words:

Blessed be Your Name
When the sun's shining down on me
When the world's all as it should be
Blessed be Your Name.

Blessed be Your Name
On the road marked with suffering
Though there's pain in the offering
Blessed be Your Name.

You give and take away,
You give and take away.
My heart will choose to say,
Lord, blessed be Your Name.

This song was our prayer as we had a time of remembering both Nancy and Tuy, our "fallen warriors," and thanking God for their lives.

During this time, the infection in my body would not budge. I had been given twelve different antibiotics, but the bacteria seemed to be resistant to them all, maybe partially due to how exhausted and run-down I was. In the end my doctor gave me an injection of antibiotics every day until I left for the airport. I had to continue taking these injections while at the conference in Chiang Mai. Dana offered to help, since he had regularly injected Nancy with pain-relief drugs. He had the dubious privilege of administering the antibiotics into my backside every day for a week. This set of antibiotics worked.

After the conference we flew from Chiang Mai to Phuket. We went to Karon Beach, which held many memories for us. With the backdrop of a spectacular sunset, one by one we described our favorite memory of Nancy, and then Dana led us in worship with his guitar. Slowly we each took a handful of Nancy's ashes and, wading into the ocean, gave thanks to God and said our final goodbye. As we started to spread the ashes, I noticed several Thais watching what we were doing, their hands together in a *wai* of respect. I am sure that they had witnessed many similar ceremonies on that beach.

As Marie grasped two handfuls of ashes, her fingers clenched tight around the remains of her friend, and she cried to God in gratefulness for Nancy's life. The waves were lapping at her legs, and the orange sun slowly sank into the horizon. A wave of emotion came from deep within her, and as she prayed loudly, deep sobs wracked her body. Cindy went to stand next to her and held her as a dam of grief burst open. I joined the two of them with Dana and Phil, and we huddled together, knee-deep in the ocean, Marie unable to open her hands.

Eventually I realized the waves were getting stronger as the tide was coming in faster. "Honey, you have to let go, or we're all going to drown!" I said, and everyone burst out laughing. With a smile, Marie threw the final ashes into the wind and sea.

The next morning when Marie woke up, she said it was as if her soul had been cleansed and touched in a deep, powerful way. It had been like losing Nancy for the first time because she finally felt free to express the deep sadness within her. While Nancy was ill, Marie was being strong for everyone else and had not allowed herself time to grieve.

After spreading the ashes, we traveled back to the States to celebrate a nephew's wedding and fulfill commitments we had made before the tsunami. We were also ready for some respite from the trauma of what had been a difficult year. I was infection-free for the first time in eight months, which was a great relief, and I needed to build up my strength. But as soon as we landed in America, we heard the news. Hurricane Katrina had hit, and New Orleans suffered badly from the storm. I immediately started receiving phone calls from YWAM Mercy staff in the US who knew I was in the country, asking if I could take a trip to see the devastation and help coordinate relief.

This time I was able to say no. "I am confident that you know what to do. If you need any input, just give me a call, but I need to rest," I said. Despite saying that, I did end up helping to coordinate some of the churches in Memphis, advising them on what their response could be. Not getting involved on the ground turned out to be a wise decision.

While we were still in the US, a major earthquake hit Pakistan-administered Kashmir on October 8, 2005. The official death toll was over seventy-five thousand people. We were concerned for the children of many teams and other partner agencies who went to an international school close to the worst-affected area. We changed some travel plans in order to fly there and begin work with the equivalent of We Love Thailand in Pakistan.

Very quickly a small group of like-minded organizations assisted in uniting twenty organizations to coordinate a response. The first problem to tackle was communication, since Internet and mobile phone lines were not reliable. An Internet technology agency helped us with a VSAT (Very Small Aperture Terminal). This satellite dish connects with low-flying satellites to provide high-speed Internet. A technology organization put the VSAT in two Kashmiri hospitals that had not been totally destroyed, which happened to be the two in which we had contacts.

The second phase was to start rebuilding the houses that had been destroyed and then provide something for people to do who had lost everything. One partner we were working with began manufacturing bricks to be used in the rebuilding of homes.

A quilting project for women provided both employment and protection from the cold. Winter was coming, and the government feared that those who had not died in the earthquake would not survive the winter because of lack of shelter and warmth.

The government told us that forty-one villages were still blocked off five weeks after the earthquake. Rocks had fallen on the roads, making them impassable. As the military brought in earth-moving equipment, we recruited volunteers from all over the world to come and serve. Kashmir, like Aceh, had been closed to foreigners, but in this time of crisis the borders were open, and our volunteers came to look after the sick and help rebuild the lives and homes that had been shattered.

After a few weeks in Pakistan and Afghanistan, Marie and I were once again back in Bangkok, meeting and consulting with We Love Thailand and Cinta Aceh. Near the Phuket airport in southern Thailand, we were working with a group of Muslim fishermen who had lost more than thirty fishing boats. The first time we had met this group, they were depressed and in shock. It seemed like all of the tsunami assistance was going elsewhere. But now with the help of WLT, they were on their way to rebuilding their boats. One day one of the fishermen asked what seemed like a strange question: "Does We Love Thailand work in Pakistan?"

"No," I told him, "this is a consortium just for Thailand."

He seemed disappointed and a bit sad.

"Why do you ask?" I said.

He replied, "Some of us know how to rebuild houses, and we thought if WLT worked in Pakistan, we could go with you to help rebuild Pakistani homes lost in the earthquake, like you have helped us rebuild here."

I was amazed at how the message of loving God and loving your neighbor was coming through loud and clear.

In another Muslim village, I was talking to a seventy-eight-year-old Muslim fisherman whose boat had been destroyed. I asked Mustafa how WLT had assisted him. He said, "They helped me rebuild my boat and also introduced me to Isa." (Isa is the Arabic name for Jesus.)

"Really, how did that happen?" I asked.

"These people didn't know me or my family and yet they came to help us. I asked them if they had any special meetings that I could attend," Mustafa said.

Mustafa was told there were no special meetings but the group did meet to worship God once a week and he was welcome to come. When Mustafa came and heard more of the gospel, he understood it was because of Isa that these people came to help his people. He wanted to know Isa too.

"I follow Isa now," he told me with a big smile on his face.

It had been quite a year. Between the two of us, Marie and I had traveled to Phuket ten times, Aceh six times, Pakistan and Afghanistan twice, Switzerland, Finland, Brazil, and the US. Tuy had died, and I had had surgery. In the middle of everything our home was robbed. One morning, we had held a tsunami planning meeting in our living room and had driven to our office in the afternoon. During that time thieves had broken in and gone upstairs to the bedrooms, pulling out drawers, moving mattresses, and taking Marie's most valuable jewelry. It was horrible to experience having had someone uninvited in our home, but we knew that in the end this was just stuff—material possessions that had emotional and sentimental value. We were just thankful that no one had been hurt and the house was not trashed.

As the months went by, Bangkok and the rest of Thailand seemed the most stable place to be, but we were wrong. On September 19, 2006, the Royal Thai Army staged a coup d'état against the government of Prime Minister Thaksin Shinawatra. It was the first coup in fourteen years. We were shocked and deeply disappointed. Thailand was seen as a key democratic country in Asia and Southeast Asia, and since the last coup in 1992, a strategy had been put in place to prevent something similar from happening.

The coup took place less than a month before nationwide elections to the House of Representatives. Since Prime Minister Thaksin and some of his senior leaders were in meetings outside the country, the military canceled the upcoming elections, dissolved parliament, banned protests and all political activities, suppressed and censored the media, declared martial law, and arrested cabinet members.

The good news was that the coup was relatively peaceful, with no loss of life. The situation did not affect our daily life too much, but we knew where it was wise not to be. We kept off the streets and made sure our staff were safe and in their homes before the evening curfew. Providentially, a day before the coup we had moved our office to a former staff house a few doors down from our home, and we no longer had to drive the streets of Bangkok to get to work. This made life much easier and meant we could go to the office even during the coup.

On New Year's Eve en route to dinner, our coworker Kim Quinley called. "Where are you?" she asked after Marie said hello.

"In the car, just by the American embassy. We're headed to a restaurant near there for dinner," Marie told her.

"We just heard that bombs have gone off in different parts of Bangkok. Be careful," Kim said.

No one knew if there were any more bombs about to explode.

We did not see anything and hadn't been near any of the explosions, but three people died and thirty were injured. While it was never confirmed who planted the bombs, the episode brought a new dimension of concern to what was happening in our city, and it also reminded us that we are not immune to the things that affect the people we serve. We had narrowly missed the tsunami and now the bombs, but we knew more than ever that the safest place to be is in the center of God's will. Our times really are in God's hands, and when it is our time to die, hopefully we will be ready. We had a deep peace that we were where God wanted us to be. Despite the dangers, "wars and rumors of wars," or whatever natural disaster hit, we were aware that God was with us and would never leave us. He would help us, and as He comforted us, He could show us how to comfort others.

WE HAVE ALWAYS had incredible people working behind the scenes in support, administration, and finances to make all of our programs and projects succeed. One such person was Nelly.

In 1986 I spoke at a gathering in the Netherlands to a group of staff, students, and friends of YWAM Heidebeek. I spoke about the refugees and the need for workers, particularly in the support and administrative areas. A white-haired Dutch accountant, Nelly van Acker, responded to that call and came to join us in Bangkok in 1987. She was a woman of detail and loved what she did. Nelly was such a gift to us in those early days. Since we were working in rural areas where it was next to impossible to get receipts, Nelly created systems that assisted all of our teams. She helped us develop good processes and good reporting. Because we were increasing our work with the various arms of the UN, we were getting more project monies and had to do more reporting and provide more audited financial statements. At one point, we needed to perform three different audited statements for three UN agencies in a single year. Nelly was a wonderful friend and prayer warrior, a woman who operated with excellence in integrity and transparency. Her outreach while she was serving out of our YWAM Mercy office was to visit international prisoners in Bangkok several times a month. Nelly worked with us at YWAM Relief Services for seven years and then went on to work with Hagar in Cambodia for another seven years before she retired to New Zealand.

After the tsunami hit Southeast Asia, Marie called Nelly and asked her to prayerfully consider coming back to help us in accounting, since we were gearing up for We Love Thailand and Cinta Aceh as well as increasing our workload. Nelly would be training others in the setting up of systems and overseeing their work. She came out of retirement and helped to set up accounting systems and train nationals in Vietnam, Thailand, and Indonesia.

One of the prisoners in Bangkok whom Nelly had visited was from Indonesia. Yunus had been arrested for drug possession and sentenced to twenty years in prison. He had been a Christian back in Indonesia, but the temptation to make some quick money by running drugs had been too great for him, and he was arrested. He repented of his crime and recommitted his life to God while in prison. Nelly helped him to grow in God. She also wrote to his family in Indonesia to let them know that she was visiting him and to keep them up-to-date. Because the family was poor and it was too difficult for them to come to Bangkok to visit him, Nelly would be a point of contact and communication.

In June 2005, we received an e-mail from Astrid, daughter of Yunus. The family had heard that Yunus had died of a stroke while in prison, and they asked if we could check on him. Yunus had been in prison for eighteen years. The family had been told it would cost them one thousand US dollars to transport his body back to Indonesia. Since they did not have the money, Astrid asked if we could ensure that Yunus had a Christian funeral in Thailand and then send pictures to show the family. Nelly had just returned to work with us in our tsunami response.

Our office was able to provide the money for the transportation of Yunus's body back to Indonesia. Nelly worked with the Indonesian embassy to get all the paperwork done for the transportation of a coffin and a body from Thailand to Indonesia. I was returning from a trip and had gotten an e-mail from Nelly, who asked me to come straight from the airport to the police morgue, where we would prepare Yunus's body, put it in a coffin, and have the police take it to the airport.

When I arrived at the morgue, Nelly was preparing Yunus's body, washing it, getting new white clothes for the trip, and, with the help of the staff on duty, placing it into the coffin. Nelly and I prayed that God would welcome Yunus into the place He had prepared for him. We said a few short prayers for the family in Indonesia and asked that God would walk with them during this time of grief. I took a few pictures of the body to send to the family in case there were any problems, and then the Thai police staff had to quickly take the coffin to the airport.

The wonderful part about being in an international mission is that we were able to call some of our leaders in Indonesia, and these leaders attended the funeral with the family to comfort them in their time of grief. The family was amazed and very grateful to have these unexpected guests at the funeral. Typical of this servant and woman of God, Nelly visited the family shortly afterward on her way to Banda Aceh.

In July 2007, as we finished our audit, Nelly said that she was going to the doctor because she had a nagging back pain that she had noticed a few months earlier on a visit to her family in the Netherlands. Since Nelly did not travel with a cell phone, we became concerned when she did not show up for dinner that night. She finally arrived looking quite pale and in shock. The doctor had told her she had stage-four lung cancer. We couldn't believe this, since Nelly had never smoked and was in good health. Much to the delight of our Thai neighbors, at seventy-six years of age Nelly still rode her bicycle regularly in our Thai-Chinese subdivision.

We prayed that God would touch Nelly and heal her. Nelly returned to New Zealand for treatment and to be with her children. Our dear Nelly went to be with the Lord on December 4 that same year. Her death was extremely hard on all of us, especially Marie. Nelly had been a gracious teacher and mentor, a woman who was easy to talk to, and a loved and respected friend.

EIGHTEEN

Doing the Next Thing

Action without vision is only passing time, vision without action is merely day dreaming, but vision with action can change the world. —NELSON MANDELA

BACK IN 1992 I had invited Dr. Ian Campbell, head of the HIV/AIDS unit of the Salvation Army, to address the YWAM Global Leadership meeting in India on this global issue. We learned about how the Salvation Army developed training materials for churches and worked with government and international agencies. Many of our YWAMers had family members who had died or were dying of AIDS. We started to have DTS students who were HIV positive, and as a mission we were sending outreach teams into places of high risk. The situation needed to be addressed—we needed to train our staff and to meet the needs of those affected and infected in any way we could.

The work continued. In 2005 approximately forty YWAM schools were running in Africa, but few had any training or teaching on HIV/AIDS as a part of their three-month lecture phase. As a mission we had to get to and stay on the cutting edge and be relevant to what was going on in society. The first step was to develop HIV/AIDS training and guidelines for all staff, students, and schools. The next was to have a conference to educate ourselves and to strategize about the best ways to respond to the need.

Uganda seemed the obvious place to start, since the country had been successful in tackling the issue. It had previously had the highest prevalence of HIV/AIDS in sub-Saharan Africa, but President Yoweri Kaguta Museveni had started a public service campaign, educating his people on safe sex and how HIV is transmitted. The two-year program worked better than he had imagined, and the percentage of HIV/AIDS in the country dropped dramatically. The First Lady of Uganda, Janet Museveni, became a spokesperson and represented the women of Uganda around the world.

YWAM Uganda was led by Sam and Irene Kisolo, an exceptional couple with fifty children—four of their own and forty-six adopted since 1991, many of the children orphaned by HIV/AIDS. YWAM staff in Uganda had adopted approximately three hundred children orphaned by HIV/AIDS and had started the Foster Family Network for Ugandan families to adopt more children. A gifted public speaker and natural leader, Sam was also on the HIV/AIDS government task force.

I had first met Sam in 2003 in Uganda. We were watching a youth organization perform dances and dramas to bring HIV/AIDS awareness.

"You see that girl in blue?" Sam asked.

We were both in the front row, and I looked at the young girl he was pointing to.

"Her name is Shifa. She's ten, and she recently lost both parents to AIDS. She is living alone in the center of Jinja and is very vulnerable," Sam explained. Sam had also learned that Shifa's sister had recently died of an AIDS-related illness.

"What can we do?" I asked.

"Tonight we will have a family meeting to pray and ask God if we should invite her into our family," he replied.

I was very impressed, knowing how large Sam's family was already. It would mean sacrificing space and committing to feed, clothe, and educate another girl when Sam and Irene had very little themselves.

The next day I was very interested to hear what their decision was. "What did your family say?" I asked over breakfast.

Sam turned to me with a big grin that lit up his whole face. "We are going to invite her into our home," he said.

I had felt God say that if Sam told me they were taking Shifa, God was asking Marie and me to trust Him for the finances to support her. When I told Sam this, he smiled, grateful for any assistance we could give. Shifa finished high school and a tailoring course at a technical school, completing an internship at a local clothing factory. Thanks to Sam and Irene's heart of compassion and willingness to act, Shifa has seen that God has a future and a hope for her to prosper and succeed.

Back in Bangkok, I contacted Sam about the idea of having a YWAM HIV/AIDS conference in Uganda. Sam got things moving, inviting First Lady Janet Museveni to speak at the conference, which was held at Hopeland, a YWAM base set in eighty acres outside of the town of Jinja on Lake Victoria.

As we started worshiping God on the first day of the conference, tears came to my eyes. I knew that we were in for a special time with God and each other. This was holy ground, and these people were anointed servants, men and women of God from various countries in Africa and Asia who were full of love and compassion, reaching out to serve those with HIV/AIDS. They spoke of working with people who were suffering and the pain they themselves faced in seeing so many die. Many staff displayed little or no emotion when they talked about this. It was as if they were numb and needed healing from what they had experienced.

We divided the conference into small groups, those who had worked with people who died and those who had not. We then blended the groups to allow those who had walked through suffering and death to tell their stories while the others listened and then sometimes asked questions about what was being said.

The Ugandan woman who spoke in my group had seen twenty people die in the past year. The whole group wept as we heard her story. The women in turn was deeply touched by simply being listened to, and we saw how powerful it was for someone who has gone through such deep pain to be heard and understood. It is similar to crisis debriefing—when the emotional and rational sides of one's brain come back together after the shock that one has just faced. The power of empathetic listening is amazing.

As a response to the stories, someone came up with a very tangible idea. Everyone wrote on twelve-inch pieces of bright red ribbon the names of the people he or she had known and had served who had died of HIV/AIDS. The ribbons were then tied together. That evening we honored those who had died by stringing the now very long piece of ribbon with thousands of names on it several times around the room. Every participant was holding up this long train of red ribbon. Then we gave thanks and worshiped God through many tears.

The conference presented incredible speakers. One of them was Dr. Matthias Cavassini, part of our adopted Swiss family who heads up the HIV/AIDS unit in Lausanne, Switzerland. Matthias attended a YWAM DTS in Hong Kong in the mid-eighties where he first learned of HIV/AIDS. One of his eleven roommates was HIV positive. As Matthias became good friends with the man, his interest in AIDS grew. Matthias kept in contact with this friend and visited him in the US before the man died of AIDS in the early nineties.

After the three-month lecture phase in Hong Kong, Matthias and his team went on outreach to the Phanat Nikhom refugee center in Thailand. One day after returning from the camps, we were on the veranda talking about poisonous snakes. As we were talking, I looked up. Above Matthias's head was a five-foot "two step" snake—if you are bitten, you can take maybe two steps before you die.

Matthias thought I was joking but quickly realized I was not. We killed the snake by knocking it off the beam with a bamboo stick and then cutting off its head with a shovel. As it lay dead on the floor, we noticed a big swelling in the middle of it.

"Let's open it up and see what the snake ate!" Matthias said, already showing signs of wanting to enter the medical field.

When we slit the snake open, we found it had eaten a plastic bag. The snake had tried to get some nourishment from whatever was in the bag. That would have taken a long time to digest!

Dr. Matthias used another story at the conference about snakes to explain the HIV/AIDS virus, since our Ugandan medical staff visited area clinics, churches, and families. "Cobras are very deadly, but if you place a light bamboo stick on a cobra's head, just that small amount of pressure will keep the cobra from moving," he said. "The cobra will act like it is dead, or at least sleeping."

Matthias went on to say that taking HIV/AIDS medication is like placing a stick on a cobra's head. The cobra is very much alive, and if you remove the stick, you could easily get bitten. This HIV/AIDS medication has to be taken every day for the rest of one's life or the virus can return even stronger and more deadly. Before we left one HIV/AIDS clinic, we could hear the staff recounting the cobra story to patients coming into the clinic for their medication. It was very important for patients to hear and remember such stories so they could keep themselves strong in the fight against AIDS.

Dr. Matthias and I visited a young African woman in her twenties. The woman was on the verge of death but did not take any HIV/AIDS medication because she did not want anyone to know she was HIV positive. This was and sometimes still is common among those who carry the stigma of being HIV positive. We prayed with her that God would comfort and be present with her. She passed away within the next few days.

Another speaker at the conference was the Reverend Canon Gideon Byamugisha. In 1992 he was one of the first African church leaders to openly admit that he was HIV positive at a time when AIDS was seen as the "disease of sinners." In 2000 he founded the Africa Network of Religious Leaders Living with or Personally Affected by HIV/AIDS. At the conference he spoke a powerful message of what had happened when he told his bishop in the Anglican church of his status. Canon Gideon expected to be ostracized by both his leader and the church. But he was wrong. The bishop took him in and looked after him as a son and, more important, asked him to be a spokesperson within the Anglican Church for those who were HIV positive.

Ugandan First Lady Janet Museveni spoke to this group of three hundred YWAMers like an apostolic mother. She challenged us that this is the time for YWAM to have a greater impact on the youth of the world, on the poor, and on those affected by HIV/AIDS. She called us to renew our efforts in and around Jinja and throughout Uganda and to deepen our partnership with local agencies as well as the government.

She spoke this challenge in front of her regional and district government leaders, with whom we talked over lunch about what that partnership could look like.

The outcome of the conference was a deeper outreach partnership with government, Muslim, and Christian organizations. Orphaned children were taken into YWAM homes around the world, and foster families in Uganda also took in children. Additionally, teaching and training was developed for churches and DTSs to better serve those with HIV/AIDS.

Sam and I subsequently attended UN meetings in New York, where he spoke powerfully to a regional African leaders workshop about YWAM's response to HIV/AIDS in Uganda. The issue required us to speak frankly about sex, a subject not talked about in many of our schools and churches. This led to the next issue that seemed to explode into our lives: human trafficking and modern-day slavery.

GOD CONTINUED TO speak to us, opening our eyes to see the injustices, the vulnerability, and the exploitation around us. Being based in Thailand since 1980, we knew and worked with women in the sex industry, as well as women and children who were at risk of being sexually abused, sold, or forced into brothels and involuntary labor. But until I read David Batstone's book *Not for Sale*, I had no idea of the extent of the injustice that was happening in virtually every neighborhood of the world.

I was at an HIV/AIDS conference in Malaysia with Sam Kisolo when I finished reading Batstone's book. "You have to read this book, Sam," I said, passing it over to him.

I particularly wanted Sam to read the book because there was a whole chapter on Uganda's child soldiers and because Sam was involved in helping these children. Joseph Kony had conscripted thousands of young children into the Lord's Resistance Army, forcing them to kill their parents or be killed themselves. Young girls were raped, beaten, killed, or kept as slaves. I was shocked to learn about indentured slaves, generational debt, forced labor, and those enslaved by the sex industry. Over the next few days Sam and I talked and prayed about this troubling subject.

David Batstone, a professor of business at the University of San Francisco, would dine with his wife two or three times a month at an Indian restaurant near Half Moon Bay, a coastal town about twenty-five miles south of San Francisco. As they enjoyed the meal, they were served by Indian teenage boys and girls, whom they assumed were children or relatives of the restaurant owners. After visiting the restaurant and enjoying the food for twelve months, the Batstones were shocked to read in their local newspaper that the restaurant owner had been arrested for trafficking over five hundred young people from India.

David was stunned that this criminal activity had been going on in this neighborhood restaurant. It made him question what else was happening in his city, his state, and all around the world.

"We didn't go looking for modern-day slavery, it came looking for us," he said in the book.

David was given leave from the university to research the issue. He conducted hundreds of interviews with women and young girls in Thailand, Cambodia, India, Uganda, South Africa, Peru, and Eastern Europe. In Uganda he interviewed children who had been kidnapped to become child soldiers of the Lord's Resistance Army. Both Thailand and Cambodia were full of stateless children trafficked from China, Laos, Vietnam, and Myanmar and working in bars and brothels and begging on the streets. In India, David saw an entire village of indentured slaves from four generations working in a rice mill. The owner made them work eighteen-hour days and enslaved them with small loans and interest that they could never, in a lifetime, pay back.

In his research, David found that even the hands of the police in San Francisco were tied. The police could not conduct a simple Google search on suspected trafficking sites without a court-ordered warrant. In reaction to this, David directed his university students to conduct the research and deliver their findings to local police. The results were hugely successful: the police arrested several traffickers and became more engaged in anti-trafficking activities.

I knew I had to meet David or to somehow get YWAM Mercy Ministries to partner with his work training people to recognize trafficking and slavery—even in their own backyards—and to become smart activists, knowing what to do and who to go to when they uncovered something.

Tim Svoboda, YWAM San Francisco leader, arranged a meeting with Dr. Batstone and me in January 2009. We sat for nearly two hours as we compared notes and I listened to David's story. I was deeply impressed with how Dr. Batstone was leveraging students, connecting business and faith communities, government and law enforcement, and media and technology to bring light and engagement to end global slavery. Before we separated, I asked David to attend Call2All in Hong Kong the following June and present this message about combating global slavery. He agreed.

Call2All is a movement of churches, denominations, and business and mission organizations that mobilize about 80 percent of the missionaries in the world. The movement is committed to fulfilling the Great Commission and the Great Commandment in this generation. I was coleading the Call2All Compassion/Justice Network, and I asked David to speak, lead a workshop, and talk about what Not For Sale was doing in this fight against slavery.

Three thousand people, half of them from mainland China, met in Hong Kong for Call2All. David addressed the entire congress in addition to leading several workshops on ending modern-day slavery and human trafficking. At a luncheon on compassion and justice, one hundred people showed up for the seventy-five places we had. As we were arranging the chairs and tables for this overflow crowd, I saw a young woman in her late twenties whom I suspected was Khmer, so I greeted her in the Khmer language. Her name was Dary.

"How do you know my language?" she asked with a surprised smile.

I explained that I worked with Khmer refugees for many years in Khao-I-Dang and other camps along the Thai-Cambodian border.

At this Dary's eyes lit up. "I was born in Khao-I-Dang!" she exclaimed.

Dary went on to tell me her story. Her parents and older sister had escaped to the border after living under the Khmer Rouge. Khmer refugees who were Christians in Khao-I-Dang took them in and cared for them as a family. That love and care from fellow refugees spoke deeply to them, and Dary's parents became Christians. It was a difficult period, since they moved many times to different refugee camps. Dary's family was repatriated to Cambodia in 1993 to their home province of Banteay

Meanchey when Dary was eight years old. They planted rice for a couple of years and then, because there was no church in that province, Dary's family moved to Battambang Province, where there were two churches. Dary's father became one of the pastors for a few years. The family then moved to Phnom Penh so that Dary's father could attend a Bible school.

Dary rebelled against her parents, running away from home. When she was at her lowest point, she reached out to Jesus, asking Him to forgive her and come into her life. She wanted a relationship with God for herself, not just a life of faith handed down from her mother and father. From that moment she was transformed. She was reconciled with her parents and attended a YWAM DTS in Phnom Penh to learn more about God. There she met Martin from Norway, and shortly after the school ended, they married. After their DTS, God spoke to Martin and Dary to go to Siem Reap and work with women and girls who had been sold into the sex trade. The couple established an NGO called White Doves. They were now participating in this Call2All congress to see how they could connect with other Christian and missions groups to better serve these women.

After hearing her story, I asked Dary if she would share with those at this luncheon how she had come to know God and start White Doves and about the challenges of trafficking in Cambodia. She needed some encouragement, but she eventually agreed to do so if I would stand with her. Through tears, she shared her story, and the Holy Spirit spoke to many of us personally.

This was a perfect example of the practical teaching of Jesus—to simply love God, love your neighbor as you love yourself, and be available to do what God asks you to do. Dary had done just that in serving the vulnerable in Siem Reap. I ended the session with the words of Jesus for these one hundred participants: "Go and do likewise." If all of us do just one thing, we can make a difference globally.

At the same time that Call2All was meeting, six hundred YWAM leaders were convening from Asia and the Pacific. We brainstormed with some of those leaders on how to collaborate between YWAM and Not For Sale (NFS). One decision was to increase our education and awareness through holding an NFS Investigative Academy (later called Abolitionist Academy) specifically for YWAM leaders. Right after

Christmas, Marie and I joined twenty-four others in San Francisco to attend this academy.

The NFS Academy is two weeks long and is aimed at educating and equipping people with smart activist tools to tackle trafficking around the world. Marie and I knew we could not recruit people to fight trafficking if we were not educated ourselves. The academy highlighted the need, the most shocking statistic being that there are more slaves on the planet today than there were in the time of William Wilberforce.

In 1787 Wilberforce took up the charge for which he is known today: the fight to abolish the slave trade throughout the British Empire. Legislation to abolish the slave trade was rejected in the British Parliament twenty-three consecutive years, but a bill was finally passed, and the law enacted, in the twenty-fourth year—just days before Wilberforce died.

I knew that God was asking us, through our relationships and networks, to raise up twenty-first-century abolitionists like Wilberforce and to do our part as a mission to fight to stop this global problem.

YWAM leaders and DTS students from twelve countries joined Marie and me in San Francisco at the academy. Each day we heard from different groups. The police had set up anti-trafficking task forces in forty of the fifty American states, and a representative from a local law enforcement agency came to explain what the agency was doing. The next day an FBI agent spoke about the agency's involvement and how we can collaborate. Then we heard from aftercare agencies who explained the journey to healing and wholeness after a trafficked person is set free.

We met a group called the SAGE (Standing Against Global Exploitation) Project, former male and female prostitutes who speak at seminars to men who have been arrested for buying sex. These men are given a choice: go to jail or attend this intense seminar. The seminars include teaching on valuing women and the respectful treatment of women. To date over ten thousand men have gone through the First Offender Prostitution Program (aka "john school"), and 72 percent of those men have not been arrested again for sexual violations.

We were significantly impacted during the academy when we visited a Filipina woman who had been trafficked. Carmencita "Chie" Abad had been working for a bank in the Philippines, trying to support her twelve younger brothers and sisters. Because her job didn't pay her quite enough, when she was offered employment in Saipan with the promise of a high salary and attractive benefits, she quickly accepted the offer.

Chie got to Saipan, her passport was taken, and she was forced to work with five hundred other women in a sweatshop that posed as a garment factory. The women were paid one dollar an hour and had an impossible quota to meet each day. If they did not meet it, they would be forced to work overtime without pay.

Chie lived and worked in the factory for five years. When she finished with each day's strenuous work, she would return to her squalid living conditions—thirty women crammed into small rooms, stacked in bunk beds four high, everyone sharing one tiny bathroom. Because of her banking background, she was given more responsibility off the sewing line. She became very angry when another of the Filipina workers was not allowed to go home for her father's funeral. She tried to organize the first union in the factory but lost by a few votes. Having raised her head above the crowd, she was noticed and fired. Chie knew she was up against incredible odds, but that did not stop her. She found a lawyer and decided to fight for her right to a decent livelihood and for the rights of her coworkers.

Saipan is part of the Commonwealth of the Northern Mariana Islands (CNMI), a US territory consisting of fifteen tropical islands belonging to the Marianas archipelago in the western Pacific Ocean. Chie realized that the twenty-five thousand women from Taiwan, China, the Philippines, and Korea who had worked in the garment factory sweatshops were owed back pay for the minimum wage they had never received. The US minimum wage was $8.05, and as a US commonwealth, CNMI was subject to the minimum wage laws. But the women had received only one dollar per hour. Chie filed suit against the garment factories and won. The case brought international shame and condemnation on retailers who used these exploitative practices, and Chie received six years' back pay and $24 million in lost wages for the twenty-five thousand former and current garment workers of Saipan. It was an amazing victory against forced labor.

Chie had persevered for over eight years and had won the case only a month before our NFS Investigative Academy started. This was an unlikely story from such a soft-spoken woman, and it showed what can be accomplished through perseverance, commitment, and collaboration.

While Marie and I were at the academy, we were thinking about Thailand, the country God had called us to. As with the AIDS issue, human trafficking was something that had been hidden for too long. Now the truth was coming to light, and our mission required that we respond, pray, and obey God in what we should do.

Youth With A Mission celebrated its fiftieth—jubilee—year in 2010, and we knew it was a significant time for us. Jubilee in the Old Testament meant the cancellation of all debts, the release of all slaves, the return of all properties bought, the distribution of justice, the rediscovery of family, and the vision of *shalom*. Jesus' message of jubilee was to bring the gospel to the poor, justice for the vulnerable, liberation from sin, poverty, and slavery, and to bring marginalized groups into belonging and acceptance in an integrated manner. We saw how this was significant in our efforts with human trafficking. God was anointing us afresh and calling us to set the captives free in this jubilee year and beyond.

YWAM has twenty-five thousand DTS students a year in over 140 countries. More than one hundred YWAM outreach teams come into Thailand each year. YWAM's desire is to see these students and teams trained to pray, to know what slavery looks like, to educate those they have come to serve, and to engage in innovative solutions.

Many of YWAM's ministries reach out to women and children at risk and to those in the sex industry. For example, the MST Project in Bangkok reaches out to male sex tourists. Chris Lenty began MST when he discovered the need to show God's love to this often despised population. It became apparent that as we focused on the global issue of slavery, we would begin to see how nations could be discipled, since this issue touches all spheres of society—government, law enforcement, education, media, health care, business, sports, and the faith community.

In October 2009 at the YWAM Indo-China/Philippines Regional Leadership Team gathering, one thing we had done tangibly was to pray, commit ourselves, and sign the Bangkok Covenant to unite together under God and declare that we are willing and ready to be used by Him to stop human trafficking and slavery. What made the covenant even more significant was that we met a few streets away from the Patpong district in Bangkok, where many girls and women are lured, tricked, or forced to sell their bodies for economic gain. The cry of our hearts was that we would be part of bringing this to an end.

In the covenant we considered all forms of slavery—child soldiers, people in forced labor, and victims of generational debt. Then we listened and heard the heart of God. We wrote down what we felt Him say: *These are your sons and daughters and families. Open your eyes and see. I hear their cries. I see their tears and pain. I love them and have another dream for them. You are a part of that dream. I am not for sale. You are not for sale. No one should be for sale.*

With the leaders of YWAM Indo-China and the Philippines, we made a solemn vow to ask God what He wanted us to do for the long term as well as for the coming months. We agreed to pray weekly for those enslaved and trafficked and to communicate to all of our staff and students and friends this covenant we had made and to act upon what God says to us.

After agreeing on the covenant, we prayed to receive the same anointing that was on Jesus when he said in Luke 4:18, "The Spirit of the Lord is upon me, because the Lord has anointed me. He has sent me to preach good news to the poor, to proclaim release to the prisoners and recovery of sight to the blind, to liberate the oppressed."

NINETEEN

The Issue of Our Time

Defeating human trafficking is a great moral calling of our time.
—CONDOLEEZA RICE, former US Secretary of State

YWAM INITIATIVES WERE operating around the world—the Hope Campaign, Because Justice Matters, Justice Acts, Sex + Money, in addition to a variety of special-interest DTSs. We were also collaborating with Call2All, TearFund UK, Soul Action, World Evangelical Alliance, the Lausanne Movement, and the Global Prayer Networks. However, in the months following the Not For Sale (NFS) Investigative Academy in San Francisco, our teams of YWAMers rose to a new level of shining the light into the darkness covering human trafficking.

Saskia Wishart from Canada was one of these YWAMers. A fiery twenty-one-year-old with a passion to make a difference, she had come to the NFS Academy from YWAM's Media Village in Cape Town, South Africa. Saskia's eyes were opened at the academy. After the training

Saskia knew what she could do to become a smart activist and make a difference where she lived. Returning to Cape Town, she contacted her local police force and met with them, telling them what she had learned about trafficking. Amazingly, the policemen listened to Saskia.

South Africa was getting ready to host the World Cup soccer tournament in June 2010. The Cape Town arena needed a trial run to see if the facilities were ready for the Games, and this gave Saskia and the team at Media Village an idea. They wanted to use the venue for the Global Day of Prayer, birthed in South Africa but now a worldwide event, and also to communicate about and pray against modern-day slavery and human trafficking. The authorities agreed to use the Global Day of Prayer to test the facilities. Fifty-five thousand people showed up to worship God, pray for the World Cup, and pray against slavery and human trafficking. Serious prayer was needed because sixty thousand women and children were expected to be trafficked during World Cup events. On the Global Day of Prayer, millions from 220 countries gathered in their own nations to humble themselves and pray.

In 2010 South Africa formed its first organized crime unit to investigate human trafficking. The unit was called "the Hawks," aptly named after the bird with the sharpest eyesight, as that is what is needed in fighting this crime—sharp eyes to see and bring a light to that which has been hidden.

One day Saskia was handing out information cards on the streets of Cape Town with a team when she met a young sex worker named Angela. After asking Angela a few questions, Saskia realized that she was a victim of trafficking. Having been taken from her home in Zimbabwe on the promise of a good job, Angela was now being forced to work as a prostitute in Cape Town.

Saskia was tempted for a moment to take Angela to her car and out of harm's way. But Angela's Nigerian pimp, who was driving around the corner, would have seen, and the results could have been serious or even fatal. Instead of taking action on her own, Saskia approached the local vice squad and identified Angela as a victim of human trafficking. The police were able to intervene and take Angela to safety and refer her to the proper service providers.

To the untrained eye Angela could have been seen as a common prostitute, but she was actually the victim of a terrible crime. With Saskia and the team's help, the Hawks were able to rescue forty-five human trafficking victims and arrest fourteen traffickers around the time of the World Cup. All the victims were female, and a third of them were under the age of twenty.

The NFS training encourages smart activists to glean information from communities, networks, classified advertisements, and online forums. When sufficient information has been gathered, the police are notified. Not For Sale and YWAM are not in the rescue business, since that requires trained professionals. It is important to remind our enthusiastic students that we are not the police but we can collaborate and assist law enforcement to the best of our ability. Anti-trafficking is serious and dangerous work, and we are not suggesting any YWAM teams put themselves in harm's way or danger.

Following on from Abolitionist Academies, Not For Sale has introduced a three-day Backyard Academy, which shows participants what slavery and anti-trafficking look like. These trainings can accommodate up to four hundred people. Not For Sale has also established Montara Circles, where up to fifty CEOs and business leaders provide innovative business solutions for at-risk communities.

The momentum continued as Not For Sale saw how prayer is a foundational and central component in the faith community for the beginning of our actions. Marie and I spoke at Christ Church Bangkok on the first Freedom Sunday, the first Sunday of Lent—a day to inform, pray, and act to set people free from slavery—and followed this up with a workshop for forty people in the city.

A teacher in the service asked me to visit her school. I agreed and spoke to a class of twelve- and thirteen-year-old international students about the slavery issue. The students' parents were CEOs of local garment factories and other companies, lawyers, and business owners—people who can play a key role in abolishing slavery. It is amazing what children understand about child labor. They care about injustices done to other children and want to do something. I would have loved to have been at one of the dinner tables that night to hear families talk about what had happened at school that day and discuss the questions that were raised.

Since reading *Not For Sale*, meeting David Batstone, and becoming an NFS board member, I have seen numerous confirmations that extreme poverty produces vulnerability and vulnerability is a step away from exploitation such as trafficking, forced or indentured labor, and using children as soldiers. Slavery is a significant issue, and when we use our networks to partner with government, business, media, faith communities, and others, we can bring about change. We are called to love God and to love our neighbor—particularly the poor and vulnerable—as we love ourselves. We are also called to love our enemies.

We expanded this collaboration to include Micah Challenge, Business as Mission, One Voice Prayer for Global Poverty, and grassroots organizations, in addition to developing working relationships with government agencies. We convene gatherings that shine a light on issues of extreme poverty, vulnerability, exploitation, and trafficking so that YWAM and its partners around the world will see what slavery looks like in their backyards and be moved to prayer and action. This journey has sent me on visits to New Zealand, Australia, Philippines, Korea, Germany, Czech Republic, Ukraine, Colorado Springs, Cincinnati, San Diego, Los Angeles, Cambodia, and Thailand. Slavery affects us all. It is in virtually every neighborhood. If these were our children, brothers and sisters, we would not be silent or inactive.

Will it take us twenty-four years as it did William Wilberforce to make a significant difference in abolishing slavery in the twenty-first century? I don't think so, not today, if we use the strengths and talents that God has given us. We also have the use of global communication, including social media and technology, and are working across all sectors of society. In addition, the missions movement has joined together with the global prayer movement. With our presence in over 170 countries with hundreds of thousands of young people concerned about this issue, collaboration and partnership going to new levels, and the prayer movement lasering in on this issue, we should be able to expose and stop this dark activity and the greedy from preying upon the vulnerable.

A leader from YWAM Colorado Springs heard me speak on trafficking at a YWAM regional conference in Chiang Mai in January 2010. She asked me to speak at their staff conference on this subject three weeks later. I prayed and felt it was right to go, thinking how unusual it was for me to have a week available at such short notice. Once again the power of story presented an opportunity for God to speak to a group of people who were ready to listen and act on what He said. After some research we learned that Colorado Springs is a hub city for trafficking across the United States. From that gathering, YWAM Colorado Springs held a Not For Sale Backyard Academy in October 2010 for three hundred people. The base became active in the city and in partnering in other nations to stop this evil. They continue to hold annual symposiums on anti-trafficking to bring together NGOs, faith communities, business, and government to better cooperate.

I was invited to speak at Herrnhut, Germany, a few miles from the border of the Czech Republic. Herrnhut was the location of the Moravian revival two hundred years ago that began with artists, refugees, criminals, and the disabled. The Moravians, led by Count Zinzendorf, sent out hundreds of missionaries, many to the Caribbean, willing to sell themselves into slavery in order to reach other slaves with the gospel. They also started a prayer chain that went on for one hundred years to release a new global movement of missionaries. Now, all these years later, a group of YWAMers were eager to lay down their lives as the Moravians did, to end extreme poverty and modern-day slavery.

The Herrnhut YWAMers are artists and musicians who want to use those gifts to reach the unreached. God wants to use us all by our applying our gifts and strengths in obedience to what He asks us to do. The YWAMers told me that the goal of their base was to be part of ending extreme poverty, but having focused on the creative arts, they knew very little about mercy ministries, justice, and social work. As I started to talk about trafficking, it struck a chord with the group, who knew that this was something God was asking them to act on.

The next day we went on a prayer trip into Czech Republic, now a member of the European Union (EU). Forty students were split into two groups of twenty to pray and see what God showed them. On the border, so close to their YWAM base, we saw trafficked women from China, Vietnam, and Cambodia who were openly offering their services as sex workers. We then visited the town in Czech Republic where YWAM Herrnhut was going to begin an anti-trafficking ministry. Forty of us met outside a church in three feet of fresh snow to bring the needs of the trafficked women before our Heavenly Father, asking for His help. The road that ran past us was the main trafficking route being used to transfer Eastern European women farther into the EU, to Hamburg, and on into Amsterdam.

From Herrnhut I was scheduled to travel to Kona, Hawaii, for the President's Gathering (PG), a meeting of the leaders of forty of the largest YWAM bases around the world. I realized it was a perfect opportunity for David Batstone to come and speak on slavery and how Not For Sale and YWAM, who were positioned globally, could collaborate and end human trafficking in our lifetime. David's speaking at PG had one problem: David had been asked by members of Parliament in Australia to speak at this same time about Not for Sale and modern-day slavery. After some persuasion on my part, he agreed to come to Kona and spoke powerfully to these global leaders. He also spoke to the YWAM Kona community at their Thursday night meeting. Afterward many key conversations confirmed that this rallying call was being heard. We also found out that about an hour away from the YWAM base, a port was being used to traffic many victims into Honolulu and then on to the West Coast of the US.

In Kona, we had lunch with YWAM leaders from Australia. This led to an invitation for an eighteen-city tour for David to educate and engage Australians about the human trafficking issue. YWAM locations opened up their bases to local government and businesspeople to hear David's message. The tour was a huge success and led to YWAM teams working on Not For Sale projects in northern Thailand, Peru, and South Africa as well as to a proposal for a Not For Sale–YWAM ship to integrate outreach in health care and anti-trafficking awareness to Papua New Guinea and Southeast Asia.

My earlier meeting in Herrnhut led to our speaking in a four-day YWAM anti-trafficking conference in Hamburg in November 2010. I spoke on poverty as a breeding ground for vulnerability and exploitation. David Batstone and Mark Wexler, cofounders of Not For Sale, came and challenged the six hundred young people to open their eyes and ears and use their skills to end slavery and bring about better futures for the exploited of our world.

Momentum was rising in the media as well. After discussions with Not for Sale and other anti-trafficking groups, CNN announced that in 2011 it would launch the CNN Freedom Project, focused on ending modern-day slavery and human trafficking. They wanted to highlight innovative responses and stories on the ground from anti-trafficking NGOs like International Justice Mission, Not For Sale, ECPAT, Free the Slaves, and Polaris. In November 2011 Anna Coren of CNN Hong Kong spoke at our first Asia Pacific Forum on Human Trafficking, cosponsored by Not For Sale and YWAM in Chiang Mai. She explained to the three hundred participants how simple it was to get stories about human trafficking aired on CNN. Also, this forum highlighted other media events like MTVExit and screened "Charcoal Slaves," an episode from Al Jazeera's eight-part documentary series *Slavery: A 21st Century Evil.*

At the second Not For Sale Asia Pacific Forum on Human Trafficking in July 2012 in Manila, a synergy of government, business, faith communities, and NGOs was represented by the five hundred participants from twelve countries. Bishop Efraim Tendero hosted this forum with Not For Sale to mobilize the pastors and leaders of over thirty thousand churches to engage in this global effort. Philippines President Benigno Aquino, who stated that one of his major goals in office was to stop human trafficking in the Philippines, sent a personal representative to communicate his message at this forum. The Visayan Forum, International Justice Mission, and other major NGOs in the region discussed new strategies for attacking the business models of traffickers. With all of them working together, making their contribution, we again saw that ending this global travesty in our time is possible.

President Barack Obama spoke in September 2012 to the Clinton Global Initiative on human trafficking and modern-day slavery, raising the bar for involvement from all sectors of society. We as people of faith have a central role to play in ending this evil in our generation.

On numerous occasions, the Gospels record that Jesus looked on the crowds or on an individual, was moved with compassion, and then acted. At other times, Jesus simply said to His disciples, "You give them something to eat." Matthew 14:14 says, "He had compassion for them and healed those who were sick." Matthew 15:32 states, "I feel sorry for the crowd. . . . I don't want to send them away hungry." Then Jesus miraculously multiplied the loaves and fishes. In Matthew 20:34, Jesus was again moved with compassion. When two blind men would not keep silent, He touched their eyes and at once their disability was healed. In Mark 1:40–41 a beggar with leprosy says to Jesus, "If you want, you can make me clean." Jesus responds, "I do want to."

Reaching out to the vulnerable and outcasts of His day who were rejected by all, Jesus acted. Whether it was the widow, the orphan, the sick, the prisoner, the disabled, the prostitute, or an enemy, Jesus saw the need, was moved with compassion, and acted. He says to us in John 14:12, "I assure you that whoever believes in me will do the works that I do. They will do even greater works than these because I am going to the Father."

Now it is our turn to bring our eyes and see, be moved with compassion, and act in that same spirit of Jesus.

TWENTY

To Love and Obey

A prayer in which we are not open to bring part of the solution will never be answered.
— C. B. SAMUEL, teacher and advocate of the poor in India

AS MARIE AND I have considered the stories we recounted in this book, a deep gratefulness has welled up in our hearts time and time again—to God, to our family, to our friends, to fellow journeyers, and to our fellow leaders and coworkers in YWAM and in the body of Christ.

"We walk backward into the future, our eyes fixed on the past." This old Maori proverb speaks of reflection and yet forethought and reminds Marie and me that our lives have been touched and influenced by the many people, situations, and difficulties that we have faced.

We are just ordinary people who have tried to listen to God and to love and obey Him by doing the next thing that He asks us to do. Many people have walked along the way with us and have touched and blessed our lives. We are eternally grateful for where our lives have intersected.

In 1979 our journey took a clear path when we saw the face of a little girl that brought the plight of the refugees alive to us. God continues today to open our eyes to see the poor, the vulnerable, the exploited—widows, orphans, prisoners, the sick, disabled, outcast, lonely, destitute, and elderly. He asks us a simple question: "Will you serve them for Me?"

"Bring your eyes and see—then you will believe," says the Somali proverb. We know that this is true. When we see, we have to act. Out of that action, we recognize that God is at work.

Many people need to see the gospel before they will hear its message. What would happen if, today, God's people simply loved Him and obeyed Him by performing hundreds of millions of random acts of kindness? What would be the practical outcome of loving our neighbor? Maybe these simple ways are the greater things Jesus was talking about because all of them are expressions of love.

Many servants, models of love and faith on our journey, have helped us to see more clearly. We are grateful to God for each of them and stand on their shoulders and follow their paths of obedience. God has used "normal" people to be a voice for those without one, a touch to the untouchable, and a listening ear to those otherwise not deemed important enough to be heard. Prayer warriors, activists, and accountants have been standing in the gap and continue to strike a match or shine a light on injustice.

In 2013, YWAM Thailand celebrated its fortieth anniversary, including eighty-plus ministries ranging from reaching university students to working in the slums to serving the rural poor. More than 120 outreach teams with over twelve hundred volunteers served in over 150 ministry locations. YWAM internationally is well-positioned to make both short- and long-term impact as it works in over fourteen hundred locations in more than 170 countries.

God's heart has never changed. It is for all people to "taste and see that He is good." We want to see the Great Commission fulfilled in our lifetime. We in the body of Christ have the resources and the people to make a difference. God said in Deuteronomy 15:4, "There won't be any poor persons among you because the LORD will bless you in the land that the LORD your God is giving you to possess as an inheritance." How about that for a bodacious goal? There should be *zero* poor among you.

In his book *Generous Justice,* Timothy Keller writes, "God's concern for the poor is so strong that He gave Israel a host of laws that, if practiced, would have virtually eliminated any permanent underclass." The Old Testament called this "the Year of Jubilee."

Poverty is not God's design. Jesus made this very clear to the expert of the law when he held up the Good Samaritan, a man from an enemy ethnic group, as an example and told the lawyer in Luke 10:37 to have mercy on those in need.

Our journey is far from finished. During the past few years we have often been asked about retirement. Retirement . . . what's that? Why would we stop doing what we love doing? With God's help and direction, good health, and continued passion for what He has called us to do, we plan to be working and serving God for decades to come, seeing and multiplying a new generation of young people fulfill their destiny in God.

And what about you? Will you be one who will "bring your eyes and see," one who will believe and act? Life continues to be exciting, full of highs and lows, but the highs far outweigh the lows, and the blessings far outweigh the sacrifices. Because you have gifts, talents, and strengths to contribute, don't miss one thing that God has for you.

Many years ago we were asked what our family verse was. Marie and I looked at each other—we didn't have one. The conversation inspired us to ask the Lord for a verse. What He gave us sums up the vision and dream of our lives. Written in old Vietnamese script, it is hanging in a prominent place in our living room: "He has told you, human one, what is good and what the LORD requires from you: to do justice, embrace faithful love, and walk humbly with your God" (Micah 6:8).

As Jesus said in Luke 10:37, may we all go and do the same.

Afterword: One Person Can Make a Difference

THE LATE GREAT William Wilberforce was one of those people. Wilberforce was born in Hull, England, in 1759 to a prosperous upper-middle-class family, who had high hopes that he would increase the family fortune. After graduating from St. John's College at Cambridge in 1779, he was elected as a member of parliament from Hull just a few days after his twenty-first birthday in 1780. He became close friends with William Pitt, who in 1783 went on to become the youngest-ever prime minister of Great Britain. He also came to know John Newton, the author of the hymn "Amazing Grace" and a former slave-ship captain who had become an Anglican priest. Newton encouraged Wilberforce that he could serve God in politics and make a difference. Wilberforce's work led to the passing of the Slavery Abolition Act.

Wilberforce devoted himself to other causes and campaigns—child-labor limitations, prison reform, health care, and the promotion of righteousness in public life. Although he enjoyed a successful political career, Wilberforce credited his success to God's will rather than his own merits.

We need to see not only the government sector impacted by young men and women but also business, education, health care, faith, sports, media, technology, police, and law. If one person can have such an impact as William Wilberforce, with God's help, you can too.

Other people have made a difference, and we have learned much from their lives and writings. Here are a few of them.

William and Catherine Booth, founders of the Salvation Army, impacted three million homeless poor in the UK. In 1890 William Booth raised this question in his book *In Darkest England and the Way*

Out: "Is it not time? There is, it is true, an audacity in the mere suggestion that the problem is not insolvable that is enough to take the breath away. If after full and exhaustive consideration, we come to the deliberate conclusion that nothing can be done and that it is the inevitable destiny of thousands of Englishmen to be brutalized into worse than beasts by the conditions of their environment, then so be it." The Salvation Army continues its mission to end extreme poverty today, serving the destitute worldwide.

Bob Pierce, founder of World Vision, led a 1950s effort to reach out to the war-orphaned children of Korea. World Vision now serves tens of millions of children across the globe.

David Bussau founded Opportunity International Australia and cofounded the Opportunity International Network, which provides microfinance to millions of small businesses today.

George Müller (1805–1898) cared for over ten thousand orphans in his lifetime and started 115 schools that provided education for more than 120,000 students, most of them orphans.

Millard and Linda Fuller (1935–2009) founded Habitat for Humanity and today have provided homes for millions of people in thousands of communities.

Paul Brand (1914–2003), a surgeon to the untouchables, was one of the first surgeons in India to appreciate that it was not leprosy that caused the rotting away of tissue but the loss of the sensation of pain that caused these deformities.

Mother Teresa wrote many books, including *A Gift for God*. Her daily prayer was "Dearest Lord, May I see You today and every day in the person of the sick and whilst nursing them, minister to You. Though You hide yourself behind the unattractive disguise of the irritable, the exacting, the unreasonable, may I still recognize You and say, 'Jesus, my patient, how sweet it is to serve You.'"

Vishal Mangalwadi, author of *The Book That Made Your World: How the Bible Created the Soul of Western Civilization*, profoundly writes about what transformation of a nation looks like and the influence of one book upon society. He dedicated his book to the Honorable Arun Shourie, Indian member of Parliament, whose criticism of the Bible prompted the writing of the book.

Special Thanks

Every man [and woman] is a bundle of his ancestors.
—RALPH WALDO EMERSON

OUR ANCESTORS CAME from Cornwall in the twelfth century and other English/Irish settlements. One of our relatives was given license for seven years to help discover (via the North Passage) China, Cathay, the Moluccas, and other regions of the East Indies. Other relatives, the first Englishmen to land on the shores of America, came to America with Sir Francis Drake in 1577 on the *Golden Hind*. They were just ordinary people—farmers, government workers, pastors, businesspeople, prisoners—both poor and well-to-do. We are grateful for these generations who have helped shape, influence, and contribute to our lives and others.

Our grandparents lived in the rural south of the United States. They were poor and worked hard on the land. They lost children from illness and disease. They didn't finish school, but they understood about learning, growing and developing, the love of family, hospitality, laughter, relationship, honesty, hard work, playing and having fun, and enjoying life in the midst of challenge and difficulty. They were generous, and they always made room for one more. They were men and women on a spiritual journey who loved God and their neighbors. We are grateful for their example.

Our parents loved God, loved us, and worked hard to provide opportunities for us to develop and succeed, often at a significant sacrifice. They were examples of faithfulness in marriage and commitment to family, which included celebrating historical passages around good food with neighbors and extended family. They introduced us to God and encouraged us in our journey to follow Him, whatever or wherever that meant. Mimi and Papau, Marge and Hap, we remember and honor you with grateful hearts.

Our brothers and their wives have made us a blessed family, and we are grateful to all of you for continuing to model loving, committed relationships. Thank you for your commitment to God and faithfulness to each other and to family. Thank you for loving us so completely and helping us to follow what we believe to be the call of God to us. You have stood with us in our victories and in our mistakes. We have laughed and cried together. We love being *family* with you! You have supported us and have stood with us in amazing ways. Thank you to Ron and Sheila, David and Pam, John and Debra, and Thomas and Frances.

We have loved, as our own, our ten nieces and nephews and their spouses, plus multiplying grandnieces and grandnephews. We treasure many special, fun memories and trust for more times to come. You have allowed us into your lives, though you really did not have much of a choice! We are so proud of the adults you have become and the precious families you have established.

The parents of our seventeen godchildren have made our quiver full by trusting us with your treasures, continually helping us to connect with them through the years and miles of separation. Our hearts and lives have been richer by loving your children and being involved with them. Thank you to our "special children" for your love and acceptance and for passing your relationship with us on to our continually increasing number of grand-godchildren!

So many dear friends, near and far, have walked this journey with us. Your love, support, and friendship have sustained, encouraged, and challenged us like cold water to a thirsty soul.

We would not have been able to do what we have done without the support of our ministry partners. Your strengthening prayers and practical love have been expressed in friendship, belief in us, and generous provision. We thank God for you.

To those with whom we have followed, worked, led, and served together in YWAM: thank you for giving us the opportunity to grow, develop, learn together, take risks, make mistakes, laugh together, have fun, become international and see God's global kingdom, to walk in openness, and be challenged to obey God in whatever He has asked.

Thanks to all of you with whom we have collaborated and partnered. This world is a smaller and better place because of you, your business, your church, and your organization. Thanks for the difference you have made and the joy we have had in participation with you. You have brought your strengths to the table and let us bring ours for a greater synergy and impact.

To the poor, the refugee, the widow, the homeless, the prisoner, the sick, the vulnerable, and the exploited of our world, you have changed our lives, our culture, and paradigms forever and given us the opportunity to work together, to change circumstances, and to have a different future. We remember you!

Lastly, thank You, Father God, for Your example in loving Your creation in sending the Lord Jesus to come among us as a servant—thinking of the other and particularly the vulnerable as just as important as ourselves—and in Your amazing humility in partnering with us. Our desire is to bring joy to Your heart.

Resources for Action

10,000 Women: www.goldmansachs.com/citizenship/10000women/index.html
Al Jazeera documentary series: www.aljazeera.com/programmes/slaverya21st
centuryevil/2011/10/2011109135233564570.html
All Girls Allowed: www.allgirlsallowed.org
Call2All Compassion/Justice Network: www.call2all.org
Call2Business: www.call2business.org
Chab Dai: www.chabdai.org
CNN Freedom Project: http://cnn.com/freedom
ECPAT: www.ecpat.net
Free the Slaves: www.freetheslaves.net
Free2Work: www.free2work.org
Freedom Sunday: www.freedomsunday.org
Global Prayer Movement for the Poor: http://onevoice.tearfund.org
Global Slavery Index: www.globalslaveryindex.org
Half the Sky Movement: www.halftheskymovement.org
Hearing the Heart Cry of the Orphans of the World: http://waitingforafather.com
International Justice Mission: www.ijm.org
Jubilee Centre: www.jubilee-centre.org
Make a Stand: http://makeastand.com/company/viviennes-story
Micah Network: www.micahnetwork.org
Mother's Choice: www.motherschoice.org
MTVExit: www.mtvexit.org
NFS Slavery Map: www.slaverymap.org
Not For Sale: www.notforsalecampaign.org
One Voice Prayer Movement: www.onevoiceprayer.net
One: www.one.org/international
Opportunity International: http://opportunity.org
Polaris: www.polarisproject.org
Poverty Cure: www.povertycure.org
Relationships Foundation: www.relationshipsfoundation.org
Slavery Foot Print: http://slaveryfootprint.org
Soul Action: www.soulaction.org
Tearfund International Learning Zone: http://tilz.tearfund.org
TearFund: www.tearfund.org
The Freedom Registry: www.freedomregistry.org
Walk Free: www.walkfree.org
World Relief: www.worldrelief.org
World Vision: www.worldvision.org
YWAM Mercy Facebook: www.facebook.com/groups/4288972901
YWAM Mercy: www.ywam-mercy.org

Steve and Marie, graduation photos, 1968

Prom dates, 1968

Wedding day, August 14, 1971

*Application
photo for
YWAM
Switzerland
SOE, 1973*

*Chalet-
a-Gobet,
Switzerland*

*"The Last
Commandment"
multimedia set,
1975*

Lem Cavassini, 1979, and later with Marie, 2013

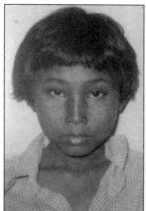 

KID Camp, 1981

John and Tove's refugee camp wedding, January 1984

*Traditional
Thai greetings
from refugee
children*

*Steve and
the YWAM
HIV/AIDS
delegation
with Ugandan
first lady Janet
Museveni,
2007*

*Saveth and
Savi Uy in KID
Camp and later,
in Cambodia,
2013*

Herat,
Afghanistan,
May 2008

Not For Sale
Investigative
Academy, San
Francisco,
2009

With Martin
and Dary
Mydland, 2010

YWAM Thailand's 40th Anniversary

Marie and Yvonne Dos Santos, 2013

Steve, David, John, and Ron Goode, 2004; Marie and her brother Thomas Bentley, 2012

Steve and Marie, 2012